Gender and Race through Education and Political Activism:

The Legacy of Sylvia Helen Forman

Dena Shenk, Editor

Published by the American Anthropological Association/
Association for Feminist Anthropology

Published by the American Anthropological Association
4350 North Fairfax Drive, Suite 640
Arlington, VA 22203-1621

Cover photo: Carol B. MacKnight, 1976.

Library of Congress Cataloging-in-Publication Data

Gender and race through education and political activism : the legacy of
  Sylvia Helen Forman / Dena Shenk, editor.
    p.   cm.
  Includes bibliographical references.
  ISBN 0-913167-75-4
  1. Forman, Sylvia Helen, 1944 or 5-1992. 2. Ethnology.
3. Feminist anthropology. 4. Social advocacy. 5. Racism.
I. Shenk, Dena.
GN21.F62G46 1995
305.42—dc20   95-42693
                                                 CIP

To Sylvia,
forever a force in my life.

Dena

Contents

Preface

Sylvia Forman died at the age of 48 on March 1, 1992, leaving behind many colleagues, students and friends through whom she imparted her legacy to the world within the field of anthropology. Sylvia was a scholar, a teacher, a mentor, an anthropologist and a very special human being. The chapters that follow include a collection of her own work and that of 10 of her former students. Through this collection, both the range of career paths being followed by her students are highlighted, while at the same time, common themes are evident in their work.

This volume developed out of a session which was organized for the AAA meetings in November 1992. In organizing that session, I contacted many of Sylvia's former students whose addresses were listed in her telephone directory. We arranged to meet for lunch before the session -- representatives of the overlapping generations of graduate students who had worked with Sylvia. Many of us had never met previously, because our graduate studies at the University of Massachusetts spanned 1976 through 1992. As we prepared for the symposium and waited for our lunch, we shared stories about our memories of Sylvia. We laughed as we developed a true sense of community, realizing the strength of her presence among us. We talked about our own work and the papers we were to present and identified bridges and connections. Most of us were pleasantly surprised at the themes that became apparent as we presented our papers. Carole Hill and Kay Warren offered cross-cutting observations as discussants. The session hung together better than we had dared to hope and we moved on to the hotel bar to continue the discussions. It was at that time that we were encouraged to pursue the publication that you now hold in your hands. Attempts were made to contact many of Sylvia's former students, inviting them to prepare chapters based on their own work which could be part of this volume. As themes developed and the volume took shape, I worked with each contributor to develop a cohesive set of essays.

Among her students, as you will see from those represented in this volume, there is a broad variety in the range of research topics, theoretical and methodological approaches, and modes of presenting and arenas for disseminating their work. That is appropriate and important to note, because Sylvia did not attempt to influence or shape her students' agendas. Rather, she taught us how to do anthropology effectively, whatever our interests. The following quote from one of her former students makes this point:

> Sylvia Forman supported me in my then unpopular approach -- different though it was from her own. But not long before she died she cautioned me not to emphasize reflexivity too much, lest people think I was trying to be fashionable... "even though I know you've been doing it all along" (B. Johnston, personal communication).

This points also to the fact that Sylvia did not "graduate" or stop working with and advising her students until she somehow sensed that we were ready to be "independent scholars." That was generally many years after we had in fact, earned our doctorates and moved on. She continued to offer advice and keep in touch with most of us. In the personal reflections offered by Ralph Faulkingham (chapter 17), he mentions the personal notes which Sylvia wrote to former students, as well as colleagues and friends in her final days.

This is the legacy of Sylvia Forman. Chapter 1 is an introduction to the volume by Kay Warren, reflecting on the major themes in Sylvia's writing and the research of her former students as represented in chapters 7 through 16. Chapters 2 through 6 are both published and previously unpublished works by Sylvia herself. These chapters represent her own efforts in the key areas in which she worked: her ethnographic research in Ecuador (chapter 2 and 3), her emphasis on education (chapter 3, 4 and 5), race (chapter 5) and gender (chapter 5 and 6). The final chapter is an essay about Sylvia's life and career by Ralph Faulkingham, her longtime colleague in the Department of Anthropology at the University of Massachusetts and close personal friend.

Sylvia was a scholar in the true sense of the word, but she did not publish more than a few articles and reports throughout her career. Her emphases were instead on education and political activism. She chose to focus her energies in the classroom and in working with students broadly, outside of the classroom as well. It was through education and political activism in other arenas which she believed that anthropology could change the world. It seems most appropriate therefore, that this volume includes her own work, and contributions from her students. It is through her students that Sylvia's lasting impact on the field of anthropology will likely be felt. Sylvia's strengths were her ability to formulate ideas and concepts, her insistence on collaboration and clearly on action. She truly believed that through education and the practice of anthropology, we could restructure the world.

The themes that become apparent in both her own work and that of her students are the focus on the issues of gender and race. Her emphasis was grounded in the strong belief that political activism should be an integral element of both one's professional work and personal life and the corollary that we can change the world through education. Thus her professional impact on the lives of others and the field of anthropology came through her work in several spheres -- in the Department of Anthropology at the University of Massachusetts where for 20 years she was recognized as a dedicated and demanding teacher, her own fieldwork in Andean Ecuador, the American Anthropological Association (AAA), the Association of Black Anthropologists (ABA) and the Association for Feminist Anthropology (AFA). Her work in each of these spheres is represented in chapters 2 through 6 of this volume.

These themes pervade her own work and that of most of the students who chose to work with Sylvia. Or is it perhaps more accurate to say, those students who Sylvia chose to work with her. As one of her early graduate students, I can state from personal experience that Sylvia was dedicated and demanding. She attracted a certain type of student, as Ralph Faulkingham explains in the closing chapter. To me this mutual selection is captured in the feeling that we all shared as we sat around the table at lunch preparing for the session at the AAA meetings. A diverse group of women, but clearly all self-motivated and all moving along our career paths and through our lives with the imprint of Sylvia Forman's hand on our shoulders, or, more accurately for some, her foot offering a kick from behind. A gentle (or not so gentle) nudge, a reformulation of a concept, a burst of intellectual energy. Somehow Sylvia was able to ascertain what each of us needed in terms of support or pressure, and she provided it in appropriate measure.

Her students' chapters are organized chronologically in terms of when we each worked with Sylvia and the themes evident in Sylvia's work are also clear in ours. Several of the chapters deal primarily with gender issues, including those by Libbet Crandon-Malamud, Dena Shenk, Melba Sánchez-Ayéndez, Lisa Markowitz and Irma McClaurin. Sue Taylor and Sue Hyatt focus on issues of race. David Nixon and Sue Hyatt focus on education and Barbara Johnston on political activism. There are also underlying themes, for example methodological issues are discussed by Barbara Johnson and Sue Taylor. It is interesting to note that the work of three of Sylvia's early graduate students deal with aging issues, although this was not a special interest of hers. This emphasizes the fact that Sylvia worked with each of us to focus our own interests and concerns. As Kay Warren discusses in her introductory chapter, there is thematic convergence of the essays along three sets of issues.

When Sylvia knew she was dying of lung cancer, she took action to begin a scholarship fund to enable Third World students to study anthropology. She established the *Sylvia Forman Third World Scholarship Fund* to provide a means in perpetuity of funding one or more scholarships per year for individuals from Third World countries to pursue graduate study in anthropology at the University of Massachusetts. She recognized that anthropology's very *raison d'etre* -- of understanding and interpreting the course, nature, and significance of human diversity -- provides a means through education to promote global peace, justice, and security. Sylvia understood that most Third World students do not have access to graduate study in anthropology, because there are so few university programs in anthropology in their countries. Moreover, scholarships for Third World students to pursue anthropology in the United States are rare. Finally, out of her own experience as a professional and teacher, Sylvia appreciated that American graduate students and their counterparts from other cultures -- and more broadly the profession as a whole -- would benefit greatly from an ongoing active collaboration in and out of the classroom between peoples of the First and Third Worlds. Sylvia's initial bequest of $100,000 provided the foundation upon which to build her scholarship program, which has been augmented through memorial gifts. Donations to *The Sylvia Forman Third World Scholarship Fund* can be made to the Fund at the Department of Anthropology, Machmer Hall, University of Massachusetts, Amherst, MA 01003-0020.

Sylvia Forman, your memory lives on in the minds and lives of your students and through your work in the field of anthropology. It is with great appreciation that I applaud the efforts of the Association for Feminist Anthropology, for publishing this book and for developing the Sylvia Forman Student Paper Award. The AFA "dedicate(s) its paper prize competition to (Sylvia's) memory and hopes that her spirit of challenge and activism will inspire the essays submitted in her honor" (AFA column in *Anthropology Newsletter* 36(5):14). In particular, Mary Moran helped get this project to publication.

There are many other people who helped. AAA Director of Publications Rick Custer has been a consistent source of encouragement and advice throughout the process of developing this volume. Ralph Faulkingham assisted by gathering files and photographs. My husband, Kenneth Quilty, not only offered his usual support, but also prepared the camera-ready manuscript for publication. He did it with his usual patience, dedication and attention to detail. And we both lived to tell about it! This project was a source of great pleasure and excitement, generated by the challenge of working with many of Sylvia's former students. This volume is a result of all of their hard work. For me, the project has indeed been a labor of love and I offer it as a token of my appreciation -- to Sylvia.

Dena Shenk

On Sylvia Forman, Intellectual Progeny,

and American Struggles: An Overview

Kay B. Warren
Princeton University

In the 1970's, Sylvia Forman and I were young professors together in the Five College system which included the University of Massachusetts at Amherst, Mount Holyoke, Smith, Amherst, and Hampshire colleges. We shared students and colleagues, found ourselves active in Anthropology and Latin American Studies, and were captured by the intensity of feminist studies and the politics of the times. In 1982, I left the Valley to become the founding director of Women's Studies at Princeton, where I am currently the chair of the Anthropology Department. My recent research has focused on violence, Mayan public intellectuals and cultural resurgence, and realist representations of Latin America in U.S. and English mass media.

The Many Preoccupations of Sylvia Forman's Anthropology

Sylvia Forman's work crossed many conventional divides: academic and applied, antiracism and feminism, research and activism, international and domestic, theory and pedagogy. To the core, Sylvia was a materialist, an activist, and a humanist. Her writing and teaching were motivated by a quest to interrogate social inequality: racial, gender, class, and international cleavages. She called on anthropologists to use their analytical skills to unmask the systematic reproduction of inequality in international development and domestic educational systems. Her anthropology was a study of constraints: from the ecology of the rural Andes, reflected in the vertical organization of social life, to bureaucratic power structures throughout the world, which channel life chances and create societies resistant to change. When Sylvia wrote of constraints, it was often an experience-distant portrayal; there were few individuals and little personal volition, but rather faceless overdetermining structures.

But there were other sides to her anthropology: Sylvia's work foregrounded human ingenuity in a world animated by political dilemmas. For Sylvia, the Andes could not be captured by a singular model of exchange between zones at different altitudes because local communities mixed reciprocity and market relations in different ways. They bred an array of specialized animals and crops and created a variety of social networks to make the most of fragile, challenging physical environments. Andean patterns of reciprocity were mediated by the nuances of verticality, political structures near and far, and social relations through which cooperation was channeled. Sylvia emphatically disagreed with those who saw in Andean communities a timeless, universal form of cooperative or collective organization.

The issue was how rural populations might improve their lives in the face of the damaging politics of national development bureaucracies with their poorly elaborated policies for the countryside. Flatlanders -- international or national development experts -- were destined to fail themselves and the people they allegedly served if they imposed top-down models that ignored local ingenuity and the lessons of verticality. The more promising alternative was an interactive model of development which would take seriously local knowledge and expertise and would share the powers of decision making.

Although Sylvia expressed a gritty combination of realism and cynicism, she was an optimist when it came to arguing that research and social criticism could make a difference. In her lectures and publications, she demonstrated a dedication to unraveling institutional power structures as well as an idealism that the seeds of a better way are already present, though often drowned out by existing arrangements. The role of anthropology is to formulate research that reveals the big picture of constraints and ingenuity, to urge flatlanders (in all their guises) to respond to local knowledge, and to find a route for activist research, for praxis. Her impulse was post-orientalist: one needs to scrutinize the culture of the development experts -- their anti-traditionalism -- as well as the culture of local communities. That meant one had to scrutinize American culture and anthropology for their contributions to social inequality.

When her gaze turned to the U.S., Sylvia took on the issues of democracy and education. How well she (and her coauthors, Carole Hill and Barbara Johnston) anticipated today's debates about the clashing politics of equity versus individualized personal responsibility. The bottom line was the tension between public fairness and private gain, between the collective and individual good. She worried about the implications of America's mistrust of government control at all levels, coupled with our dependency on large centralized bureaucratic structures. She saw the rebirth of individualism and the bureaucratic principles of efficiency and functional rationality as powerful legitimizers of contemporary patterns of inequality. For Sylvia, American democracy needed wider citizen participation (not more elaborate structures of representation), a questioning of intolerance in the face of cultural diversity, and a commitment to public welfare. Democracy should aim for an educational system self-conscious about its role in the reproduction of inequality and aware of the benefits of being student-rather than teacher-focused. Her contributions called for a renewal of debates about the meanings of democracy, a critique of the top-down policies of bureaucratic elites who leave little room for grassroots involvement in decision making, and a recognition that the contradictions in American democracy mean that justice will always be a struggle. Awareness of these tensions, she argued, allows for constructive change. We need her optimism now.

Finally, Sylvia subjected the discipline of anthropology to this critical method and joined with others to discuss the ways in which our profession structures and replicates patterns of inequality. Criticism entails praxis. It needs wider networks to pressure for change. The Association for Feminist Anthropology has turned out to be an enduring and very active intergenerational organization. The Race and Gender Workshops at the annual AAA meetings were for Sylvia another opportunity to build bridges and challenge the status quo. These meetings were extraordinarily important to Sylvia: there she was just months before her death, stealing a quick smoke before joining others to help moderate what turned out to be her last Race and Gender Workshop. Finally, she invested a great deal of her career working with the next generation to insure that this would be a diverse multiracial, multicultural profession with strong international and national representation.

From Students to Colleagues: Routes to a Committed Anthropology

If you knew Sylvia, you understand why her students, now professionals, are tough and independent. In anthropology, our students are a special sort of progeny, unusual because the relationship is not based on the accident of birth but rather is a result of two individuals -- professor and student -- finding each other and taking each other seriously. Often it is not an uncontested relationship -- not with Sylvia Forman at any rate. But the goal is clear: to see two creative minds unfold, to watch a graduate student find her own voice and to find one's own changing as well. Anthropologists such as Sylvia make their convictions evident by supporting students who pursue high risk projects in areas novel to anthropology. Sylvia worked to break down barriers and to widen the voices and issues represented in the discipline. She was proud when students became colleagues. Think of it, she was a fiercely independent person who knew the practice of anthropology was not just doing one's own research and writing but also investing in other people so the academy, the canon, and wider social worlds would have to change.

We see in these articles a committed anthropology. Because the essays focus on the real-world consequences of the tensions anthropology documents, the authors speak from a concrete, problem-confronting perspective. Consequently, this research can be used to anticipate some of the effects of current shifts in U.S. social policy. Readers can trace the likely implications of cutbacks in federal funding for social services, the disestablishment of affirmative action for jobs where minorities are underrepresented, skepticism about rehabilitation through prison education, geopolitical isolationism which leaves less funding for international development efforts, and ambivalence about social criticism produced in the academy.

Gender, race, and ethnicity -- not as transcendent identifications but as dimensions of identity embedded in culture, class, generation, rural and urban divides, and social policies -- appear as cross-cutting concerns in many of these analyses. The essays personalize gender and ethnic relations; they show how identities are the product of wider social struggles and conflicting meanings forged in institutional and local practices. Case studies demonstrate ways in which individuals and institutions generate a politics of exclusion, despite mandates and public commitments to meet the needs of all citizens. Scholar-activists illustrate their attempts to become involved in projects to transform institutions and their cultural arrangements, to legitimize grassroots activism independent of larger institutions, and to communicate people's own stories to wider audiences.

A benefit of these approaches and the international scope of the volume is that readers will be able to see echoes of American development dilemmas in other countries and vice versa. Clearly the "West"/"Rest" dichotomy so prevalent in development studies needs to be challenged by a humanistic approach to social tensions in contemporary society at home and abroad. Here it is fine-grained ethnography -- not structural analysis -- that reveals the nuances of ingenuity and tragic conflict in people's lives.

There are many ways to read this collection. The route I want to pursue is one that notes (surprisingly, since this was not planned) the thematic convergence of these essays along several sets of issues: the formal and informal structuring of elder care, the social dilemmas of international development, and anthropology's role in reproducing/unmasking inequality. These essays have synergistic ways of speaking to each other.

Research on Aging: The Culture of Informal Networks and Formal Institutions

Dena Shenk demonstrates that life-transforming lessons can be learned through cross-national comparisons of conceptions of aging, strategies for fostering adult in(ter)dependence, and national policy. In comparing rural Denmark and Minnesota, she reveals ironies in both systems' patterns of elder care. The judgments women make about mobilizing personal sources of support or, alternatively, using institutionalized services reflect contrasting responses to aging in the two countries. Her discussion of the meanings formal institutions have for people's lives and the preoccupations elders have about privacy and control is fascinating. In Denmark, women seek privacy through impersonal services; in the U.S., women worry about losing control when they rely on institutional help. Shenk's critique of the U.S. system for its built-in blame-the-victim mentality -- because social services are thought of as a measure of the failure of an individual's personal networks to meet needs, not as a right to be exercised by all -- becomes more compelling when it is seen as one choice among other alternatives. This puts the underutilization of social services in the U.S. in new perspective, especially as both countries face cutbacks in programming.

Sue Perkins Taylor pursues the issue of underutilized elder services by urban minorities in the U.S. Her approach to the heterogeneity within our nation traces the ways social relations and cultural attitudes mediate elders' participation in federally financed programs designed to reach those in the greatest social and economic need. This analysis shows that poverty is not a unitary experience which generates a universal set of needs. Taylor organized separate discussion groups of minority elders and service providers in Cincinnati with the goal of diagnosing the problem of underutilization and offering workshops for staff members to give them access to other perspectives in their social system. The results of the focus groups were telling. Service providers, who are overwhelmingly white, attributed low minority participation to African Americans' lack of interest in social programs (as opposed to meals, for instance) and to a life before retirement of few social activities outside of work. By contrast, African American elders were more concerned with the age differences between providers and clients. They were put off by providers' attitudes that stereotyped their cultural interests and produced uninteresting programming. And they felt that some African American elders were not particularly interested in being around other seniors. Clearly, to maximize scarce resources social service staffs need to hire minorities and stress outreach, and elders need to be involved in designing activities. How one does this in racially and ethnically mixed communities remains the challenge, especially in a climate of cutbacks in social services. Taylor warns that in the past when states were given autonomy to define those in greatest need of services, the result was an unequal distribution of funds and unmet needs in some communities.

Melba Sánchez Ayéndez completes the trilogy of articles on elder care by looking at the informal support networks crucial to the welfare of Puerto Rican women in lower income Boston families. These intergenerational networks channel emotional support and interdependence. Sánchez Ayéndez explores the grounding of this philosophy of care in daughters' sense of responsibility to support their mothers for the sacrifices they made in the past when they raised their children. Her analysis finds that direct financial support is not necessarily the key issue that binds generations together; rather, if they can, mothers offer day care and meal preparation for their grandchildren when daughters are at work, and daughters routinely help their mothers with emotional support, nursing, and assistance with transportation and communication. Sánchez Ayéndez avoids idealizing the pattern by noting that, while the lines of support are mutually beneficial, middle-aged daughters come under great stress with multiple family obligations, and receive little relief in day-to-day responsibilities from their brothers. Women enhance their autonomy and responsibility when they commonly refer to men as *"como niños"* (literally "like boys"; that is, as grown-up children) who lack the emotional maturity and endurance women exhibit in the family. In part this is a tactical rebalancing of women's subordinate place in gender politics, yet it may lead to bitter disappointment as adult brothers fail to do their fair share of daily reciprocities in the support of their mothers.

Research on Anthropology and the Mismeasurement of Development

Libbet Crandon-Malamud shows us that solutions to development problems must cope with radical shifts in the nature of the problem itself. In her insightful research on Honduras, she makes the case for longer-term anthropological research to show the volatile nature of the realities in which people live and the consequences of sudden shifts in the structure and experience of conflict. Her tough lesson is that redistributive programs, such as agrarian reform in Latin America, sound great but need to be studied for their uneven consequences. (Knowing Libbet, she would have offered the same warning about today's discussions of democracy as decentralization.) In her ethnographic case study of Costa Rica, we see another instance of the social production of meanings that stigmatize certain sectors. In this instance, she reveals how structural changes undermined women's enterprises and resulted in their being personally labeled incompetent in an environment where local branches of larger organizations competed for external resources. This analysis raises important issues about women's internalization of wider tensions and conflicts displaced onto them, and the ways in which the "family" in family values is subject to atomization by wider social forces at great cost to women. The analysis also suggests that decentralized decision making is shaped by the politics of competition for resources allocated at higher levels and, thus, is not necessarily more sensitive to local needs.

Lisa Markowitz examines the institutional neglect of women agro-pastoralists in the Bolivian Andes who take care of herds of sheep and alpacas while men are in charge of the cattle. Women have wide extra-domestic managerial responsibilities, including the supervision of the juvenile work force in small-animal herding and the balancing of herding with competing crop and forage demands that change over crop cycles. While agricultural extension programs do not exclude women by definition, they do in practice through decisions about meeting times, travel schedules, language choice for agricultural publications, and male staffs (which creates potential problems with women's husbands). Information on animal care in women's areas of responsibility simply does not get to them, given the organization of nonformal education in agro-pastoralism as a masculine enterprise. This analytical framing, though insightful as a development critique, silences other issues and social dynamics. One wonders if Bolivian women have additional development priorities, muted by the interplay of national and local political structures, and if informal women's groups operate below the surface and across communities, as they do in Peru. The story of women's marginalization is incomplete and potentially disempowering without their responses and informal practices. On the basis of research on other parts of Bolivia and Peru, one also wonders about the importance of cross-regional networks created by the urban migration of some extended family members and the rural deployment of others. Older men and women are often left by their extended families to manage land and animals in an Andean form of elder care. Depending on urban political economies and family dynamics, men and women in the parental generation may lead largely urban lives, except for harvests and festivals. Their children may be sent back to their grandparents for child care or on to urban schools for opportunities not available in rural communities. These decisions are mediated by wider social fields, so, though they clearly have implications for gender politics, they are not exclusively male-female problems.

Irma McClaurin continues consideration of the issue of gender and the mismeasurement of development with an examination of the pervasiveness of women's groups and collective action in the multiethnic state of Belize. Although there are hundreds of local groups with their own leadership and agendas, most would not even register in official accountings because they have not sought money from the state or NGOs. In terms of conventional measures of success established by the development community, they would simply fail to register. McClaurin suggests an alternative way of understanding these groups and their impacts: women's own judgments about the ways in which their lives have changed and their joint sense of an active questioning of conventional female roles. Women value new forms of socialization, and they have found ways to cut down on male hostility toward their activities: invite the men and create novel options to socialize and cooperate as couples. Women phrase their needs in the language of widening educational and work opportunities, not explicitly in the language of gender inequality. Many mobilize along the existing ethnic contours of regions and communities. They respond to personal concerns about women's economic dependence, underemployment, domestic conflict, and a political economy that creates different life chances for sexually active boys and girls. This reevaluation of informal organizing is very useful. One wonders, however, about possible parallels to the pressures Crandon described, which over time corroded women's common purpose in Honduras, and about how pan-community networks in Belize deal with or evade racism. Is there an emergent consensus about women's common concerns, a development discourse that erases important differences in culture, social relations, and the social history of ethnic groups in this multi-ethnic state? Will this gendered consciousness serve as a basis for wider grassroots organizing and also, perhaps, for state intrusion to regulate community life through social policies that recreate difference and hierarchy?

Research on the Dilemmas of the Discipline and its Practitioners

Although it has become common to hear caustic dismissals of reflexive anthropology, four of these essays show how anthropologists and anthropology benefit from being included in the analytical framing. They offer strikingly different avenues for understanding and critique.

Susan Hyatt is concerned with the political implications of the ways ethnographers have historically directed their inquiries into urban African American life in the U.S. In classic research -- which formulated the culture of poverty, the street corner genre of ethnography, and Black family studies -- anthropologists reproduced images of ghettos set apart from white society and each other, and imagined an assumed norm from which African Americans were deviant. This tendency was reinforced by using more optimistic language to define crises of white poverty. Thus, regardless of their personal politics, these studies substantiated and naturalized the dominant view of racial hierarchy as inevitable. Hyatt's project as a white anthropologist is to interrogate anthropology, to

> examine [ghetto] ethnographies as a discursive field within which the poor, the Black poor in particular, were constructed as particular kinds of subjects under the scrutiny of white anthropological gaze, and to understand how those constructions reflected and upheld ... "the social" ... as a domain that could be governed through purposeful planning and regulation, rather than by force (p. 187).

Her question for anthropologists is how our work promotes particular policy agendas which might stand in tension with our political convictions. Her article explores alternative formulations -- such as community organizing and civil rights activism -- which were framed out of the analysis by these ethnographers and might have created alternatives to their disempowering narratives. Her remedy is the self-conscious analysis of the ways power is always at play so as to overdetermine the language of social analysis and reproduce hierarchies consistent with technologies of social control. This is troubling critique of a discipline which sees itself producing independent social criticism.

Barbara Rose Johnston sees room for the invention of language that will change people's consciousness of inequality. Her activist struggle as an anthropologist has been to gain recognition of the connection of human rights abuse and environmental degradation. Rights work by environmentalists has tended to focus on constitutions, legislation, and human rights conventions. Johnston argues that environmental racism is evident in the selective victimization of certain groups who are exposed to environmentally hazardous conditions at much higher rates than other groups. Her aspiration has been to use analytical strategies and case studies drawn from anthropology to bring into focus this unrecognized problem for policy makers so they would see the issue as one with a collective impact, not just another instance of individualized harm. The essay discusses her attempts to mobilize the American Anthropological Association and the Society for Applied Anthropology in order institutionally to influence the UN Subcommission on Human Rights and redirect international law in this area. She offers an anthropological strategy to challenge the status quo which appropriated international rights languages -- in this instance, the language of collective rights promulgated by indigenous movements -- for new issues. Johnston worries about measuring her efficacy in institutional terms at the same time as she has found evidence of the changing awareness in academic, human rights, and development circles. Here we see that discursive practices are not static but rather influenced by global flows of political critique.

David Nixon offers another form of self-reflexivity: a case study of teaching anthropology in a prison environment. As we have seen with discursive practice in the last two essays, Nixon finds that education cuts two ways: it calls for a submission to authority and it can be used as a resource by prisoners who attempt individually to rebuild their sense of identity and quality of life under the most difficult of circumstances. After judgment, stigmatization, and incarceration, inmates are subject to localized power structures and status hierarchies which they must master to survive. Nixon argues that the rebuilding of complex identities with a moral dimension is crucially important for prisoners. But anthropological teaching in prisons needs to be grounded in the practice of education and in the multiple identities -- internal and external -- that students (and disruptive guards who resent educational opportunities for prisoners) bring into the classroom. Nixon found that anthropology was an interesting if novel sounding board for these students. The teacher's challenge is to find locally appropriate ways of responding to students' concerns without validating aggressive behavior and to make space for different points of view without triggering violent disagreements. Tactics for responding to these dilemmas included appropriating prisoner conventions for ways to mark safe spaces for disagreement.

Finally, Barbara Johnson developed an interactive, collaborative methodology in her work in Israel with the immigrant Cochin storyteller Ruby Daniel. In her bi-cultural writing, Johnson aims to recapture the intimacy of their dialogic production of Ruby's life story from years of discussions, exchanges of drafts Ruby wrote, and a cross-national process of editing. Like the earlier writers of oral traditions in her family, Ruby wants to communicate her own knowledge and heritage to the next generation. She also uses the collaboration to contest in print her family's historical stigmatization as descendants of "freed slaves" who did not merit full rights to the synagogue in their South Indian Jewish community. Ruby imagines a heterodox audience for her work: South Asians including those who mistreated her family, Israelis of European origin who know little of South Asian Jews beyond their Eurocentric prejudices, international researchers interested in the Cochin Jews, and young relatives in Israel. In this ethnography of writing, Barbara Johnson became part of the story, without the story losing its focus on the protagonist. What Barbara so successfully captures is Ruby's engagement in the writing and editing process (that is, where the compiling and editing was frustrating, where the collaborators found the interweaving of Ruby's memories and old family stories to be a successful narrative practice, and when Ruby cared about editing decisions or not), Barbara's changing questions about the politics of the collaboration, and the role of readers as a third partner in the ultimate shape and aesthetics of the work.

These essays illustrate diverse framings of common issues and thus the limitations inherent in any one framing. For me, the grey area between stark alternatives allows for an insightful, contradictory blend of anthropology. Here opposites coexist: the power of damaging discursive formations overlaps with histories of individual and collective ingenuity. At times, all anthropologists are like the Puerto Rican women in Boston who shrug and refer to men as *"como niños."* That is, we find ourselves operating with mixtures of resistance, complicity, and subversion, where the same act carries multiple meanings that may or may not be in our control. As anthropologists, we may choose to narrate the blend in different ways, and so we must question the rationales of our choices and recognize the traces of subversive interpretations present in our ethnographic descriptions.

Throughout these essays, we see the ways in which social ideologies of difference and hierarchy are generated by institutions and ideologues who are very self-conscious about their political choices. Additionally, anthropology pursues the internalized patterns of daily activity in local communities, discursive practices there as well, that often without thinking stigmatize in ways that reinforce power differentials. We also find vibrant social criticism in the daily lives we seek to understand. These essays demonstrate the importance of Sylvia Forman's optimism that social action and critique can be used in wider partnerships (with some flatlanders but not with others) to rethink and challenge existing social arrangements. Or at least to set the record straight so echoes of prejudice can be seen in new arenas of American struggle.

Anthropology is sometimes complicit in replicating invidious patterns; yet, it is also a source of projects for deconstructing received wisdom and for answering Barbara Rose Johnston's insightful question: Who is to say what version of reality is real? As the authors of these essays demonstrate, the answers to this question are political, empirical, and terribly important.

Taken by Stephen Nichols, 1988.

'Verticality': Concept and

Practice, Past and Future[1]

Sylvia Helen Forman

An earlier version of this chapter appeared as "The Future of the "Verticality" Concept: Implications and Possible Applications in the Andes" (In *Actes du XLII Congress International des Americanists*, Paris: Societe des Americanists, 1978, Volume IV:233-256) which was reprinted in *Human Impact on Mountains*, (edited by Allan, N.J.R., G.W. Knapp and C. Stadel, NJ: Rowman and Littlefield, 1987). The revised version which appears here was published in *Papers in Honor of Richard B. Woodbury* (edited by J. Cole and R.B. Thomas, Research Report #29, Department of Anthropology, University of Massachusetts, 1993:145-164.) It is reprinted here with the permission of the Department of Anthropology. It was listed as "in press" on the final version of Sylvia's vita.

In confronting complex and urgent issues of social and economic development, the Andean nations must confront particular versions of development problems: versions that are shaped by cultural, geographical and ecological features unique to the Andean region.[2] Many of the special elements of their development problems derive from the mountainous terrain of these countries and from the interaction of the agricultural traditions of their highland areas with the policy orientations of development programs. In this paper, I explore some implications which the concept of "verticality" and related ethnographic data on the economic and ecologic integration of Andean communities have for addressing the diverse problems of highland agricultural development, now and in the future.

In examining this topic I first briefly review the general framework of Andean ecology and the model of vertical adaptation. I then outline one perspective on the problems of economic development in the Andean highlands. Finally, I discuss some of the implications and possible applications of "verticality" and related ethnographic information in treating Andean development problems.

Andean Ecology and Verticality

It has long been recognized that high mountains present difficult environments for plant and animal life, and for human societies (Peattie 1936; Tosi 1960; Troll 1968; Winterhalder and Thomas 1978). Nonetheless, humans have found it worthwhile to exploit mountain environments, and have developed cultural mechanisms that permit and facilitate such exploitation. About six percent of the world's population lives in highlands (Webber 1979:3; see also Eckholm 1975:764). In Ecuador, Peru and Bolivia, about half of the population lives in the sierra.[3]

In a general way the Andes, like other high mountain systems, present a picture of ecological zones that vary with increasing elevation above sea level. But the vertical ecozones of the Andes are not simply strata which duplicate, with rising elevation, the global bands of latitudinal variation (Tosi 1960; Troll 1968). Rather, there is immense variation among and within the ecozones of the Andes (Basile 1974; Brunnschweiler 1971; Cuatrecasas 1968; Heath et al 1969; MAB 1974; Pulgar 1946; Thomas 1979; Tosi 1960; Troll 1968; Webster 1973). This extreme degree of localized and regional variation is a function of the interplay of such factors as elevation, latitude, geologic and edaphic conditions, steepness and orientation of slope, temperature, wind and precipitation patterns, mountain mass and relief of terrain (Gade 1975; Peattie 1936; Tosi 1960; Winterhalder and Thomas 1978). To exist in the highlands, people must cope with the manifestations of these variables as local patterns of climate, terrain, soils and biotic distribution. Both the specific situational variations and the overall vertical structuring of them have great impact on the life-ways of humans living in the Andes.

The "verticality" model represents an effort to understand cultural adaptations to and utilization of the vertical zonation and extreme environmental variability of the Andean region. As proposed by Murra in his ethnohistorical studies, the model treats both cognitive and behavioral levels of response. The perceptions, knowledge and values of highland inhabitants and their economic and political activities and institutions are viewed in the context of their ecological situations (Murra 1975).[4] Murra states his main thesis this way:

> The andean universe was conceived by its inhabitants as an aggregate of floors ordered "vertically" one on top of the other, forming a macro-adaptation, a system of ecological relations distinctly andean. Ascending the landform to more and more elevated altitudes, the inhabitants had to confront continuous changes of climate, fauna and flora.
> Along the mountain range, communities and ethnic groups always had endeavored to control the greatest number possible of micro-climates. Regions which it was not possible to reach in one day's walk, or by seasonal migration, were populated by groups of permanent colonists.... (1975:204) [my translation].

In another discussion, Murra refers to "archipiélagos verticales" and examines five ethnohistorical cases of simultaneous control over vertically arranged ecological "islands", even under quite distinctive sets of conditions (1975:60-61). His examples illustrate the nature and operation of indigenous control of multiple vertical zones in small communities, larger regional ethnic groups, and states (*reinos*) of large scale. He emphasizes that vertical control of a maximum possible number of ecological zones was an ideal -- as well as a practice -- of a range of Andean societies, in different geographic regions, of very different scales of economic and political complexity and he goes on to note that such distinctions among Andean social groups inevitably implied other differences in the institutional forms of their verticality (1975:60).

Sylvia in the field in highland Ecuador, 1970.

Since Murra outlined the ethnohistorical framework of the verticality model, many ethnographic studies have illustrated that access to distinct ecological zones is still very important to highland agriculturalists and that significant variations in the organization of verticality still exist among *campesino* (small scale farmers and herders) communities and ethnic groups in the Andes (see for example Basile 1974; Brush 1973, 1977; Burke 1971; Carter 1965; Collins 1984; Custred 1973,[5] 1974; Dorsey 1975; Flores 1968; Love 1989; Mayer 1974; McCorkle 1987; Mitchell 1976; Orlove 1974, 1977; Webster 1971; Weismantel 1988).

Drawing on a range of ethnographic examples, as well as on Murra's model, Brush (1974) has distinguished three types of ecologic integration of peasant groups in the Andes: compact, archipelago, and extended. His first type, "el tipo compacto," is found where a set of very different vertical ecological zones occur in close proximity to each other and are accessible to the members of a community directly, without requiring major travel or extensive exchange with other communities (Brush 1974:292-293). "El tipo archipiélago," the second type, is basically that delineated by Murra (1975), in which the ecological zones utilized by a social group are more or less distant from each other and separated by unused areas (Brush 1974:293-294). Access to the different zones requires extended travel (several or more days) and sometimes involves establishing permanent colonies from the home community in diverse sites. Because such colonists remain members of their home community, the modes of exchange that characterize the archipelago type of vertical control are reciprocity and redistribution, rather than commercial trade. In the third type, "el tipo extendído," each community involved exploits directly only one or a few of the ecological zones in a region, specializing in certain products. Access to needed products of other ecological zones comes through exchange among communities based in different ecozones. Such exchange may take a variety of forms, including barter and marketing (Brush 1974:294-295; also see examples in Burchard 1974; Casaverde 1977; Custred 1974; Flores 1975, 1977, 1985; Markowitz mss.; Mayer 1971; Orlove 1974; Webster 1973).

In a comparative discussion of cultural/ecological patterns in mountain environments, Rhoades and Thompson (1975) suggest that two broadly defined types of adaptive strategies may be distinguished. Their "generalized" type "involves a single population which, through agro-pastoral transhumance, directly exploits a series of microniches or ecozones at several altitudinal levels," while in their "specialized" type

> a population locks into a single zone and specializes in the agricultural or pastoral activities suitable to that altitude, developing elaborate trade relationships with populations in other zones which are also involved in specialized production (Rhoades and Thompson 1975:547).

Both of their types are found in the Andes, although communities with "generalized" adaptive strategies may or may not rely on pastoralism in addition to agricultural pursuits.

My own research, in the central highlands of Ecuador, and other recent studies (e.g., Collins 1984; Love 1989; Markowitz mss; Orlove 1987) indicate that under contemporary economic conditions -- of increased cash cropping and wage labor, improved transportation, and expanded capitalist market penetration -- more traditional forms of exploitation of vertical ecozones have declined in prevalence or even disappeared in much (or most) of the Andean region. Current "mixed" types of verticality may involve direct access to one or a few ecozones by members of a campesino community, combined with indirect access to other resources through exchange with communities based in different ecozones or, increasingly, through commercial marketing.

Custred has pointed out that we need to take two approaches to the study of human life-ways in the highlands:

> One is to investigate adaptations to specific vertical life zones, the other to examine the uses made of the entire range of such zones and the role this has played in shaping the social and economic patterns of mountain populations (1973:50).

The verticality model -- or "ecological complementarity" in more recent usage (Shimada 1985) -- represents the general principles of past adaptive strategies of social groups in the highlands. Ethnographic data provide a complementary set of descriptions of how specific local groups exploit the ecozones (and other economic options) available to them. I return to these two levels of study in my discussion of possible applications of verticality to agricultural development.

Some Andean Problems of Development

In addition to exhibiting a great degree of local variability, the Andes, like other high mountain regions, are a most fragile ecosystem (Billings 1979; MAB 1974:21ff; Thomas 1979).

> When the environment starts to deteriorate on steep mountain slopes, it deteriorates quickly
> -- far more so than on gentler slopes and on plains. And the damage is far more likely to
> be irreversible (Eckholm 1975:765).

In montane environments, such phenomena as deforestation, poor agricultural practices, over-grazing of pastures, and improper irrigation very rapidly lead to decline in soil fertility, erosion, and soil compaction. Highland erosion has the direct effect of leaving the eroded land partially or entirely unusable for agriculture, forestry, animal husbandry, or even tourism. It further has secondary effects of major importance. It leads, in particular, to greater damage from earthquakes and landslides, local loss of water for agricultural and domestic use (due to increased surface run-off), periodic flooding of down-stream lowland areas, and reduction of hydroelectric and irrigation capacities through silting of lower river courses and of lakes and reservoirs (Eckholm 1975; Hewitt 1976; Ives 1979; MAB 1974:21, 119; 1975:9-10, 117-18).

Such irreversible and dangerous damage to the Andean ecosystem, and its surrounding watersheds and plains, is not an abstract or distant matter. Significant erosion and soil deterioration has taken place already. Current practices of agriculture, pastoralism and forest utilization -- founded in population growth, agricultural intensification, and capitalist development endeavors -- continue to reduce the life-support capacity of the highlands and to threaten the usefulness of adjacent lowlands.

The fragile nature of the highland environment and the ramifications of continuing damage to it constitute serious problems in themselves. They also stand as the necessary background for understanding some of the other development problems of the Andean countries. I outline certain aspects of these problems below. But first I must note that the view I present is far from a complete picture. Indeed, our current knowledge does not encompass all the interrelated social and environmental problems of Andean change and development (see Ives 1979; Salomon 1985). Further, my sketch here does not attempt to express all of the complexities and local variations of the difficulties of development in the Andean agro-pastoral sector, nor does it adequately represent the systemic nature of these problems (i.e., the feedbacks among the components and levels of the problems). My discussion is based on an assumption that economic development is a necessary, and feasible, goal of the Andean countries and, moreover, that one major aspect of Andean development must be improvement in the quality of life of the small producers, the campesinos, in the context of their agricultural and pastoral communities.

One crucially important issue in Andean development is population. While it probably cannot reasonably be said that the Andean countries are presently over-populated, it can be noted that they are likely to be so within the next couple of decades, since their population growth rates are high.[6] The pressure of increasing population, now and in the future, creates increasing demands for food, housing, fuel, and jobs, and also for social services. There are also pressures for improving the living standards of this growing population -- so demands for increases in goods and services rise at higher rates than the rate of population growth itself.

Food production, in particular, is not increasing sufficiently rapidly in the Andean countries (Anderson 1975; Orlove 1987; World Bank 1988). Efforts to expand production of food (and of fiber and wood), in the context of inadequate inputs and infrastructure, contribute to overuse and misuse of the highland ecosystem.

As noted above, damage to the mountain environment is already marked and is continuing to be aggravated. Such environmental deterioration undercuts contemporary efforts to raise the level of agricultural production and to improve the quality of life of the poorer portion of the population. Moreover, because much of this damage is either irreversible or reversible only over long time periods, it also bodes very badly for the long term capacity of the highland ecosystem to contribute to the support of increasing populations in the Andean nations. On-going degradation of the highland environment will inevitably exacerbate existing problems of poor nutrition and poor health in rural areas, migration to urban areas, and under- and unemployment.

It appears that the Andean countries are caught in a "vicious circle," in which increasing population and demand for food and for cash income mean more pressure on the land, with resultant environmental deterioration and lowered agricultural output, yet more pressure on remaining arable land, and so on around. One effect of this cycle is relatively rapid depopulation of rural areas of the Andean highlands.[7] Clearly that outcome is not desirable: it not only means that crucially needed land and labor are removed from food production, but it also creates new problems of the urban resettlement and employment of the displaced campesinos. Since the Andean countries do not have, and in the immediate future do not seem likely to have, an industrial base large enough to employ a significant percentage of the peasantry, it seems both desirable and necessary to have a large proportion of their populations remain in primary agricultural activity.[8]

One possible way to break this positive feedback system is to have the death rate increase; but this is an undesirable, and humanely and politically untenable, approach. Another possible way to escape the vicious circle is to decrease the rate of population growth by lowering the birth rate. This is certainly a component of any eventual solution. But there is good evidence that people do not voluntarily control their fertility until their standard of living reaches a certain minimum level (see Rich 1973).[9] The living standard necessary for reduction of population growth through voluntarily controlled fertility is well above that of most of the rural population of the Andean countries. The conclusion is that the campesinos' standard of living will have to be improved by some means before their birth rate declines.

Yet another possible way to break the circle is to make massive inputs of technology (of industrial and/or green revolution sorts) into the highland agricultural sector. However, this tactic also presents problems: the costs of importing technology, the feasibility of employing such technology in the highly variable mountain ecosystem, the potentially deleterious effects of such technology in terms of pollution and further environmental deterioration (Alexander 1974, IUCN 1968; Johnson 1972; Jorgenson 1971; Schumacher 1975; Sternberg 1973), and the potential conflicts between the technological inputs and existing social organization (Coutu and King 1969; Kottack 1990; Thiesenhusen 1974). More moderate inputs of agricultural technology are not likely to lead, by themselves, to sufficiently increased levels of production, and would still present many of the same problems as massive inputs.[10]

From the perspective of this discussion, the general problem might be phrased: how, without doing irreparable damage to the highland ecosystem, can the quality of life of the highland population be improved to such a level that people will continue their farming enterprises and that their rate of population growth will decline? Stabilizing the population would alleviate some of the increasing pressure on the mountain environment and permit maintaining it in such condition that it could continue indefinitely to provide needed resources for human use.[11]

While the more obvious and urgent problems of development in the Andean nations can be expressed in terms of factors such as poor nutrition, lagging agricultural production, underemployment, erosion, etc., less obvious problems arise from the very efforts to deal with these primary issues. These secondary problems derive from the development process itself when, due to corruption, misunderstanding, bias, lack of relevant information, or poorly elaborated policy, development programs ignore problem areas or take actions that create new sources of difficulty or exacerbate existing ones. Certain aspects of the ideas, attitudes and behaviors of political leaders of the Andean countries and of national and international development planners and agencies stand out as past and future sources of these secondary development problems.

There is a general tendency among development agencies in the Andean countries (as elsewhere) to use the industrialized western countries as direct models for development, rather than creating approaches which are better adapted to local features of resources, ecology and culture (Kottack 1990; Sternberg 1973).[12] While environmental degradation has come to be recognized as a major set of problems in the industrialized countries, many planners and political leaders in the Andean nations are not urgently concerned with conservation and anti-pollution issues (IUCN 1968; MAB 1975:22; Sternberg 1973).[13] And, while there is some increased interest recently in indigenous agricultural methods and in intermediate technology, there still is continuation of the tendency among Andean development specialists to prefer "hard" to "soft" technology, commercial to subsistence crops, larger-scale capital-intensive to smaller-scale labor-intensive productive institutions, novel to traditional agricultural methodologies (see Gade 1969:49; Sternberg 1973; Tendler 1975; Thiesenhusen 1974). The development agents are more impressed by and concerned with encouraging agricultural development in the "easier" coastal regions than in the highlands (Tendler 1975:313-337; Wetering 1973:5, 8). This fact may be related to the negative image that most Andean developers seem to have of highland peasants in general and of Quechua- and Aymara-speaking Indian peasants in particular (Forman 1972; Tendler 1975:282-283). In addition, most development planners are and think like "flat-landers." That is: they conceive the problems of agricultural (and other economic) development in the

Andes as though the environment were horizontally rather than vertically arranged and as though it were homogenous rather than immensely varied (see Rhoades and Thompson 1975:548-549).

Such concepts and attitudes of development agents can and do generate many sorts of new problems, ranging from extreme balance-of-payments deficits and external debts (for imported food and technology) to loss of genetic variability of plants and animals (as species are decimated or traditional crops are dropped from production [Gade 1975; IUCN 1968:83; NSF 1989]). Inappropriate development strategies also lead to enormous waste of international and national resources in specific projects that are doomed to failure because of their designs and to unproductive disruptions of traditional agricultural systems.

Given the fragility of the Andean environment and the human costs of creating new problems or aggravating old ones, it is clear that research to improve our knowledge of the highland ecosystem and the human place in it should precede or at least accompany development activities. A number of anthropologists, geographers, and ecologists have underlined the current limitations of our understanding both of the natural conditions of the Andes and of the human ways of dealing with those conditions (Custred 1973:49-50; Dickinson 1971; Heath et al 1969:388-389; Ives 1979; Jorgenson 1971; MAB 1974, 1975; Momsen 1971; Salomon 1985). But at the same time, much valuable information, about the ecological and cultural complexities of the highlands, already is available for use in development planning (see Browman 1987a). This information could and should be utilized by development planners to help them achieve a thorough-going recognition of the special problems of the highlands and an understanding that these problems may be enlarged rather than reduced by programs designed for other ecological and social situations.

Murra makes a relevant point when he says that in the Viceroy Toledo's _reducciones_ (in the 16th century) "the patterns of vertical ecologic control were ignored, thus reducing the resources available and permanently impoverishing the Andean economy" (1970:9). It appears that current efforts at economic development in the Andean countries similarly ignore -- or even oppose -- ecological complementarity, and related pertinent data and concepts, and hence are on the threshold of even more thoroughly damaging the environmental and economic underpinnings of the highlands.

Implications and Applications of "Ecological Complementarity"

There are both general and specific ways in which anthropological concepts and ethnographic data may be applied in Andean rural development. The most general application is probably a precondition to the effective implementation of any others; it concerns the expectations and ethnocentrism of those managing the development process. Some of the attitudes of development planners have been mentioned above. The first step here is to present some general responses to them.

Preference for western industrial models has been, and largely still is, strong among Andean developers. Yet we know that industrial, modern, scientific ways -- i.e., hard technology, capital-intensive ways -- of doing things are not the only ones and, indeed, may not be the most desirable or effective approaches in many circumstances (Evans 1979; Schumacher 1975). Moreover, economically rational development does not necessarily mean the same thing in all times and all places (Popkin 1981; Schumacher 1975; Skinner 1976, esp. pp. 5, 19). The subsistence orientation of peasants can be preferable to a commercial orientation under many conditions (Nietschmann 1971; Sternberg 1973). Family-size farms are often more productive (per land unit) than larger operations (Thiesenhusen 1974).

Peasants, including Quechua- and Aymara-speaking Andean campesinos, seem to be viewed by development agents as ignorant and irrationally conservative. Of course, since their economic situations are generally precarious, peasant producers do tend to be conservative, but their resistance to change is not automatic and, especially in such matters as agricultural practices, must often be seen as rational and even wise given their knowledge of the resources available to them (see Rhodes and Thompson 1975:548-549). Indeed, their understanding of their environment and its limitations is usually far more profound than that of externally-trained development workers (e.g., Gladwin 1979). Moreover, peasant conservatism should not be viewed as refusal to innovate and experiment. The evidence is conclusive that they are creative and proactive about change when economic and cultural conditions are appropriate (Johnson 1972; Mayer 1985:53; Thiesenhusen 1974).

Given the above, the starting points for the application of ethnographic data and the verticality concept to Andean development must be: (1) an appreciation for the adaptations already made by highland agriculturalists (and their ancestors) to their unusual environment, and (2) a willingness to consider seriously routes to rural development that are non-ethnocentric and non-industrial, in terms of values and models of rationality as well as in terms of scale and type of technology.

The verticality model, in its most general form, tells us that access to and exploitation of multiple vertical ecozones -- either directly or indirectly through exchanges -- is the Andean cultural method for achieving a tolerable subsistence level in an unpredictable, fragile, and complexly heterogeneous environment. Inherent limitations on agro-pastoral production in any one ecozone are made up for by the utilization of more than one vertical zone. Although Murra (1975) has shown that verticality has operated as an integrating principle on scales as great as the indigenous Andean kingdoms, I think that in application to modern problems of rural development, the verticality model will be most useful on the levels of the local community and region.

Ethnographic information on the ways that verticality actually operates indicates that specific adaptations (in the forms of crop mixes, types of livestock, or systems of exchange) enable the exploitation of a wide range of ecozones, with some kind of optimal usage pattern for each ecozone being exploited (Brush 1973, 1977; Burchard 1974; Carter 1965; Custred 1973, 1977; Dorsey 1975; Flores 1968, 1975, 1985; Harris 1985; Heyduk 1974; Mayer 1971, 1974, 1985;

Mitchell 1976; Orlove 1973, 1974; Vallée 1971; Webster 1971, 1973). The nature and extent of ecological complementarity in a given community or region in the Andes is, then, a function not only of the vertical ecozones available, but also of social organization and of the human manipulation of plants and animals, tools and productive techniques in interaction with the environment.

There is no question about the need for increased agricultural productivity in the Andean countries. There seems to be general agreement that increased production should -- or will have to -- come about primarily through more effective use of existing farm and grazing lands, rather than through the opening of new land (Coutu and King 1969; Sternberg 1973; Thiesenhusen 1974). Generating greater agro-pastoral yields in the highlands requires some changes in productive methods. Among the requirements are: improved crop and livestock varieties, maintenance of soil fertility, control of crop pests, and conservation of arable land and water resources. But these requirements must be fulfilled within the bounds of the campesinos' economic and ecologic circumstances. Ethnographic information on specific adaptive features of highland agriculture and pastoralism can be used as a foundation for determining appropriate changes, and I draw on such data in the discussion below. The suggestions made in this discussion are far from exhaustive of the possibilities. Rather, and apart from any intrinsic merits they may have, they are meant primarily to indicate *types* of development approaches that could contribute to raising the standard of living of Andean small-scale agro-pastoralists and to increasing highland agricultural productivity without great cost and without further damaging the highland ecosystem.

Livestock

The camelids, especially the llama and alpaca, have long been an important component of multiple ecozone exploitation in a large area of the central and southern Andes. Camelids are adapted to life at elevations up to almost 5000 meters. Because they can eat the coarse grasses available as pasture at high elevations, camelids are the crucial intermediaries in human exploitation of very high elevation ecozones -- *páramo* and *puna*[14] -- that cannot be used effectively for crop production (Browman 1987b; Custred 1973:19-20; Flores 1975: 300-301; Webster 1971:177). While some other livestock, particularly sheep, can be raised at high elevations, "the llama is the most efficient converter of altiplano vegetation to live animal weight" (Stouse 1970:138).

The llama and alpaca provide Andean campesinos with fiber, bone and hides, meat and fat, transport, and dung for use as fuel and fertilizer (Custred 1973; Flores 1975; Markowitz mss; Orlove 1977; Stouse 1970; Webster 1971; Winterhalder et al 1974). Improved yields from camelid herds -- in terms of greater reproductive efficiency, higher quality fiber, and more meat production -- could contribute significantly to improving the diet and/or increasing the cash income of many campesino families. There has been research on camelid breeding and husbandry carried out since the 1960's (IVITA 1972; PAL 1988), but there is undoubtedly a need for much more. Further, there is a strong need for effective dissemination of the results of camelid research to small-scale pastoralists (Kuit 1990:12-130). To allow camelid herding to decline is to forfeit the option of exploiting certain of the available ecozones.

To benefit fully from increased yields of fiber and meat, Andean pastoralists must be able to exchange camelid products for other goods. Such exchange requires more effective marketing mechanisms and infrastructure than now exist. Both producers and consumers would gain from legal means, with appropriate sanitary measures, for marketing camelid meat. Improvement of fiber quality and yield needs to be backed up by marketing mechanisms that encourage campesinos to market partially and completely finished wool products as well as raw wool, control the quality of marketed wool, and insure prices which reflect an adequate return for peasant labor.[15] In some regions marketing camelid products might involve some exchange among communities in different vertical ecozones as a first stage (e.g., exchange of raw wool for agricultural produce) and commercial marketing as a later stage (e.g., finished wool products for cash). In regions where pastoralists do not traditionally engage in any agriculture, camelid (and sheep and cattle) dung is sometimes sold or bartered to agricultural communities. Increases in herd size and/or improvements in transportation or marketing means in these regions might lead to increased distribution of dung for fertilizer and fuel. This would not only profit the pastoralists, but would be important in communities in which people cannot afford to purchase other fuels or chemical fertilizers.

In conjunction with efforts to improve yields from camelids, several steps are necessary to insure that pastoralists receive benefits from increased production without endangering the delicate puna and paramo environments. In recent decades in some areas, population growth has led to increased herd sizes and to overgrazing (Guillet 1987; Tosi 1960:130-142). Overgrazing lowers the productive capacity of pastures, makes water control more difficult, and leaves pasture lands vulnerable to erosion. Improving the quality of pasturage, by seeding and using irrigation where possible, and encouragement of cultivation of fodder would contribute to increasing livestock yields and would alleviate some of the danger of overgrazing.

Despite their efficiency in using puna and paramo ecozones and the value of their products, camelids are not evenly distributed throughout the Andes (Gade 1977).[16] Improved breeding and more effective husbandry methods might make camelids attractive (re-) introductions to regions where they are not now raised, opening to the campesinos of those areas opportunities to exploit ecological sectors that are presently of marginal utility.

Cultigens

While some Andean campesino groups specialize in pastoralism, a far greater proportion engages in a combination of livestock and crop production and many rely almost entirely on crops. Successful agriculture in the highlands requires a diversity of crops (to match the diversity of ecozones) and certain types of crops that are suitable for cultivation at higher elevations and under specific ecological conditions.

A number of tubers, legumes and grains are native Andean domesticants and are well adapted to specific highland ecological conditions. Important among these native cultigens are: tarwi (*Lupinus mutabilis*), a legume; oca (*Oxalis tuberosa*), melloco (*Ollucus tuberosus*), mashua (*Tropaeolum tuberosum*) and many varieties of potatoes (*Solanum* spp.), all tubers; maize (*Zea mays*), quinoa (*Chenopodium quinoa*) and canihua (*Chenopodium pallidicaule*), grains (see Milstead 1928; NRC 1989; Pulgar 1946:110-120). While some food plants have been introduced historically into Andean agriculture with success -- particularly barley, wheat and fava beans -- and while it may be that some other crops might still be introduced,[17] there is much to be said in favor of heavy reliance on the indigenous highland crops in efforts to increase agricultural productivity.

The native Andean cultivars constitute a fund of plant genetic variability and of indigenous agricultural knowledge that it is crucial to preserve for the future (Gade 1969; NRC 1989; Rowe 1969; Sternberg 1973). In the Andes, and elsewhere (NRC 1989:15), these crops hold great potential for improving diet and nutrition and for enabling exploitation of ecozones that are not suitable for the production of other species. In addition, some of the traditional Andean crops have significant potential for commercial export. With appropriate research and improvement in stock and production techniques, some of the native crops, which are already adapted to local environments, could contribute greatly to the effort to increase agricultural production in the highlands. Unfortunately, most of the native crops have not been the subjects of agricultural research efforts (NRC 1989; Thiesenhusen 1974).

"At the time of the Spanish conquest, the Incas cultivated almost as many species of plants as the farmers of all Asia or Europe" (NRC 1989:1). Many indigenous crops were replaced by European species at the demand of the Spanish rulers. Of the thirty or more traditional crops which continued in cultivation into this century (NRC 1989:3), many recently are declining in or being dropped from production (Brown 1987; Gade 1969, 1970, 1975; Leonard and Thomas 1988). They are being displaced, in some cases, by introduced species which have higher yields under ideal conditions (but often have lower or no yield when conditions are not optimal), or which are in more demand in the market. In other instances, shifting ("modernizing") dietary preferences (see Orlove 1987) or difficulties of preparation of the native crops lead to reduction in their cultivation.

Canihua (or kaniwa), for example, is one of the traditional crops whose production is limited and declining. Yet it is of great potential value in highland agriculture:

> Perhaps no other crop is so resistant to the combination of frosts, drought, salty soil, and pests, or requires such little care in its cultivation. At the same time, few grains have such a high protein content as does canihua (13.8%), surpassing quinoa (12.3%), wheat (12.0%), barley (9.7%), or maize (9.4%) (Gade 1970:55).

Canihua grows at very high elevations -- in protected sites as high as 4500m. Its resistance to frost, drought, and pests makes it an excellent form of crop insurance in higher ecozones. Because it has different nutrient requirements from potatoes and other tuber crops, it can successfully be planted the year after a field is used for tubers. Canihua can be eaten as a whole grain or can be made into flour. Its major drawback is that the covering of the seeds must be removed, by soaking in water and rubbing, before the grain can be consumed (NRC 1989:134). Quinoa, a close relative of canihua, is almost as hardy and as nutritionally valuable as canihua. But its seed-coating contains a very bitter saponin and thus it shares the problem requiring laborious processing.

Limited research to date indicates that these chenopoids can be improved by selective breeding for non-bitter varieties and for increased yields (NRC 1989:124-161; IUCN 1968). Availability of improved varieties could lead to increased production of these crops by small farmers. Both quinoa and canihua could be used within the Andean countries to improve nutrition. Moreover, there is a developing, "gourmet," export market for quinoa.

Tarwi, a legume, is another native crop which is disappearing from cultivation despite significant potential as a source of protein and oil. Tarwi can be grown up to elevations of about 3600m. Like canihua, it serves as an insurance crop, as it is more resistanttent to cold and insects than maize or fava beans. Like other legumes, tarwi is a nitrogen-fixer and releases nitrogen to the soil. Thus it fits as a form of fertilizer into a rotation pattern in which it is planted the year before tubers, maize or beans. While tarwi is an excellent source of protein, its seeds contain a bitter (and mildly toxic) alkaloid that must be extracted by soaking for several days. Again, improved varieties, bred for greater yields and a non-bitter seed, could be developed and would lead to increased cultivation. (See Gade 1969; NRC 1989:181-189.)

Tarwi, quinoa and canihua serve as examples of the potential value of native highland food plants. They and other Andean crops, particularly the tubers (see Rowe 1969), should be the subjects of intensive research and selective breeding to enhance their ecological adaptations, eliminate their limitations, and expand their planting range (NRC 1989). To a far greater degree than introduced species, these crops can form the bases for more intensive high elevation agriculture. That they are primarily subsistence rather than commercial export crops, or that they are associated with Indians (Gade 1969:49; NRC 1989:11), are not reasonable grounds for agricultural research and development agencies to ignore them.

Agricultural Practices

Increased and improved use of fertilizers is another important component in the effort to intensify highland agriculture. Andean peasants are well aware of the importance of fertilizer application, but few of them can afford to purchase chemical fertilizers. Traditionally they use the dung of camelids, sheep and cattle on their fields. However, quantities of dung from domestic animals are not adequate for intensified agricultural production.

Composting of animal dung and vegetable matter, for use as fertilizer, does not seem to be a fully developed practice among Andean agriculturalists. This probably is due in part to the fact that at high elevations the rate of organic decay is very slow (Cabrera 1968). But even if decomposition is slow and incomplete, composting would improve the quality of organic fertilizers and make more efficient use of potential fertilizer materials. The techniques of composting are relatively simple and inexpensive and could be easily incorporated by campesinos. Research might indicate some methods for improving rates of decomposition, even in colder areas, and point to mixtures of compost materials which would provide the organic and mineral elements needed in specific local soils. Increased application of composted material would contribute directly to increasing crop yields and would facilitate more intensive cultivation by compensating for reduced fallow periods of fields.

A major reason for the apparent lack of attention to composting is the emphasis placed on the value of chemical fertilizers by many professional agronomists, who share some of the pro-industrial, anti-traditional biases mentioned above. Yet both Chinese and U.S. agricultural experience -- as well as that of the Andean farmers -- illustrates the value of organic fertilizers (Champeau 1975; NAS 1975; Wade 1975). Moreover, organic fertilizers are less likely than chemical ones to contribute to water pollution, and they are far less expensive. Manure and compost not only supply nutrients for crops, as do chemical fertilizers, but they also provide organic matter, which is the basis of biological activity, to soils. Organic matter improves soil structure and water retention and also helps bind the soil, lessening erosion (Winterhalder et al 1974).

Reduction in the amount of crop loss due to insect pests and plant diseases would also help increase highland agricultural yields. One possible partial solution to the problem of insect and disease damage is the development and dissemination of pest-resistant varieties of crops. Another possible tactic is the use of naturally occurring controls, such as predator insects. Both of these approaches require much more intensive research on highland cultivars and their parasites than has been undertaken so far. Chemical pesticides, of course, are yet another possible approach to reducing crop damage. But chemical pesticides are very expensive -- especially by the standards of Andean farmers -- and most of them are dangerous to use and are ecologically harmful and polluting. If pesticides are to be used, even in limited quantities, the safest and least expensive ones should be chosen. One of the safest pesticides known is pyrethrum. It is made from the flowers of *Pyrethrum aureum*, a plant which grows at elevations up to at least 3000 m and is already cultivated in limited quantities in the Andes. If local processing facilities were available pyrethrum production could be increased. This would be of direct economic benefit to pyrethrum growers and would make a relatively safe pesticide available to small agriculturalists at much lower prices than imported chemical ones.[18]

Intensification of highland agriculture is also predicated on adequate land and water resources. Maintenance of soils and of water supplies in the Andes requires prevention of erosion and of surface run-off of water. The best means for controlling erosion on steep slopes is to terrace fields. Terracing of arable slopes was extensively practiced by the pre-conquest societies of the highlands, but has largely disappeared from the Andean peasants' repertory of agricultural practices.[19] The re-introduction of terracing, in those regions where steepness of slope and local ecological conditions call for it, is urgently needed to prevent further erosion and enhance control of water for agricultural purposes. It has also been suggested that in some regions the traditional practice of building and cultivating raised fields could be reinstated to dramatic effects in terms of crop yields (NRC 1989:8-12).

As the lack of forests in the Andes is known to be a primary cause of soil erosion, reforestation is seen already as a necessity. All the Andean countries have initiated reforesting efforts in the highlands. However, a number of problems are involved in reforestation. One of these is the issue of which land should be reforested and under what sorts of arrangements with rural communities (Budowski 1968:161). In this regard, there is a need for greater integration into forestry planning of information about the existing land use and ownership patterns -- including verticality practices -- of local campesino communities. Possible campesino uses of forest products also needs consideration in planning reforestation.

The employment for reforestation of already eroded land and of zones too dry or too steep for farming is an obvious option. But forest development cannot be planned in isolation. The possibilities, in some areas, of interspersing or combining pasturage and forests deserves greater attention. In many parts of the Andes, population pressure has led already to the use of marginal ecozones for agriculture. If reforestation efforts were joined with efforts to improve and intensify farming in optimal areas, more marginal zones might be turned to tree production, to the benefit both of the campesinos and the environment.

Another issue in highland reforestation is the types of trees to be used. Emphasis to date has been on the use of eucalyptus and secondarily of certain pines (Budowski 1968:159-160). Apparently little attention or research is being devoted to the possibilities of using native highland trees -- including food-producing species -- for reforestation, despite the fact that they are adapted to local ecological conditions and could be improved to suit specific ecological and cultural needs (NRC 1989; Sharp 1970).

The principles of drawing on local traditions and resources in developing culturally integrated technology which is low-cost and ecologically safe can be extended to a number of areas that relate directly to enhancing the living standards of Andean small agriculturalists. For example, local variants of improved stoves for burning dung, wood and straw could be developed. This same approach might be used in many other ways: to improve means of storing foods for better preservation and less loss to rodents, or to design a cheap, simple grain milling machine that could be powered by streams or in integration with irrigation works. Even manufacture and introduction of small-scale mechanized agricultural tools, such as simple corn-huskers or small garden tractors or rototillers, are feasible. The main determinants of success for these kinds of efforts to develop the rural highland economy are the devotion of sensitive attention to the productive traditions, needs and limitations of campesino agro-pastoralism and the integration of planned changes with each other as well as with the existing culture and ecology.[20]

Policies and Programs

Ethnographic information on patterns of traditional exploitation of specific ecozones is particularly valuable as a basis for planning specific kinds of changes in agricultural practices, crops and technology. When ethnographic data of this kind are subsumed in the more general model of verticality, a range of broader possible applications becomes evident. The verticality model -- informed by information on historical and contemporary campesino life-ways -- has significant implications for policies and programs of land reform, agrarian legal reform, agricultural extension, and infrastructure building that are so fundamental to increased agricultural production and improved standard of living in the highlands.

The training of agriculturalists and extension personnel should incorporate knowledge of ecological complementarity and foster an appreciation for appropriate utilization of local ecozones. At a minimum, agricultural extension work should include attention to understanding local operation of verticality and the ramifications of verticality in terms of local diversity of crops and productive techniques. Calendrical agricultural patterns (e.g., transhumance movements) which are linked to vertical integration should also be taken into consideration by extension agents. The labor demands of exploiting several ecozones dictate rural patterns of geographic movement and daily and seasonal use of time and work force. To make effective contributions to the development of campesino groups, extension agencies must be flexible and adapt their activities to the places and time made available in the highland agricultural routine -- not vice versa.

One of the most important and general possible applications of the verticality model is in land reform. There is little evidence that land reform policies in the Andean countries, over the last three decades, have had maintenance or enhancement of verticality as an explicit goal.[21] In Bolivia, land reform has been carried out sometimes in such a manner than verticality has been maintained in communities where it already existed (see Burke 1971; Dorsey 1975; Harris 1985). More generally, it seems that land reform regulations have reduced the access of communities to multiple vertical ecozones (see Browman 1987b; Mayer 1985: 69; Scott 1974:342). Indeed, Murra (1985:10) asserts that there has been governmental opposition to ecological complementarity, consistently from the early colonial period right through recent agrarian reforms.

It seems obviously highly desirable -- at least from the perspectives of the campesinos and conservationists -- to incorporate considerations of verticality into all phases of land reform planning and implementation in the Andes. In general, such application of the verticality model should mean examination of the possibilities for direct exploitation of contiguous vertical ecozones in a given locale, whether or not such a pattern of exploitation is the existing practice. Then, as appropriate, land redistribution and agrarian regulations should be compatible with optimal productive use of the ecozones available. In instances where vertical patterns of land use already exist, examination of these patterns and of their significance to a community should precede reallocation of land and help dictate the form the redistribution will take.

Incorporation of verticality into land reform programs should also include attention to local patterns of residence, communal land holding, cooperative labor, and economic exchange beyond the community (see Browman 1987b; Scott 1974:342-343). Highland communities range in settlement patterns from completely nucleated to extremely dispersed. Where members of a community are directly exploiting a set of vertical ecozones, they may have residences in more than one area (Brush 1973; Flores 1975, 1985; Webster 1973). Sometimes settlement and residence patterns may be artifacts of hacienda organization, but in other instances they can be products of long-standing local verticality practices. Where residence and settlement forms are closely linked to verticality, land reform actions should not disrupt them.

It is not uncommon in the Andes for campesino communities to possess communal lands (see Basile 1974:71; Mayer 1974; Webster 1973). However, the nature and scale of communal land holdings is highly variable, ranging from small areas of pasture to some or all of the arable land of a community, and may be derived from historical patterns or from recent legal actions (Forman 1972; Guillet 1981). The type of communal holding in a given community may be integral with practices of verticality. Land reform agencies need to determine prior and/or existing patterns of communal land holding and use before either reducing its type and extent or attempting to augment the degree of communal land use. Generalized theories that highland Indians are all communally oriented are belied by the actual diversity of cultural traditions and campesino behavior, and ought not to be blindly applied.

Similar injunctions apply in the case of cooperative labor practices. Cooperative and communal labor practices are also highly variable both in organization and degree of importance (see Carter 1965; Fonseca 1974; Forman 1972; Isbell 1974; Mitchell 1976; Orlove 1974). Such cooperative work forms as *minga* and *ayni* (see Fonseca 1974; Orlove 1974) have different bases in different regions of the highlands and can relate to some aspect of verticality as well as to the kinship and political organization of a community. In no instance, however, should they be mistaken for some general or inherent propensity for cooperative organization. Rather, their role in local production and community organization should be examined carefully before efforts are made to modify or elaborate them. The frequent failures of cooperative organizations established in connection with land reform illustrate the problems that can arise from ill-founded efforts to create collective labor institutions where they do not fit with local cultural and ecological patterns (Alberti and Mayer 1974:32-33; Browman 1987b; Brush 1973:13; Heath et al 1969:393; Orlove 1974:320; Tendler 1975; Webster 1971:179).

In areas where verticality has operated through exchange mechanisms (of market or non-market types), land reform and changes in transportation networks or commercial opportunities may either enhance or reduce access to the products of multiple ecozones (see Burchard 1974; Custred 1973; Flores 1975:309-311; Love 1989; Mayer 1971).[22] Exchange of labor (e.g., at harvest time) for food among communities may be an important avenue of access to the resources of other ecozones (Burchard 1974; Custred 1974:282-284), and ought not to be undercut by agrarian legislation (Alberti and Mayer 1974:30-33; Scott 1974:343).

In terms of raising the standard of living of highland peasants, direct exchanges among communities in different vertical ecozones may be preferable to shunting the flow of products from different zones through a commercial market in which a significant portion of the value of those products is diverted to the profits of large-scale entrepreneurs. Traditional forms of exchange could and should be supported by appropriately oriented development of rural infrastructure (e.g., roads, credit facilities, small markets, agricultural extension). The fact that campesinos aim some of their production at commercial markets does not mean that other forms of exchange (especially of subsistence products) are irrelevant or unnecessary.

Summary and Conclusions

The ethnographic and geoecological information we possess makes it clear that in the Andes we are dealing with complex and unusual environmental and agricultural conditions. Variations in the mix of topography, elevation, soils, climate, and biota make the Andean highlands a mosaic of ecological settings. Variations in social, political, economic, cultural and demographic conditions create a superimposed mosaic of human use of the diverse Andean ecozones. In the context of this complicated situation there are the linked needs of improving the quality of life of an increasing population while preventing further, eventually disastrous, deterioration of the fragile highland environment.

Given the nature and degree of the problems faced by the Andean countries in their efforts to achieve greater economic and social development, it is evident that verticality is a useful, perhaps a crucial, concept with many possible applications to setting the directions and shaping the specific elements of development programs. Ethnohistorical data demonstrate that it is possible to support a relatively large population in the Andean highlands -- as long as people are willing and able to adapt their productive practices and patterns of exchange to the vertical organization and local ecological variation of the sierra.

Application of the model of verticality in such components of development as land reform and agricultural extension would lead to programs that are less disruptive to the people and the environment than has often been the case to date. Elaboration and improvement of local crops, livestock, technologies and exchange systems hold a promise of raising the standard of living of small scale agro-pastoralists, without driving them into the cities and without irreparably damaging the fragile ecosystem of the mountains.

While in purely environmental terms it might be preferable to reduce the human population in the highlands, in social and economic terms it is necessary to utilize fully -- but not overuse -- as many of the ecozones of the Andes as possible. Full use will require diversification and intensification of small-scale agriculture and pastoralism, as well as improvement of infrastructure. I have argued in this paper that optimal development of the high altitude agro-pastoral sector can most effectively be carried out by drawing on anthropological information about past and present adaptations of Andean cultures, especially their traditional patterns of ecological complementarity.

I have also stressed the desirability of relying on local resources and small-scale technology to enhance and develop the traditional agricultural practices of the peasants.

It is true that our understanding of the Andean ecosystem and the human ways of exploiting it is still incomplete. Yet the verticality model and related ethnographic data on specific adaptations to local ecozones provide us with some sound guidelines for proceeding with rural development in the Andes.

Notes

1. This is a substantively revised and updated article, based on my earlier paper on the same topic: Forman 1978. A number of colleagues have helped me with one aspect or another of this work. I thank Karen Bruhns, Glen Custred, Patricia Lyon, George Miller, Benjamin Orlove, J.J. Parsons, John H. Rowe and Judith Tendler, again, for their assistance with the original version. Brooke Thomas has been of special assistance to the revision process.

2. Although Colombia and Chile are considered "Andean countries" for some purposes, I am referring almost exclusively to Ecuador, Peru and Bolivia when I use the term herein.

3. In both Ecuador and Peru just under half of the population lives in the mountain zone; in Bolivia about three-fourths of the population does.

4. I am citing from the 1975 collection of John V. Murra's essays. This collection is in Spanish; some of the essays included are slightly changed from their original published forms. The original references for the two chapters I draw most from are Murra 1968 and Murra 1972. The original text for the quotation translated in the next sentence is:

> El universo andino fue concebido por sus habitantes como un conjunto de pisos ordenados "verticalmente" uno encima del otro, formando una macro-adaptación, un sistema de relaciones ecológicas netamente andinas. Al ascender el asentamiento a alturas más y más elevadas, los habitantes tenían que enfrentarse con cambios continuos de clima, fauna y flora.
> Al lo largo de la cordillera, las aldeas y etnías habían procurado siempre controlar el mayor número posible de micro-climas. Las regiones a las cuales no era posible llegar en un día de camino, o mediante migraciones estacionales, fueron pobladas por grupos de colonos permanentes, dedicados al pastoreo, a recoger sal o *wanu*, y al cultivo de coca, maíz o ají. (Murra 1975:204)

5. The 1973 paper by Custred also appears, in Spanish and revised form, as Custred 1977.

6. Average annual percentages of population growth for the period 1980-86 were: 2.7% for Bolivia, 2.9% for Ecuador, and 2.3% for Peru (World Bank 1988:274).

7. Eckholm (1975:765) notes that under similar ecological problems conditions in the Eastern hills area of Nepal "as much as 38 percent of the total land area consists of abandoned fields." While the situation does not seem to be so extreme, yet, in the Andes, migration of campesinos to urban areas is an on-going pattern (World Bank 1988:284).

8. Efforts to resettle highland campesinos through colonization of the eastern lowland regions is at best a stop-gap measure and is a source of additional, new problems of environmental destruction of the rainforest.

9. While this standard of living is commonly expressed in terms of cash income, in fact availability of social services (e.g., health care) and social security are as important as cash.

10. Although it is not part of the main theme of this paper, it is still worth noting that land reform *by itself* will not guarantee significant increases in agricultural production, even though it is a necessary precondition for agricultural development in the Andes. This point is underlined by Jose Flores M. who says that Bolivian land reform "did not include in any sense the socialization of the land, because the wealth and production of the nation were and remain pitifully low, and misery cannot be socialized" (1965:130) and reiterated by Wetering when he states that land reform in Peru "is likely to make only a small contribution to the redistribution of national income... The redistribution of agricultural income alone can generate neither a rapid nor a self-sustained increase in agricultural production in Peru unless it is also accompanied by a major effort to increase the capacity to produce" (1973:9).

11. I am not entirely original in seeing the problem this way. The UNESCO "Programme on Man and the Biosphere" (MAB) Project 6, on "the impact of human activities on mountain and tundra ecosystems," which includes participation by all the Andean countries, states that the overall objective of its research effort "Should be to provide a basis for the beneficial combination of resource development and human settlement that would improve the quality of human life in mountain habitats without damaging the life-support capacity of these ecosystems" (MAB 1974:20).

12. By "planners" here and hereafter I mean to refer both to foreign personnel (e.g., from A.I.D. or the World Bank) and to nationals of Andean countries who work for national or international agencies. Some of the attitudes of planners may be partly attributed to their being from industrialized countries or having been trained in those countries, so that their development ideas are shaped by cultural frames of affluence and capitalism. Further, many of the planners who are nationals of Andean countries are members of the elites of those countries, with the class biases of the elite. However, even if individual development planners did not hold pro-industrialist views, the suggested problems would still arise from the inherent conflicts between capitalist modes of economic development and goals of social reform.

13. The lack of concern with conservation and pollution control is especially true if it appears that such concern might interfere in any way with rapid economic growth. This, of course, also remains a problem in the industrialized countries.

14. *Puna* refers to the high altitude steppeland of Peru and Bolivia (3400 to 5200 m) (see Custred 1973: 2-12). *Páramo* refers to the more humid high elevation areas in Ecuador and northern Peru (3200 to 4700m).

15. Alpaca fiber, particularly, is in demand in the U.S. and Europe and can bring high prices on the export market (Markowitz mss; Orlove 1977). Locally made Andean woolen products are also appreciated on the export market. The problems are of insuring a steady flow of such goods and of making sure that the peasant producers receive a reasonable proportion of the profits from them.

16. There is some, very small scale herding of llamas in central Ecuador, but in general both llamas and alpacas are absent in northern Peru and in Ecuador.

17. For example, some varieties of soy beans grow at elevations up to at least 2300 m, and in cool climates (Hymowitz 1969). These species could conceivably be introduced into highland Andean agriculture.

18. My information on pyrethrum comes in part through personal communication with Dr. C.S. Koehler of the agricultural extension program, Univ. of California, Berkeley.

19. Eckholm (1975:766-767) not only notes this loss of terracing expertise, but also suggests that some Andean valleys supported larger populations in the pre-conquest period than they are able to do today, because of better land maintenance and water control than now are practiced. See also Guillet 1987:86.

20. Since I completed the first version of this paper, there has been a proliferation of "appropriate technology" approaches along these lines. See for example Darrow et al (1981), Evans and Adler (1979) and the periodic publications of such organizations as International Development Research Centre of Canada and Volunteers in Technical Assistance.

21. The closest thing I know of in this vein is the provision in the Bolivian land reform law for differential redistribution according to the quality of land; see Heath et al 1969, especially the appendix.

22. One important impact of increasing use of the commercial market for food is a decline in the quality of diet as processed foods are substituted for traditional subsistence foods. See Leonard and Thomas 1988 and Orlove 1987.

References

Alberti, Enrique Mayer
1974 Reciprocidad Andina: Ayer y Hoy. In *Reciprocidad e Intercambio en los Andes Peruanos.* Giorgio Alberti and Enrique Mayer, eds. Perú-Problema 12:13-33. Lima: Instituto de Estudios Peruanos.

Alexander, Martin
1974 Environmental Consequences of Rapidly Rising Food Output. *Agro-ecosystems* 1(3):249-264.

Anderson, C. Milton
1975 Food Crisis Forces Reform of Farm Policy in Ecuador. *Foreign Agriculture* 13(30):10-11 (July 28).

Basile, David G.
1974 Tillers of the Andes: Farmers and Farming in the Quito Basin. *Studies in Geography* 8, Dept. of Geography. Chapel Hill: University of North Carolina.

Billings, W. Dwight
1979 High Mountain Ecosystems: Evolution, Structure, Operation and Maintenance. In *High Altitude Geoecology.* AAAS Selected Symposium 12. Patrick J. Webber, ed. Pp. 97-125. Boulder, CO: Westview Press.

Browman, David L.
1987a Introduction: Risk Management in Andean Arid Lands. In *Arid Land Use Strategies and Risk Management in the Andes: A Regional Anthropological Perspective.* David L. Browman, ed. Pp. 1-23. Boulder, CO: Westview Press.
1987b Pastoralism in Highland Peru and Bolivia. In *Arid Land Use Strategies and Risk Management in the Andes: A Regional Anthropological Perspective.* David L. Browman, ed. Pp. 121-149. Boulder, CO: Westview Press.

Brown, Paul F.
1987 Economy, Ecology and Population: Recent Changes in Peruvian Aymara Land Use Patterns. In *Arid Land Use Strategies and Risk Management in the Andes: A Regional Anthropological Perspective.* David L. Browman, ed. Pp. 99-120. Boulder, CO: Westview Press.

Brunnschweiler, Dieter
1971 The Study of the Physical Environment in Latin America. In *Geographic Research on Latin America: Benchmark 1970. Proceedings of the Conference of Latin Americanist Geographers* Vol.1:220-231. Barry Lentnek, Robert L. Carmin and Tom L. Martinson, eds. Muncie, IN: Ball State University.

Brush, Stephen B.
1973 A Study of Subsistence Activities in Uchucmarca, Peru. *Land Tenure Center Newsletter* 40:10-18. (U. of Wisconsin, Madison)
1974 El Lugar del Hombre en el Ecosistema Andino. *Revista del Museo Nacional* 40:277-299. (Lima, Peru)
1977 *Mountain, Field, and Family: The Economy and Human Ecology of an Andean Valley.* Philadelphia: University of Pennsylvania Press.

Budowski, Gerardo
1968 La Influencia Humana en la Vegetación Natural de Montañas Tropicales Americanas. *Colloquium Geographicum* 9:157-162. Proceedings of the UNESCO Mexico Symposium, 1966. Carl Troll, ed. (Geographisches Institut de Universitat, Bonn.)

Burchard, Roderick E.
1974 Coca y Trueque de Alimentos. In *Reciprocidad e Intercambio en los Andes Peruanos.* Giorgio Alberti and Enrique Mayer, eds. Perú-Problema 12:209-251. Lima: Instituto de Estudios Peruanos.

Burke, Melvin
1971 Land Reform in the Lake Titicaca Region. In *Beyond the Revolution: Bolivia since 1952.* James M. Malloy and Richard S. Thorn, eds. Pittsburgh: Univ. of Pittsburgh Press.

Cabrera, Angel L.
1968 Ecología Vegetal de la Puna. *Colloquium Geographicum* 9:91-116. Proceedings of the UNESCO Mexico Symposium, 1966. Carl Troll, ed. (Geographisches Institut der Universitat, Bonn)

Carter, William E.
1965 Aymara Communities and the Bolivian Agrarian Reform. *Social Science Monographs* #24. Gainesville: University of Florida.

Casaverde R., Juvenal
1977 El Trueque en la Economía Pastoril. In *Pastores de Puna [Uywamichiq Punarunakuna].* Jorge A. Flores Ochoa, ed. Pp. 171-191. Lima: Instituto de Estudios Peruanos.

Champeau, Harold C.
1975 Five Communes in the People's Republic of China. *Foreign Agriculture* 13(33):6-8.

Collins, Jane
1984 The Maintenance of Peasant Coffee Production in a Peruvian Valley. *American Ethnologist* 11(3):413-438.

Coutu, Arthur J. and Richard A. King
1969 The Agricultural Development of Peru. *Benchmark Studies on Agricultural Development in Latin America, #4.* New York: Praeger.

Cuatrecasas, Jose
   1968 Paramo Vegetation and Its Life Forms. *Colloquium Geographicum* 9:163-186. Proceedings of
      the UNESCO Mexico Symposium, 1966. Carl Troll, ed. (Geographisches Institut der Universitat,
      Bonn.)

Custred, Glen
   1973 Puna Zones of the South Central Andes. Paper presented in symposium "Cultural adaptations to
      mountain ecosystems," Annual Meeting of the American Anthropological Association. mimeo.
   1974 Llameros y Comercio Interregional. In *Reciprocidad e Intercambio en los Andes Peruanos*.
      Giorgio Alberti and Enrique Mayer, eds. Peru-Problema 12:252-289. Lima: Instituto de Estudios
      Peruanos.
   1977 Las Punas de los Andes Centrales. In *Pastores de Puna [Uywamichiq Punarunakuna]*. Jorge
      A. Flores Ochoa, ed. Pp. 54-85. Lima: Instituto de Estudios Peruanos.

Darrow, Ken, Kent Keller and Rick Pam
   1981 *Appropriate Technology Sourcebook, vol. II*. Stanford, CA: Volunteers in Asia, Inc.

Dickinson, III, Joshua C.
   1971 Research on Forests and Man in Latin America. In *Geographic Research on Latin America:
      Benchmark 1970. Proceedings of the Conference of Latin Americanist Geographers*, Vol. 1:215-
      219. Barry Lentnek, Robert L. Carmin and Tom L. Martinson, eds. Muncie, Ind.: Ball State Univ.

Dorsey, Joseph F.
   1975 *A Case Study of Ex-hacienda Toralapa in the Tiraque Region of the Upper Cochabamba
      Valley. Research paper #65*. Land Tenure Center. (Univ. of Wisconsin, Madison).

Eckholm, Erik P.
   1975 The Deterioration of Mountain Environments. *Science* 189:764-770. (Sept. 5)

Evans, Donald D.
   1979 Appropriate Technology and Its Role in Development. *In Appropriate Technology for
      Development: A Discussion and Case Histories*. Donald D. Evans and Laurie Nogg Adler, eds. Pp.
      1-80. Boulder, CO: Westview Press.

Evans, Donald D. and Laurie Nogg Adler, eds.
   1979 *Appropriate Technology for Development: A Discussion and Case Histories*. Boulder, CO:
      Westview Press.

Flores Moncayo, Jose
   1965 Objectives of Agrarian Reform in Bolivia. In *Agrarian Reform in Latin America*. T. Lynn
      Smith, ed. Pp. 129-130. New York: Alfred A. Knopf.

Flores Ochoa, Jorge A.
   1968 Los Pastores de Paratia. *Serie Anthropologia Social #10*. Mexico: Instituto Indigenista
      Interamericana.
   1975 Sociedad y Cultura en la Puna Alta de los Andes. *América Indígena* 35(2):297-319.
   1977 Pastoreo, Tejido and Intercambio. In *Pastores de Puna [Uywamichiq Punarunakuna]*. Jorge A.
      Flores Ochoa, ed. Pp. 133-154. Lima: Instituto de Estudios Peruanos.

1985 Interaction and Complementarity in Three Zones of Cuzco. In *Andean Ecology and Civilization: An Interdisciplinary Perspective on Andean Ecological Complementarity.* Shozo Masuda, Izumi Shimada and Craig Morris, eds. Pp. 251-276. Tokyo: University of Tokyo Press.

Fonseca Martel, Cesar
1974 Modalidades de la Minka. In *Reciprocidad e Intercambio en los Andes Peruanos.* Giorgio Alberti and Enrique Mayer, eds. Perú-Problema 12:86-109. Lima: Instituto de Estudios Peruanos.

Forman, Sylvia Helen
1972 *Law and Conflict in Rural Highland Ecuador.* Ph.D. dissertation. University of California, Berkeley.
1978 The Future Value of the "Verticality" Concept: Implications and Possible Applications in the Andes. *Actes du XLII Congrès International des Américanistes,* Vol IV:233-256. Paris: Sociète des Americanistes.

Gade, Daniel W.
1969 Vanishing Crops of Traditional Agriculture: The Case of Tarwi (Lupinus mutabilis) in the Andes. *Proceedings of the Association of American Geographers* 1:47-51.
1970 Ethnobotany of Canihua (Chenopodium pallidicaule), Rustic Seed Crop of the Altiplano. *Economic Botany* 24(1):55-61.
1975 *Plants, Man and the Land in the Vilcanota Valley of Peru.* The Hague: Dr. W. Junk B.V.
1977 Llama, Alpaca y Vicuña: Ficción y Realidad. In *Pastores de Puna [Uywamichiq Punarunakuna].* Jorge A. Flores Ochoa, ed. Pp. 113-120. Lima: Instituto de Estudios Peruanos.

Gladwin, Christina H.
1979 Cognitive Strategies and Adoption Decisions: A Case Study of Nonadoption of an Agronomic Recommendation. *Economic Development and Cultural Change* 28(1):155-173.

Guillet, David
1981 Land Tenure, Ecological Zone, and Agricultural Regime in the Central Andes. *American Ethnologist* 8(1):139-156.
1987 On the Potential for Intensification of Agropastoralism in the Arid Zones of the Central Andes. In *Arid Land Use Strategies and Risk Management in the Andes: A Regional Anthropological Perspective.* David L. Browman, ed. Pp. 81-98. Boulder, CO: Westview Press.

Harris, Olivia
1985 Ecological Duality and the Role of the Center: Northern Potosi. In *Andean Ecology and Civilization: An Interdisciplinary Perspective on Andean Ecologiccal Complementarity.* Shozo Masuda, Izumi Shimada and Craig Morris, eds. Pp. 311-335. Tokyo: University of Tokyo Press.

Heath, Dwight B., Charles J. Erasmus and Hans C. Buechler
1969 *Land Reform and Social Revolution in Bolivia.* New York: Praeger.

Hewitt, Kenneth
1976 Earthquake Hazards in the Mountains. *Natural History* 85(5):30-37.

Heyduk, Daniel
1974 The Hacienda System and Agrarian Reform in Highland Bolivia: A Re-evaluation. *Ethnology* 13(1):71-81.

Hymowitz, Theodore
1969 The Soybeans of the Kumaon Hills of India. *Economic Botany* 23(1):50-54.

IVITA (Instituto Veterinario de Investigaciones Tropicales y de Altura)
1972 Investigaciones del IVITA en Camélidos Sudamericanos. *Boletín de Divulgación* #10. Lima: Universidad Nacional Mayor de San Marcos.

IUCN (International Union for Conservation of Nature and Natural Resources)
1968 Proceedings of the Latin American Conference on the Conservation of Renewal Natural Resources. *IUCN Publications New Series #13*. Morges, Switzerland: IUCN.

Isbell, Billie Jean
1974 Parentesco Andino y Reciprodidad; Kuyaq: Los que Nos Aman. In *Reciprocidad e Intercambio en los Andes Peruanos*. Giorgio Alberti and Enrique Mayer, eds. Peru-Problema 12:110-152. Lima: Instituto de Estudios Peruanos.

Ives, Jack D.
1979 Applied High Altitude Geoecology. In *High Altitude Geoecology*. AAAS Selected Symposium 12. Patrick J. Webber, ed. Pp. 9-45. Boulder, CO: Westview Press.

Johnson, Allen W.
1972 Individuality and Experimentation in Traditional Agriculture. *Human Ecology* 1(2):149-159.

Jorgenson, Harold T.
1971 Basic Issues in the Process of Development in Latin America: Food-Land-Employment-Income-Environment. In *Geographic Research on Latin America: Benchmark 1970. Proceedings of the Conference of Latin Americanist Geographers,* Vol. 1:402-411. Barry Lentnek, Robert L. Carmin and Tom L. Martinson, eds. Muncie, Ind.: Ball State Univ.

Kottack, Conrad Phillip
1990 Culture and "Economic Development." *American Anthropologist* 92(3):723-731.

Kuit, H.G.
1990 *Ganadería Campesina: Estudio de Caso y Aportes para del Debate.* Juliaca, Puno, Peru: Centro de Proyectos Integrales en Base a la Alpaca.

Leonard, William R. and R. Brooke Thomas
1988 Changing Dietary Pattern in the Peruvian Andes. *Ecology of Food and Nutrition* 21:245-263.

Love, Thomas
1989 Andean Interzonal Bartering: Why Does It Persist in a Cash-Market Economy. In *Multidisciplinary Studies in Andean Anthropology*. Virginia J. Vitzthum, ed. Pp. 87-100. Michigan Discussions in Anthropology, Vol. 8. (Univ. of Michigan, Ann Arbor)

MAB (Man and the Biosphere)
   1974 Final Report, Working Group on Project 6: Impact of Human Activities on Mountain and
      Tundra Ecosystems. *MAB Report Series #14*. Programme on Man and the Biosphere (MAB).
      Paris: UNESCO.
   1975 Draft report: Regional Meeting on Integrated Ecological Research and Training Needs in the
      Andean Region. *MAB Report Series #23*. Programme on Man and the Biosphere (MAB). Paris:
      UNESCO.

Markowitz, Lisa B.
   mss. *Pastoral Production and Its Discontents: Alpaca and Sheep Raising in Caylloma, Peru*. Draft
      of Ph.D. Dissertation. University of Massachusetts, Amherst.

Mayer, Enrique
   1971 Un Carnero por un Saco de Papas: Aspectos del Trueque en la Zona de Chaupiwaranga, Pasco.
      Revista del Museo Nacional 37:184-196. (Lima, Peru)
   1974 Más Allá de la Familia Nuclear. *Revista del Museo Nacional* 40:301-330. (Lima, Peru)
   1985 Production Zones. In *Andean Ecology and Civilization: An Interdisciplinary Perspective on
      Andean Ecologiccal Complementarity*. Shozo Masuda, Izumi Shimada and Craig Morris, eds. Pp.
      45-84. Tokyo: University of Tokyo Press.

McCorkle, Constance M.
   1987 Punas, Pastures, and Fields: Grazing Strategies and the Agropastoral Dialectic in an Indigenous
      Andean Community. In *Arid Land Use Strategies and Risk Management in the Andes: A Regional
      Anthropological Perspective*. David L. Browman, ed. Pp. 57-79. Boulder, CO: Westview Press.

Milstead, Harley P.
   1928 Distribution of Crops in Peru. *Economic Geography* 4(1):88-106.

Mitchell, William P.
   1976 Irrigation and Community in the Central Peruvian Highlands. *American Anthropologist*
      78(1):25-44

Momsen, Jr., Richard P.
   1971 Mapping Spatial Factors for Development Planning. In *Geographic Research on Latin
      America: Benchmark 1970. Proceedings of the Conference of Latin Americanist Geographers*,
      Vol. 1:379-401. Barry Lentnek, Robert L. Carmin and Tom L. Martinson, eds. Muncie, IN: Ball
      State Univ.

Murra, John V.
   1968 An Aymara Kingdom. *Ethnohistory* 15(2):115-151.
   1970 Current Research and Prospects in Andean Ethnohistory. *American Research Latin Review*
      5(13):3-36.
   1972 El "Control Vertical" de un Máximo de Pisos Ecológicos en la Economía de las Sociedades
      Andinas. In *Visita de la Provincia de León de Huanuco (1562)*, Iñigo Ortiz de Zúñiga, Tomo II.
      John V. Murra, ed. Pp. 427-468. Huánuco: Universidad Hermilio Valdizan.
   1975 *Formaciones Económicas y Políticas del Mundo Andino*. Lima: Instituto de Estudios Peruanos.

1985 "El Archipielago Vertical" Revisited. In *Andean Ecology and Civilization: An Interdisciplinary Perspective on Andean Ecologiccal Complementarity*. Shozo Masuda, Izumi Shimada and Craig Morris, eds. Pp. 3-13. Tokyo: University of Tokyo Press.

NAS (National Academy of Sciences)
1975 *Plant Studies in the People's Republic of China: A Trip Report of the American Plant Studies Delegation*. Washington, D.C.: National Academy of Sciences.

NRC (National Research Council)
1989 *Lost Crops of the Incas: Little-Known Plants of the Andes with Promise for Worldwide Cultivation*. Washington, D.C.: National Academy Press.

NSF (National Science Foundation)
1989 *Loss of Biological Diversity: A Global Crisis Requiring International Solutions. A Report to the National Science Board [NSB-89-171]*. Washington, D.C.: National Science Foundation.

Nietschmann, Bernard
1971 The Substance of Subsistence. In *Geographic Research on Latin America: Benchmark 1970. Proceedings of the Conference of Latin Americanist Geographers*, Vol. 1:167-181. Barry Lentnek, Robert L. Carmin and Tom L. Martinson, eds. Muncie, IN: Ball State Univ.

Orlove, Benjamin S.
1973 A Mixed Agricultural-Transhumance Economy and Techniques of Microenvironmental Variation in the Andes. Paper presented in symposium "Cultural Adaptations to Mountain Ecosystems," Annual Meeting of the American Anthropological Association. mimeo.
1974 Reciprocidad, Desigualdad y Dominación. In *Reciprocidad e Intercambio en los Andes Peruanos*. Giorgio Alberti and Enrique Mayer, eds. Perú-Problems 12:290-321. Lima. Instituto de Estudios Peruanos
1977 *Alpacas, Sheep, and Men: The Wool Export Economy and Regional Society in Southern Peru*. New York: Academic Press.
1987 Stability and Change in Highland Andean Dietary Patterns. In *Food and Evolution: Toward a Theory of Human Food Habits*. Marvin Harris and Eric B. Ross, eds. Pp. 481-513. Philadelphia: Temple University Press.

PAL (Proyecto Alpacas)
1988 *Información de Base: Estudios sobre Camélidos Sudamericanos*, 1940-1988. Puno, Peru: PAL (INIAA-CORPUNO-COTESU/IC).

Peattie, Roderick
1936 *Mountain Geography: A Critique and Field Study*. Cambridge, Mass.: Harvard University Press.

Popkin, Samuel L.
1981 Public Choice and Rural Development - Free Riders, Lemons, and Institutional Design. In *Public Choice and Rural Development*. Clifford S. Russell and Norman K. Nicholson, eds. Pp. 43-80. Research Paper R-21. Washington, D.C.: Resources for the Future.

Pulgar Vidal, Javier
  1946 Historia y Geografía del Peru. Tomo I. _Las Ocho Regiones Naturales del Peru._ Lima:
  Universidad Nacional Mayor de San Marcos.

Rhoades, Robert E. and Stephen I. Thompson
  1975 Adaptive Strategies in Alpine Environments: Beyond Ecological Particularism. _American
  Ethnologist_ 2(3):535-551.

Rich, William
  1973 Smaller Families through Social and Economic Progress. _Overseas Development Council
  Monograph #7._ Washington, D.C.: Overseas Development Council.

Rowe, P. R.
  1969 Nature, Distribution, and Use of Diversity in the Tuberbearing Solanum Species. _Economic
  Botany_ 23(4):330-338.

Salomon, Frank
  1985 The Dynamic Potential of the Complementarity Concept. In _Andean Ecology and Civilization:
  An Interdisciplinary Perspective on Andean Ecologiccal Complementarity._ Shozo Masuda, Izumi
  Shimada and Craig Morris, eds. Pp. 511-531. Tokyo: University of Tokyo Press.

Schumacher, E. F.
  1975 _Small Is Beautiful: Economics as if People Mattered._ New York: Perennial Library (Harper and
  Row).

Scott, Christopher D.
  1974 Asignación de Recursos y Formes de Intercambio. In _Reciprocidad e Intercambio en los Andes
  Peruanos._ Giorgio Alberti and Enrique Mayer, eds. Perú-Problema 12:322-345. Lima: Instituto de
  Estudios Peruanos.

Sharp, W. Curtis
  1970 New Plants for Conservation. _Economic Botany_ 24(1):53-54

Shimada, Izumi
  1985 Introduction. In _Andean Ecology and Civilization: An Interdisciplinary Perspective on Andean
  Ecological Complementarity._ Shozo Masuda, Izumi Shimada and Craig Morris, eds. Pp. xi-xxxii.
  Tokyo: University of Tokyo Press.

Skinner, Reinhard J.
  1976 Technological Determinism: A Critique of Convergence Theory. _Comparative Studies in
  Society and History_ 18(1):2-27.

Sternberg, Hilgard O'R.
  1973 _Development and Conservation._ Erdkunde, Archiv fur Wissenschaftliche Geographie, Bank
  XXVII, Lfg. 4:253-265. Bonn. (Reprinted by the Center for Latin American Studies, Univ. of
  California, Berkeley)

Stouse, Jr., Pierre A.D.
   1970 The Distribution of Llamas in Bolivia. *Proceedings of the Association of American Geographers* 2:136-140.

Tendler, Judith
   1975 *A.I.D. and Small Farmer Organizations: Lessons of the Ecuadorian Experience.* Office of Development Programs of the Latin American Bureau. Washington, D.C.: Agency for International Development.

Thiesenhusen, William C.
   1974 What Changing Technology Implies for Agrarian Reform. *Land Economics* 50(1):35-50.

Thomas, R. Brooke
   1979 Effects of Change on High Mountain Human Adaptive Patterns. In *High Altitude Geoecology.* AAAS Selected Symposium 12. Patrick J. Webber, ed. Pp. 139-188. Boulder, CO: Westview Press.

Tosi, Jr., Joseph A
   1960 Zonas de Vida Natural en el Peru. *Memoria Explicativa sobre el Mapa Ecológico del Peru.* Boletín Técnico #5. Instituto Interamericano de Ciencias Agricolas de la OEA; Zona Andina.

Troll, Carl
   1968 The Cordilleras of the Tropical Americas: Aspects of Climatic, Phytogeographical and Agrarian Ecology. *Colloquium Geographicum* 9:15-56. Proceedings of the UNESCO Mexico Symposium, 1966. Carl Troll, ed. (Geographisches Institut der Universitat, Bonn.)

Vallée, Lionel
   1971 La Ecología Subjectiva como un Elemento Essencial de la Verticalidad. *Revista del Museo Nacional* 37:167-173. (Lima, Peru)

Wade, Nicholas
   1975 Boost for Credit Rating of Organic Farmers. *Science* 189:777 (Sept. 5)

Webber, Patrick J.
   1979 Introduction and Commentary. In *High Altitude Geoecology.* AAAS Selected Symposium 12. Patrick J. Webber, ed. Pp. 1-8. Boulder, CO: Westview Press.

Webster, Steven S.
   1971 An Indigenous Quechua Community in Exploitation of Multiple Ecological Zones. *Revista del Museo Nacional* 37:174-183. (Lima, Peru)
   1973 Native Pastoralism in the South Andes. *Ethnology* 12(2):115-133.

Weismantel, Mary J.
   1988 *Food, Gender, and Poverty in the Ecuadorian Andes.* Philadelphia: University of Pennsylvania Press.

Wetering, H. Van de
  1973 The Current State of Land Reform in Peru. *Land Tenure Center Newsletter* 40:5-9. (Univ. of
  Wisconsin, Madison)

Winterhalder, Bruce, R. Larson and R.B. Thomas
  1974 Dung as an Essential Resource in a Highland Peruvian Community. *Human Ecology* 2(2):89-
  104.

Winterhalder, Bruce P. and R. Brooke Thomas
  1978 Geoecology of Southern Highland Peru: A Human Adaptation Perspective. *Occasional Paper
  #27, Institute of Arctic and Alpine Research.* Boulder, CO: University of Colorado.

World Bank
  1988 *World Development Report 1988.* [Published for The World Bank] New York: Oxford
  University Press.

Address about Education

Sylvia Helen Forman

On May 3, 1987, Sylvia Forman wrote and presented the following address to a meeting of the Honors Program of the University of Massachusetts at Amherst. It was prepared in longhand and never typed, entered into a computer file, or even mentioned in her vita. It is included here because it provides a very clear and direct statement of her views about education and the enterprise of teaching. In her notes for the talk, she indicated the spot where she intended to include the "Mead quote" and 2 photocopied pages were attached with some penciled markings indicating the relevant quotes she intended to use. It is published here for the first time.

This address is about the future -- but let me begin in the past.

The first time I went to the small, Indian village of Nanay, high in the Andes in Ecuador, in 1968, I felt I had traveled across hundreds of years as well as hundreds of miles: There seemed to be a time warp involved -- the immediate reality in Nanay was a past-reality similar in many ways to rural life in the 1600's or 1700's. People spoke the language of the Incas. They lived in straw-thatched houses, small, built without nails, dirt-floored. Their clothing -- especially that of the women -- was of heavy woolen cloth -- made from the fleece of their sheep, woven on simple household looms. They grew crops -- a dozen varieties of potatoes, maize, quinoa, milloco -- domesticated thousands of years ago in the Andes. And they cooked those foods in clay pots identical in form to some I had seen in museums.

People in Nanay asked me why I had come to their village -- another strange *gringo* (North American), ignorant of proper behavior, unable to speak Quechua, creature of mysterious motives. Was I a missionary -- there were several already around -- But no. Was I a Peace Corps volunteer -- again, already present, though certainly peculiar -- again NO. I was a university student. Simple enough to say -- but truly without meaning to these people, I soon realized. After all, what was a university? Why would one send me to their small community? What was the point of all the silly questions I asked?

I stayed only a few months in Nanay in 1968, but returned again two years later for a research visit that lasted over a year. During that time, I learned of the details of how people in Nanay lived their lives: agricultural practices, problems of economic insecurity, what they quarreled about and how they settled disputes, religious beliefs and rituals, how marriage partners were chosen and how babies were cared for. And, how children learned all these things and more. At the same time, I began to notice changes: a house with a tiled roof, aluminum cooking pots, more store-bought clothing. One family went to work for a time in Bogota, Columbia. People had begun, some years before, to send more of their children to nearby elementary schools -- not all

41

children, but some. Now they begin to ask about the high school (colegio) in the provincial capital -- perhaps a few of the young people could go there? What effects would such action have? I left my typewriter, when I departed, for those potential high school students to use.

When I visited again, in 1974, there were several young men and women from Nanay struggling their way through the academic courses of the high school, in Spanish, and simultaneously learning the life ways of urban, Ecuador, adolescent culture. By my 1978 visit, two of these students had gone on to the University, in Quito -- one to study law and the other linguistics. And while they had in some respects become almost as mysterious to their families and friends as I had been a decade before, they were rapidly building a bridge between two worlds -- an archway across that time warp I, and they, had felt. Yet they were also doing more than -- to use a trite and rather misleading phrase -- more than bringing their community actively into the wider 20th century world -- coming to recognize the inevitability of change -- they were thinking about the future beyond, asking what the village would need, not just at the moment, but through years to come.

What did I learn from this series of observations? Also trained for the past-immediate past -- as these young people had been -- unthinking, uncritical about what and how I had been taught (cross-cultural exposure) -- and so I brought questions home -- questions about education and learning.

For all of human history, it has been the nature of culture, the universal pattern, to carefully pass on knowledge to the next, the new, generation -- how to catch that type of animal, how to form a particular crop, the proper words to use in ritual, the secret means of curing the ill. No human society fails to educate its children -- and that education is aimed at replication, at continuity, at maintaining received wisdom, tradition and values. And yet, human life does *not* remain static -- it never has for very long. People are both creative and adaptive, and so are human cultures adaptive -- people think up new ways of doing things -- pottery, metal-working, printing, newer moon-landers -- and they adjust their lifeways to changes in their environments -- weather, invasions, new diseases, urban living.

Thus, we confront a massive contradiction: education, transmission of culture (as we anthropologists are fond of stating it) is a process of ensuring continuation of the past, but life changes and we -- or our children -- must cope with the new forms.

Education in the home -- and local community -- still has the universal quality of replication -- we enable our young children to learn to speak our language, understand and adhere to our values, play the games we know. But, in our rapidly changing world, education in the formal system is a mixed bag: trying to encompass both tradition (great books) and to foster and generate discontinuities and change. The contradiction is obvious, unsettling, even painful. Educational institutions are asked to liberate and constrain the thinking of young people simultaneously, to support traditional values, but train students in new methods and technologies.

And, because our schools and colleges are social institutions, and closely connected to other social institutions -- business, government agencies, churches -- they approach this contradictory task in rigid ways. One key aspect of this is an emphasis on teacher and teaching.

> "There are several striking differences between our concept of education today and that of any contemporary primitive society; but perhaps the most important one is the shift from the need for an individual to learn something which everyone agrees he would wish to know, to the will of some individual to teach something which is not agreed that anyone has any desire to know. Such a shift in emphasis could come only with the breakdown of self-contained and self-respecting cultural homogeneity. The Manus or the Arapesh or the Iatmul adults taught their children all that they knew themselves. Sometimes, it is true, there were rifts in the process. A man might die without having communicated some particular piece of ritual knowledge; a good hunter might find no suitable apprentice among his available near kin, so that his skill perished with him. A girl might be so clumsy and stupid that she never learned to weave a mosquito basket that was fit to sell. Miscarriages in the smooth working of the transmission of available skills and knowledge did occur, but they were not sufficient to focus the attention of the group upon the desirability of *teaching* as over against the desirability of *learning*. Even with considerable division of labor and with a custom by which young men learned a special skill not from a father or other specified relative but merely from a master of the art, the master did not go seeking pupils; the pupils and their parents went to seek the master and with proper gifts of fish or octopus or dogs' teeth persuaded him to teach the neophyte . . . Thus, with the appearance of religions which held this belief in their own infallible superiority, education becomes a concern of those who teach rather than of those who learn" (Mead 1943:164, 166-167).

But we do not agree about what to teach out of all what could possibly be passed on to prepare students for the future. Now, I recognize that we *cannot teach* the future -- we do not know it and cannot foresee its specific elements. Moreover, we are bound ourselves, in large degree, to the past. However, we can draw on our knowledge of the past, and of the experiences of other cultures, to remind us that change and discontinuity are significant features of the human condition. That learning is the true core of education.

Those points, in turn, allow us to consider forms of education in which the *processes* of learning and the learner take priority, where adaptability and creativity -- rather than simply repetition and replication -- are supported and encouraged. That is, if we cannot teach the future, we can at least try to help the members of the next generation learn it as they live it.

Programs like our Honors Program here have the opportunity to engage this issue of a less contradictory form of education -- in two ways: directly, though their courses and other interactions with individual students and indirectly, by providing all of us a setting in which innovative approaches to learning can be sampled and tested and from which those can then be shared with others.

References

Mead, Margaret
    1943 Our Educational Emphases in Primitive Perspective. *American Journal of Sociology* 48:633-639.

Taken by University of Massachusetts Photographic Services, 1981.

Democratic Values and Equality:

A Short Commentary on

Educational Policy

Sylvia Helen Forman

Carole E. Hill
University of Georgia

This paper was written for and presented at the Third Annual Conference of the World Future Society - Education Section held in Amherst, Massachusetts in November 1980. The original title was "Inequality and Compliance: The Heart of American Education." Carole Hill has edited the piece for inclusion in this volume, but the content and message of the original presentation have been retained and clearly reflect Sylvia Forman's thinking on several of the themes of this volume.

Carole E. Hill (Ph.D. 1972) a cultural anthropologist, has published in the fields of medical and educational anthropology. Her major interest involves the interrelationship between policy, policy makers, and local level populations. She has been active in several professional organizations such as the American Anthropological Association and the Society for Applied Anthropology. Her activities in the former led to a friendship with Sylvia, initially through serving on the Committee on the Status of Women in Anthropology in the late 1970's and early 1980's. It was during this time that the AAA censored several departments for their hiring practices in regard to women. Their work on this committee cemented her friendship with Sylvia. She worked with Sylvia on a variety of committees and programs in the AAA, the SfAA, and other regional organizations. In the late 1980's she, along with Sylvia and Naomi Quinn spearheaded the founding of the Society for Feminist Anthropology.

Introduction

As anthropologists, we are concerned with the intrinsic cultural values in American society that provide the basis for constructing educational policies. Specifically, we are interested in the ways the educational system supports class and ethnic group distinctions. We argue that the ideology of democratic education, as represented in the words of policy makers, contradict their decisions which perpetuate cultural and social distinctions on local level. We feel that before a true democratic transformation can take place in education that assures equity in formal education for all, the contradictions between ideology, capitalism, and pluralism must be addressed on all levels of the U.S. educational system.

In order to illustrate these contradictions, we will draw upon a wide range of texts written by scholars concerned with the U.S. educational system and ideological systems. For the purposes of this paper, we are defining the educational system as formal and informal learning. In a broader perspective, education means more than just public or private schooling; it involves the total processes of socialization including learning the beliefs, values, and expected behaviors in a society.

Ideology, Democracy, and Policy

Traditionally, members of U.S. society have been ambivalent toward the future and nostalgic toward the past. The propensity of Americans to search the past for guidelines is, in reality, a search for identity. This nostalgia for the past combined with the ideology of democratic roots, tends to foster mistrust of governmental control on local levels. The argument for little governmental "interference" with local issues is a common political theme throughout the history of the U.S. This ideology conjures up an image that somehow, democratic principles are being eroded; and that more government means less individual freedom.

This ideology was described as early as 1835 by Alexis de Tocqueville (1835) who observed that the U.S. had a built-in "memory hole" in its individualism and commitment to equality of condition. These beliefs and values have a tendency to emphasize the past and, at most, the present. More importantly, they create a fear of change. Events that contradict these believed-in principles are often structured out of memory.

What then, has maintained the idea of a democratic republic through time in this country? De Tocqueville felt that laws and, more importantly, mores contribute to the success of a democracy. Mores are rooted in religious tradition and are inextricably bound to the economic, political, and educational systems. There are, however, contradictions of mores among these institutions which allow for a great deal of ambiguity in the creation, interpretation, and implementation of educational policy. Such ambiguity can be used by those in power, either on the national or local level, to create and maintain an educational system which calls upon the values of the past to legitimize inequalities in the present system.

This process often occurs under the guise of supporting the democratic way. In his ground breaking book, "*Democracy and Education*" Dewey (1916) explained the complex relationship between democratic principles and the functions of educational policy for U.S. society. A century earlier, de Tocqueville (1835) pointed out certain dangers that threaten the moral basis of U.S. democratic and equitable society. The most serious threat to democracy is the spread of material prosperity and the exclusive concern for advancing it which lead to dependency on large centralized bureaucratic structures. He states:

As social equality spreads there are more and more people who, though neither rich nor powerful enough to have much hold over others, have gained or kept enough wealth and enough understanding to look after their own needs. Such folk owe no man anything and hardly expect anything from anybody. They form the habit of thinking of themselves in isolation and imagine that their whole destiny is in their own hands. Thus, not only does democracy make men forget their ancestors, but also clouds their view of other descendants and isolates them from their contemporaries. Each man is forever thrown back on himself alone, and there is a danger that he may be shut up in the solitude of his own heart (1835:508).

De Tocqueville felt that a "soft despotism" (utilitarian individualism) would creep into the system that "would be more widespread and milder; it would degrade people rather than torment them." Such a society "does not break men's will, but softens, bends, and guides it." Such a society would take each citizen and shape her/him to its will and the government would then extend its embrace to include the whole society. According to Tocqueville, "it covers the whole of social life with a network of petty, complicated rules that are both minute and uniform, through which even men of the greatest originality and the most vigorous temperament cannot force their heads above the crowd" (1835:692).

We are not suggesting that Tocqueville's fears have been completely realized in the 150 years since he wrote about them. Rather, we use his writings as an example of someone who foresaw the disintegration of a moral basis of U.S. society and the weakening of democratic ideals within the context of a growing multiculturalism and a growing materialistic value. We argue that a form of materialism, based on individual self-interest, is rooted in our culture and is upheld by religious principles and political decisions. This self-interest has provided a context for selfish actions in all U.S. institution, including education, and, ironically in the name of democracy. Furthermore, private interest and interest groups are the major forces on the political landscape rather than a concern for the public interest, equality or, we would argue democracy itself.

Educational Policy and Pluralism

The ideology of capitalism and the bureaucracy that supports capitalistic activities guide contemporary U.S. policy. Social institutions, including educational ones, reflect the dominance of certain values and normative conceptions about social problems and their solution. These value choices and definition of existing conditions are not derived from consensual agreement of members of U.S. society, nor do they result from compromises among those persons most affected by educational policies. The most powerful groups, the ones with greater resources of class, status, and usually white, influence the definitions and framing of educational policies and the solutions to educational issues and problems in the U.S.

The existing U.S. social structure delineates the power of individuals and collectivities and the opportunities for change. We think that the "structural interest" (Alford 1976) of the powerful dominate the choices and the decision making process on all levels of education. These decisions are made as a consequence of interest-group accommodation among governmental bureaucrats and educational professionals rather than in negotiation with ethnic and minority groups themselves. In 1945, Steward Cole, Director of the Bureau for Intercultural Education warned that "National cultural unity must not be jeopardized by an exaggerated development of the forces of cultural diversity" (1945:564). This warning reflects an ideology based on control of a few white men who incorrectly assumed that their beliefs were rooted in democracy. Two years earlier, Kilpatrick and Cole wrote "The American people must learn to respect and encourage meritorious cultural differences, while at the same time insure the cultivations of over-all purposes and coordination of activities which give unitary vigor to our democracy" (1943:1). The forthcoming debate on cultural diversity in educational settings will attack these statements and question the definition of cultural knowledge, of whose culture should be taught in schools, and of the dominance of western knowledge itself. Eventually, policy choices will have to be made about what will be taught and who will teach in the educational system.

These choices will be guided by an ideology of democratic education that defines equality as a goal to be striven for "someday," but not anytime soon. Consequently, class and ethnic inequality are defined as "special problems" rather than "opportunities" in the educational system. "They" are the problem, not the system or the ideology that worked in the past and must be maintained in the present. Inequality is also maintained. This separatist policy creates the illusion that the less powerful groups are responsible for their own problems in the educational system. On the other hand, those who argue that inequality in education is a consequence of system failure, not individual failure, lay a foundation for governmental interventions to provide a more equitable educational system for all. Both the proponents of the "status quo" and those who support change through public policy believe that their position is supported by the past, by the democratic principles that lay the foundation for the country. The supporters of maintaining the present educational system argue that individuals should have a choice and governmental intervention takes that choice away. Delineating and implementing equity in education undermines the democratic process. The supporters of educational change argue that diverse cultural groups must be given the freedom to equally participate in the educational system through having a say in who teaches, what is taught, and who has the power to make educational policy decisions. Only then can the U.S. have a democratic educational system.

These contradictory ideologies will create a debate over what constitutes knowledge and this debate will occur because of the failure of educational policies that neglected to give some power to the groups that were most affected by the policies, rather than framing the issues within a "traditional text." This is really a debate over using the traditions of the past as a basis for policy making or embracing cultural and social changes in U.S. society and linking them to the democratic ideal of equity of the past for survival in the future.

Critique and Consequences of Pluralism

There are several problems with the theory of pluralism which, we feel, have served to undermine the traditional democratic principles of U.S. society. The problems with pluralism are:

(1) It equates organized representation and interest-group participation with democratic participation of individuals nullifying the significance of individual action; (2) it fosters the belief that equal access is provided all relevant parties through interest-group politics and ignores the fact that citizens who are not organized are excluded from the political process and, (3) it assumes the existence of an underlying values consensus that will make whatever results from the competitive interplay of organized interests congruent within broad areas of value agreement.

We believe instead that the groups with the most power and wealth dominate the system and, consequently, continue a paradigm that orders and relates certain selected facts into a logical framework. Their paradigm (based on the ideology and class and ethnic structure previously discussed) excludes alternative frameworks that threaten the established educational order. Policies based on the dominant paradigm tend to reflect and support the social and economic interest of the powerful in U.S. society. Established goals that seek to fundamentally change the educational system are likely to be transposed into negotiable and administrable goals that preserve the existing order in the pluralistic policy process. Change becomes a tinkering with the existing system rather than devising a foundation for a new system. The framing of policy creates an illusion of change through debating new themes based on old ideas.

Just as economic policies have never translated the traditional U.S. belief in equality into action, educational policies follow suit. In fact, economic and educational polices are inextricably bound to one another. They essentially are based on the principle of efficiency and functional rationality with a bureaucratic structure that sees to their maintenance, not principles of democracy and freedom for individuals and groups. The educational system fosters the teaching of democratic principles, based on equality. It also fosters the teaching of materialism and utilitarian individualism. The former stresses the importance of justice and fairness in public life, while the latter stresses the importance of private gain. This historic stress between the good of the individual versus the good of collectives creates contradictions and ambiguity into the ideology and politics of education and, as a consequence, perpetuates class and ethnic distinctions in local educational institutions.

Summary

We feel that until the educational power structure, (i.e., the policy makers and, for that matter, the power brokers in U.S. society) disassociates itself from the past and looks to its multicultural future, class and ethnic inequalities will continue to permeate the educational system. Changes in policies that guide what is being taught, who teaches, and who makes decisions about local school systems will be slow, at best. For true transformations to occur, democratic principles that support equality of education and economic structures, as depicted by De Tocqueville, must be put into action in the future. We must see a paradigm shift toward policies that balance the values of capitalism with those of the true democratic principles of equality. De Tocqueville expressed these sentiments in his discussion of New England as a prototype of "the American experience." He felt that, at that time, they were balancing democracy with individualism.

The new paradigm for the future of education will demand that individual growth (private) be balanced with a concern for the collective welfare and groups (public). An awareness of these contradictions in educational policy by the public and educational policy makers will, hopefully, lay a foundation for a more humane society for all its citizens. Incremental change only fosters more of the same, serves the rich and powerful and perpetuates the existing paradigm. Contemporary symbols of change remain just that -- symbols without action. By delineating the assumptions and contradictions in U.S. educational structure and policy with its face toward the past, we hope to create a useful debate about how to accomplish real change for the future.

References

Alford, Terry W.
   1972 The Political Economy of Health Care: Dynamics Without Change. *Politics and Society* 2:164-173.

Cole, Steward G.
   1945 Intercultural Education. In *One America: The History and Contributions, and Present Problems of Our Racial and National Minorities*, ed. Frances J. Brown and Joseph S. Roucek. Englewood Cliffs; Prentice Hall.

Dewey, John
   1961 *Democracy and Education*. New York: MacMillan Company.

Erikson, Erik H.
   1968 *Identity, Youth and Crisis*. New York: W.W. Norton and Company, Inc.

Kilpatrick, William and Steward G. Cole
   1943 Cultural Democracy in War and Peace. *Intercultural Education News* 4:1-2.

Tocqueville, Alexis de
   1835 *Democracy in America*. J.P. Mayer, ed. New York: Doubleday and Company, Inc.

Teaching as Praxis:

Race and Gender Working Sessions[1]

Barbara R. Johnston
Center for Political Ecology

Sylvia Helen Forman
University of Massachusetts, Amherst

After Sylvia Forman died, I inherited her collection of Association for Feminist Anthropology (AFA) notes, correspondence, and other organizational documents. Sylvia Forman was a founding member of the AFA who drew upon her vast political network to bring a number of feminist anthropologists into the initial organizing process. She wrote a series of organizing letters, created sub-committees to work on bylaws and membership, and served as the central clearinghouse during the organizational period. Following the organization of the AFA, Forman continued to play an integral role serving as interim President. Her first action following the AFA organizing meeting in 1988 was to help draft and present a resolution (during the open forum of the American Anthropological Association business meeting) calling for child care at the annual meetings. In her year of service, Forman worked on a finalized version of the by-laws, drafted ideas for a newsletter, and forged links between the AFA and other advocacy-oriented units, especially the Association for Black Anthropology (as represented by the following article). One of her ideas that eventually came to fruition was the creation of a committee structure in the AFA -- a structural mechanism that allowed issue-specific research and praxis, defined and (most importantly) funded by the Association.

Forman's AFA archive provides material evidence of her organizational style and the motivating factors that structured her political actions within the discipline of anthropology. For example, her notes for the 1989 "Teaching as Praxis: Race and Gender" workshop includes the following list of concerns:

- resisting thinking based on biological determinant models

- looking at and analyzing racism and other invidious social distinctions cross-culturally-- so social activism can be theoretically informed

- teaching separate courses vs. integrating issues into all courses

- pedagogy: what's effective when covering issues people get defensive about; and variations according to the population

- issues related to a white Euro-American teaching about race and racism.

In the personal statement she wrote when applying for promotion to Professor, (see Appendix), Forman wrote:

> I have consistently devoted much, if not most, of my professional effort and attention to teaching and advising . . . I take very seriously my teaching role outside of the classroom, especially that part concerned with students preparation of theses and dissertations . . . My service activities to the Department, University, Five College System, and the Discipline can be taken as another form of applied anthropology an effort to dedicate disciplinary expertise to the practical issues of the institutions with which I am involved . . .

These brief comments suggest the essential core that was Sylvia Forman's professional life: she was committed towards the production and the constant reformation of anthropological pedagogy, social activism, and the notion of social responsibility. In many ways Forman was the consummate applied anthropologist -- applying her intellect, her innate organizational abilities, and her gifted understanding of political structure to expose institutionalized inequities, reform and create new structures. Sylvia Helen Forman challenged and changed the structure and meaning of the anthropological discipline (Barbara Johnston).

For three years now a group of people has met at the American Anthropological Association (AAA) annual meetings to work on the difficulties of teaching race and gender issues. In 1989, Association for Feminist Anthropology (AFA) co-organizer and founding member Sylvia Forman and Association of Black Anthropologists (ABA) president Faye Harrison chaired an open forum on *Teaching Race and Gender*, with the goal of sharing successful strategies and materials. In a room crammed with people wanting to contribute their frustrations or successes, the discussion rapidly jumped from topic to topic. We commented on the structure of academia as it reflects and reproduces social inequality. We discussed ways that anthropological media can reproduce that inequality in the larger society. Participants described course outlines, recommended reading materials, and shared innovative class discussion and student project ideas. From theory to praxis and back again, we moved through our first working session with a great deal of energy, but with little substantive progress in either arena. People left wanting more.

The second year, 1990, saw the formation of two sessions: one to focus on an analysis of teaching as praxis, the other to follow up on individual issues, strategies, or complaints. These sessions were *Teaching as Praxis: Race and Ideologies of Power*, chaired by Deborah D'Amico-Samuels and Pem Davidson Buck, and an open forum chaired by Lynn Bolles and Sylvia Forman, *Teaching about Race and Gender: Courses, Curriculum, and Classrooms*. These sessions were designed to fill the diverse needs aired at the previous year's open forum. They were intended to run back-to-back, with panel presentations and open discussion followed by a focused working session where participants formed problem-specific groups which would report their findings back to the larger group. Program scheduling placed the panel presentation on Friday morning and the working session late Saturday afternoon. The Friday *Teaching as Praxis* session went over the allotted time, and some forty anthropologists, including both participants and members of the audience, continued discussion over lunch. Splitting the symposium/workshop event apart meant a loss of some of the panel participants, and more importantly, the lack of a shared experience. Many of the participants in Saturday's workshop did not have the benefit of the previous day's presentations, discussion, and analysis. Thus, time was again spent in the open discussion period of the workshop covering old ground, examining such questions as, "Why, when we say race, do we limit ourselves to discussions of Blacks and Whites"? or, "How do we incorporate race and gender issues in all the courses we teach"? A few people brought curriculum material to the session, and some copies were disseminated. A collective decision was reached to work for the formation of a national project focusing the discipline on issues of race and racism, as the recently completed gender project, and a task force created. One of the more significant and enduring contributions of the 1990 AVA/AFA effort was ABA's publication of the panel papers and synopsis of ensuing discussion (*Transforming Anthropology* 2(1), 1991).

In 1991, the Teaching as Praxis panel/discussion/workshop format was finally achieved, and the contribution to discussion was obvious to all. Comments and discussion again crossed the theory/praxis spectrum but were grounded in a shared framework established in the morning's presentations. Thus, we avoided the frustration of the previous year where workshop participants reproduced in small ways the observations and comments from an earlier, significant session. Furthermore, by providing a copy machine and asking participants in advance to bring curriculum material, people left the workshop with substantive material.

Nevertheless, in spite of the successful format, the content of our discourse was not new. In fact, many of the pivotal issues raised in 1991 had also been raised in 1990. And in 1989. And, as in previous years, the bulk of our allotted time was spent in describing race and gender inequities in the anthropological experience (material, disciplinary structures, academic structures), with little or no movement on ways to change these realities. Some of the issues raised include: How do we go about defining race and gender issues, constructing curriculum, and facilitating a learning experience when our history as a discipline has in many ways been central to the social reproduction of inequity? How do we approach race and gender inequity when our personal experience is often that of white mainstream, those born to power? Or, if we are one of the very few people of color, how do we move beyond the academic and classroom expectations that we should act as informants on the experience of victimization by "race/gender inequity." And finally, why must these questions be raised on the sidelines; why do we not find these concerns in the center of our discipline?

The issues above have been raised at each of the three workshops, addressed in the 1990 and 1991 Teaching as Praxis panels, and discussed in a previous issue of *Transforming Anthropology* by Faye Harrison (1990a, 1990b). They have been raised and addressed elsewhere, for example, in Johnnetta Cole's 1989 plenary address on racism to the American Anthropological Association. That they still need to be raised speaks to the marginalization of these concerns, to the very structure of power in our discipline, and perhaps to the relative lack of power our discipline has in the larger context of academia and society.

Three years of working sessions has demonstrated that while there are no simple answers, there are a myriad of strategies used in the effort to identify and transform the race and gender schisms in our thinking, writing, teaching, or institutions. Action-oriented discussion over the years has repeatedly recommended the following changes:

1. Restructure our approach to graduate training, including theoretical structure as well as the practical issues of recruitment and retention.

2. Design and participate in faculty training programs which deal with racism/classism/sexism in the faculty and in the curriculum, within anthropology and within academia.

3. Increase access to race/gender sensitive curriculum material.

4. Bring issues of inequity in the anthropological experience (material, disciplinary structures, academic structures) to the center of disciplinary discourse.

Suggestions to meet these needs include supporting the efforts of a graduate student-designed guide to minority recruitment and retention; sponsoring a student-designed panel on graduate training at the AAA meetings; forming a project on race and gender in the curriculum in order to analyze existing sources of bias in the literature; structuring future Race and Gender workshops; compiling and distributing curriculum material; and utilizing our diverse networks to broadly disseminate material such as the proceedings from Teaching as Praxis sessions.

Perhaps the most significant contribution of the Race and Gender workshops has been the establishment of a forum for an ever-changing mix of people to recognize and confront the insidious "isms" within our discipline. In doing so, we shape and reshape our commitment to the destruction of the "isms," as Johnnetta Cole puts it, voicing again the values and ideals which drew us into anthropology.

> Why, my sisters from around the world, what do you do about the vile, persistent, destructive stuff called racism? For those of us in the U.S. where there is a truly frightening resurgence of racism, do you as a woman feel and act on a special responsibility to fight that system of inequality? Poverty, exploitation, racism and sexism know no national borders. But while we know this is true, do we make our hard choices on this reality? Do we structure our decisions and strategies around an awareness of these realities? And are our actions shaped by a commitment to the destruction of the "isms" of the world? (Cole 1990:2-5).

The questions posed by Cole represent the very essence of anthropology. We need to ask ourselves now, and always, if our methods of teaching, our research and writing choices, our funding and hiring choices reflect a commitment to "the destruction of the 'isms' of the world"?

Note

1. Appreciation is due to Robert Painter, Deborah Rubin and Lynn Bolles for their comments and suggestions.

References

Cole, Johnetta
  1990 Proceedings of the Fourth International Interdisciplinary Congress on Women.
    I.W.A.C. Bulletin 2 (November): 2-5.

Harrison, Faye V.
  1990a Three Women, One Struggle: Anthropology, Performance, and Pedagogy. *Transforming Anthropology* 1(1):1-9.
  1990b Towards a More Critical Pedagogy: Syllabus for a Course on Historical Perspectives in Sociocultural Anthropology. *Transforming Anthropology* 1(1):18-21.

Sylvia Forman and Thomas D. ("Tip") O'Neill (former Speaker of the U.S. House of Representatives), April 14, 1982, Memorial Hall, UMass campus; taken by the University of Massachusetts Photographic Services.

Occupational Status of Women

In Anthropology Departments

Sylvia Helen Forman

The following two reports appeared in the *Anthropology Newsletter (AN)* in 1977 and 1978 (Volume 18, no. 9 and Volume 19, no. 8). Sylvia published them in her role as a member of the Committee on the Status of Women in Anthropology (COSWA). These reports represent the kind of work that Sylvia considered most important and for which she is perhaps, best known. She worked hard to change the world by using anthropology and to improve the field of anthropology by constantly evaluating and pushing the boundaries of our profession.

Report 1: Occupational Status of Women in Anthropology Departments, 1976-77

This report summarizes the results of a survey based on the *Guide to Departments of Anthropology 1976-77* and conducted under the auspices of the Committee on the Status of Women in Anthropology (COSWA) of the AAA. COSWA has sponsored several such *Guide* studies in the past, with findings reported in the *Anthropology Newsletter* (vol 16, no 4; vol 14, nos 2 and 9; vol 11, no 9); all share the purpose of monitoring the occupational status of women in the academic world of anthropology.

Although this study includes all the people listed in academic departments (but not museums) in the 1976-77 *Guide*, it must be noted that not all professional anthropologists -- not even all academically-employed anthropologists -- appear in the *Guide*. Further, while in this report reference will be made to previously published COSWA *Guide* studies, comparisons are constrained by changes of departments listed in the *Guide* over the years.

Listings in the *Guide* include the following information for almost all individuals: employing department and institution, personal name, highest degree with its granting date and institution, academic title (rank), employment status (full-time, part-time, joint appointment) and areas of specialization. Sex of individuals must be (and was in this survey) inferred from the names. I have tried to insure accuracy of such inference in cases of uncommon names by consulting with people who knew the individuals involved and/or the language from which names derived; for about 50 difficult cases, telephone calls to departmental offices were made to ascertain sex. The data have been computer stored and tabulated.

Of the 3827 people listed in the 1976-77 *Guide* and included in this study, 905 (23.65%) are female and 2918 (76.25%) are male; 4 individuals (0.1%) are unidentified by sex. Since these last cases are so few, they have been omitted from tabulations herein. All totals and statistics below are based on N = 3823. Table 1.1 presents a breakdown of the occupational statuses of these people.

TABLE 1.1. PERCENTAGE AND NUMBER OF FEMALES AND MALES AT DIFFERENT RANKS, ALL EMPLOYMENT STATUSES COMBINED, AND BY FULL TIME EMPLOYMENT STATUS AND BY PART TIME OR JOINT EMPLOYMENT STATUS

	Full-Time				Part-Time or Joint				Employ	All Combined				
	female		male		female		male		status	female		male		Total
Ranks	%	N	%	N	%	N	%	N	unknown	%	N	%	N	Number
Full	11.25	100	88.75	789	11.24	10	88.76	79	4	11.30	111	88.70	871	982
Assoc	19.71	176	80.29	717	15.00	9	85.00	51	2	19.37	185	80.62	770	955
Asst	31.16	330	68.84	729	38.24	26	61.76	42	1	31.68	357	68.41	771	1128
Lect	32.31	21	67.69	44	39.74	31	60.26	47	1	36.55	53	63.19	91	144
Instr	41.57	37	58.43	52	42.86	15	57.14	20	0	41.94	52	58.06	72	124
Research	41.38	24	58.62	34	41.38	12	58.62	17	23	39.09	43	60.91	67	110
Adjunct	11.76	2	88.24	15	30.43	21	69.57	48	4	27.78	25	72.22	65	90
Emeritus	13.16	5	86.84	33	10.00	1	90.00	9	2	12.00	6	88.00	44	50
Visiting (all ranks)	26.87	18	73.13	49	33.33	11	66.67	22	0	29.00	29	71.00	71	100
"Other"	27.96	26	72.04	67	44.44	16	55.56	20	11	31.43	44	68.57	96	140
Totals	22.61	739	77.39	2529	29.98	152	70.02	355	48	23.67	905	76.33	2918	3823
(Column no	1	2	3	4	5	6	7	8	9	10	11	12	13	14)

The information in Table 1.1 illustrates the fact that women anthropologists are not equally represented across ranks in academic departments. Given that 23.65% of those employed are women, we can note that women hold relatively high percentages of low rank appointments an disproportionately low percentages of the senior positions. In addition, more women proportionally are in part-time or joint positions than are men (the difference in these proportions-the totals in columns 2,4,6 and 8 of Table 1.1--is significant by chi-square test at P<0.001).

TABLE 1.2. PERCENT OF FEMALES HOLDING DIFFERENT RANKS AT THREE PERIODS.

Year	Full	Assoc	Asst	Lect	Instr	Research	"Other"
1971-72	10.00%	15.00%	22.00%	31.00%	32.00%	39.00%	26.00%
1974-75	11.00%	19.00%	27.00%	40.00%	40.00%	42.00%	27.00%
1976-77	11.30%	19.37%	31.68%	36.55%	41.94%	39.09%	27.36%

Note: These percentages are calculated by taking the number of women at a rank over the total number at that rank. Comparison is with Vance 1975. "Other" ranks include: emeritus, adjunct, visiting, curator, fellow, lab technician, field archaeologist and associate and those unknown.

While the number of women in the profession has grown and the percentage of women employed at lower ranks has increased since 1971-72, the percentage of women in higher ranks (full, associate and emeritus professorships) has not grown significantly. Table 1.1 presents a condensed comparison of percentage of women at different ranks over time. The only rank at which the increase in proportion of women employed is statistically significant is Professor (for Assistant, the change in portions of females and males from 1974-75 to 1976-77 is significant by chi-square test at P<0.05 and the change from 1971-72 to 1976-77 is significant by chi-square test at P<0.001).

TABLE 1. 3. PERCENTAGES OF FEMALES AND MALES REACHING DIFFERENT RANKS BY 1976-77 BY COHORTS OF YEARS IN WHICH THEY RECEIVED DOCTORAL DEGREES.

PhD Cohort Years	Full and Emeritus	Assoc	Asst	"Other"	Total number in cohort by sex	
1975-79						
female		2.86	80.95	16.20	105	
male	0.47	7.5	71.4	20.66		213
1970-74						
female	1.30	19.90	65.80	12.96	301	
male	2.73	32.15	56.50	8.66		843
1965-69						
female	13.90	55.50	17.50	13.14	137	
male	25.74	59.70	6.80	7.70		544
1960-64						
female	56.45	22.60	3.20	17.70	62	
male	71.65	22.10	1.25	4.98		321
1955-59						
female	60.50	30.20	0.0	9.30	43	
male	81.30	8.91	0.0	9.79		235
1950-54						
female	60.90	17.40	0.0	21.70	23	
male	92.20	3.60	0.0	4.20		166
1945-49						
female	50.00	40.00	0.0	10.00	10	
male	97.87	0.0	0.0	2.13		47
1940-44						
female	62.50	12.50	0.0	25.00	8	
male	92.70	0.0	0.0	7.30		41
1935-39						
female	66.70	16.67	0.0	16.67	6	
male	84.60	0.0	0.0	15.40		39
1930-34						
male	100.00	0.0	0.0	0.0	0	12
1925-29						
female	0.0	0.0	0.0	100.00	3	
male	66.67	0.0	0.0	33.33		6
≥ 1924						
female	100.00	0.0	0.0	0.0	1	
male	0	0.0	0.0	0.0		0
PhD year unknown						
female	0.0	0.0	66.67	33.33	3	
male	12.00	16.00	28.00	44.00		25
female total					702	
male total						2492

That women are not represented in adequate proportions at higher ranks is further illustrated by examining percentages at different ranks by cohorts receiving the doctorate at different periods. Table 1.3 summarizes this information and shows that women are not progressing through the academic ranks as rapidly as men. This pattern is persistent over the last 8 years (see other COSWA _GUIDE_ reports). Under Assistant Professor in Table 1.3, we can note again a recent gain for employment of women. For the 1965-69 and 1960-64 cohorts, women appear to be reaching the Associate Professor level more quickly. However, females overall achieve the Associate, Full and Emeritus Professorships with a notable and continuing lag behind their male colleagues from the same doctoral degree cohorts.

It has been found in previous COSWA _Guide_ studies that the more prestigious and important anthropology departments have had the poorest records of employment of women at senior ranks. This pattern also still persists. The major anthropology departments show a tendency to hire "their own" in general, but they hire and promote their own male graduates to a greater extent than their own female graduates (see Table 1.5).

Table 1.4 presents the figures on production of PhDs by sex and by 2 categories of departments: 14 major departments, defined as those which have granted doctoral degrees in anthropology for the longest period, and all others listed in the 1976-77 _Guide_. (The 14 major departments are: California-Berkeley, California-Los Angeles, Columbia, Harvard, Michigan, North Carolina, Pennsylvania, Yale, Wisconsin, Chicago, Stanford, Arizona, Washington and Illinois.) As Table 1.4 shows, 57.55% of the women now listed in the _Guide_ have received their doctoral degrees from the 14 major departments, as compared with 54.90% of the men. These figures represent a small increase in the proportion of women gaining their degrees from the 14 departments, as compared with 54.90% of the men. These figures represent a small increase in the proportion of women gaining their degrees from the 14 departments over the last 8 years. Women have received 22.80% of the PhDs granted by these 14 departments. The percentages given in Table 1.4 provide a background for examining the information in Table 1.5.

TABLE 1.4. PERCENTAGES AND NUMBERS OF PhDs BY SEX AND BY THE 14
MAJOR DEPARTMENTS AND ALL OTHER DEPARTMENTS.

	Female			Male			Female & Male	
	number	row %	column %	number	row%	column%	number	column%
14 major depts	404	22.80	57.55	1368	77.20	54.90	1772	55.48
all other depts	298	20.96	42.45	1124	79.04	45.10	1422	44.52
all depts combined	702	21.98		2492	78.02		3194	100.00

Table 1.5 illustrates the fact that women are less well represented in the senior ranks at the 14 major departments than in general, although they are relatively well represented at the Assistant Professor level. Women with PhDs appear in disproportionately high percentages in the Researcher and Adjunct ranks at the 14 major departments and in the Lecturer, Instructor and Researcher ranks at the other departments.

TABLE 1.5. NUMBER AND PERCENTAGE OF FEMALE PhDs BY RANK AT 14 MAJOR DEPARTMENTS AND AT OTHER DEPARTMENTS, AND BY DEGREE GRANTED FROM 14 MAJOR DEPARTMENTS AND FROM OTHER DEPARTMENTS.

Ranks	Employed by others			Employed by 14 major			Total % & No at rank	Total % & No of all PhDs (male & female) at ranks:		
	degree from 14 major	degree from others	total % & No at rank	degree from 14 major	degree from others	total % & No at rank		14 major	others	all
Full	8.4%	4.41%	12.81%	3.7%	3.2%	6.9%	11.46%	48%	26.46%	29.49%
	(61)	(32)	(93)	(8)	(7)	(15)	(108)	(216)	(726)	(942)
Assoc	11.88%	8.42%	20.3%	8.54%	6.1%	14.64%	19.78%	18.22%	29.45%	27.86%
	(96)	(68)	(164)	(7)	(5)	(12)	(176)	(82)	(808)	(890)
Asst	15.95%	15.16%	31.11%	26.2%	8.74%	34.94%	31.51%	22.89%	32.22%	30.9%
	(141)	(134)	(275)	(27)	(9)	(36)	(311)	(103)	(884)	(987)
Lect	27.1%	8.3%	35.4%	18.2%	0.0%	18.2%	32.2%	2.44%	1.74%	1.85%
	(13)	(4)	(17)	(2)	(0)	(2)	(19)	(11)	(48)	(59)
Instr	13.3%	33.3%	46.6%	0.0%	0.0%	0.0%	46.67%	0.0%	0.55%	0.47%
	(2)	(5)	(7)	(0)	(0)	(0)	(7)	(0)	(15)	(15)
Research	34.88%	11.63%	46.51%	60%	0.0%	60%	47.92%	1.1%	1.57%	1.5%
	(15)	(5)	(20)	(3)	(0)	(3)	(23)	(5)	(43)	(48)
Adjunct	8.96%	11.94%	20.9%	33.3%	16.7%	50%	23.29%	1.33%	2.44%	2.29%
	(6)	(8)	(14)	(2)	(1)	(3)	(17)	(6)	(67)	(73)
Emeritus	11.77%	2.94%	14.71%	0.0%	0.0%	0.0%	11.11%	2.44%	1.23%	1.41%
	(4)	(1)	(5)	(0)	(0)	(0)	(5)	(11)	(34)	(45)
Visiting (All ranks)	13.56%	11.86%	25.42%	8.3%	8.3%	16.6%	23.94%	2.67%	2.15%	2.22%
	(8)	(7)	(15)	(1)	(1)	(2)	(17)	(12)	(59)	(71)
"Other"	11.7%	18.33%	30.03%	25%	0.0%	25%	29.69%	0.89%	2.19%	2%
	(7)	(11)	(18)	(1)	(0)	(1)	(19)	(4)	(60)	(64)
Totals	(353)	(275)	(628)	(51)	(23)	(74)	(702)	100%	100%	100%
								(450)	(2744)	(3194)
(Column No	1	2	3	4	5	6	7	8	9	10)

Note: The percentages in columns 1, 2 and 3 were created by taking each number, at a rank, over the number at that rank in column 9; for columns 4, 5 and 6, each number at a rank over the number at that rank in column 8; for column 7, number at each rank was over the number at that rank in column 10.

Table 1.6 presents a breakdown by sex and subdisciplinary specialty of those employed anthropologists who have doctoral degrees. Women are rather evenly distributed across the cultural/social, physical and linguistic subfields, but are underrepresented in archeology.

This survey of the 1976-77 *Guide* reveals the same pattern of occupational status of women that earlier studies have demonstrated. There has been an increase in the proportion of women hired at junior levels. But women are still relatively excluded from senior academic ranks, especially in major anthropology departments, and they still make up too large a share of the part-time and joint appointments and of the non-professional ranks. Finally, women anthropologists progress less fully and less rapidly than their male colleagues through the academic ranks and to the associate and full professor levels.

TABLE 1. 6. PERCENTAGES OF FEMALES AND MALES,
WITH DOCTORAL DEGREES, BY SUB-DISCIPLINE

Subdisciplines	Female		Male		Female & Male	
	Row %	Col %	Row %	Col %	Col %	Row #
Cultural/social	24.90	64.53	74.99	56.74	56.90	1817
Archaeology	12.85	11.68	87.15	22.31	19.96	638
Physical	21.82	11.25	78.18	11.36	11.32	362
Linguistic	27.34	9.97	72.27	7.42	8.01	255
"Other"	14.75	2.56	85.25	4.17	3.81	122
All subdis-ciplines	21.97	100.00	78.02	100.00	100.00	3194
	N = 702		N = 2492		100.00	

Report 2: Occupational Status of Women in Anthropology Departments, 1977-78

This report is one of a series based on the *Guide to Departments of Anthropology* (of the AAA) and sponsored by the AAA Committee on the Status of Women in Anthropology (COSWA).[1] All of these studies share the purpose of monitoring the occupational status of women in the academic realm of anthropology.

This study is based on the 1977-78 *Guide* and includes all the people listed in academic departments (but not museums) for 1977-78. While my discussion below of the results is couched in general terms, it must be remembered that the numbers presented are not all-encompassing since not all professionally employed anthropologists -- nor even all those in academic departments -- appear in the *Guide*. It should also be noted that comparisons to previously published *Guide* studies are constrained to some extent by changes in methods of analysis used and in departments listed in the *Guide* over the years.

Listings in the *Guide* include the following information for almost all individuals: employing department and institution, personal name, highest degree with its granting year and institution, academic title (rank), employment status (full-time, part-time or joint appointment) and areas of specialization. Sex of individuals must be and has been inferred from their names. To insure the accuracy of such inference in cases of uncommon names, I have made extensive consultations, including direct inquiry to employers. All data have been computer stored and tabulated.

Of the 3,974 people listed in the 1977-78 *Guide* and included in this study, 965 (24.28%) are females and 3,009 (75.72%) are males. (Seven individuals could not be identified by sex; since these cases are so few, they are omitted from the total above and from all tabulations.) Table 2.1 presents a breakdown of the occupational ranks and statuses of these people.

TABLE 2.1. PERCENTAGE AND NUMBER OF FEMALES AND MALES AT DIFFERENT RANKS, BY ALL EMPLOYMENT STATUSES COMBINED, FULL-TIME EMPLOYMENT STATUS, PART-TIME EMPLOYMENT STATUS AND OTHER (JOINT AND UNKNOWN) EMPLOYMENT STATUS.

Ranks	Full-Time				Part-Time				Other (joint & unknown)				All Combined				
	female %	N	male N	total % at rank	female %	N	male N	total % at rank	female %	N	male N	total % at rank	female %	N	male N	total % at rank	Total number
Full	11.48	108	833	27.78	14.29	3	18	6.46	7.06	6	79	32.44	11.17	117	930	26.35	1047
Assoc	20.88	205	777	28.99	25.00	5	15	6.15	20.83	10	38	18.32	20.95	220	830	26.42	1050
Asst	33.07	339	686	30.26	41.67	15	21	11.08	33.33	15	30	17.18	33.36	369	737	27.83	1106
Lect	45.16	28	34	1.83	48.48	32	34	20.31	33.33	3	6	3.44	45.99	63	74	3.45	137
Inst	39.06	25	39	1.89	45.95	17	20	11.38	50.00	1	1	.76	41.75	43	60	2.59	103
Research	35.16	32	59	2.69	45.45	15	18	10.15	28.57	6	15	8.02	36.55	53	92	3.65	145
Adjunct	16.67	3	15	.53	32.08	17	36	16.31	32.00	8	17	9.54	29.17	28	68	2.42	96
Emeritus	13.95	6	37	1.27	9.09	1	10	3.38	0.00	0	4	1.53	12.07	7	51	1.46	58
Visiting	33.33	20	40	1.77	28.00	7	18	7.69	20.00	2	8	3.82	30.53	29	66	2.39	95
"Other"	26.73	27	74	2.98	34.78	8	15	7.08	10.00	1	12	4.96	26.28	36	101	3.45	137
Totals	23.41	793	2594	100%	36.92	120	205	100%	19.85	52	210	100%	24.28	965	3009	100%	3974
column #	1	2	3	4	5	6	7	8	9	10	11	12	13	14	15	16	17

Notes: (a) "other" ranks include: curator, lab technician, fellow, field archaeologist and research assistant. (b) Calculation of percentages: percentages in column 1, for example, are calculated by dividing an N in column 2 by the sum of Ns in columns 2 and 3 for that row; and the percentages in column 4, for example, are calculated by dividing the sum of the Ns in columns 2 and 3 in a given row by the sums of columns 2 and 3 in the Totals row. The same procedure is followed for each employment status type.

As the contents of Table 2.1 illustrate, the 24.28% of anthropologists who are female are not distributed across academic ranks or employment statuses in the same pattern as men. Women continue to be employed in disproportionally greater numbers at lower ranks and disproportionally smaller numbers at higher academic ranks. These differences in female and male distribution are statistically significant (P<.005) for the ranks of full, associate and assistant professor, and lecturer and instructor.[2] Also, women hold a disproportionally large share of part-time positions.

While the overall number and percentage of women in the profession have grown more or less steadily for some time, that growth is not reflected in the proportions of women employed at higher ranks. There has been no significant change in the proportion of women at the full professor rank since 1971-72 (see table 2.2). Although there was no significant gain in the proportion of women at the associate rank between 1971-72 and 1976-77 (Forman 1977), there is a notable increase in the number of women at this rank between 1971-72 and 1977-78 (see Table 2.2; chi-square test of difference in numbers of females and males at this rank between 1971-72 and 1977-78 is significant at P<.03). However, this recent gain does not change the general picture.

TABLE 2.2. COMPARISON OF NUMBERS AND PERCENTAGES OF FEMALES
HOLDING DIFFERENT RANKS IN 1971-72 AND 1977-78.
(1971-72 FIGURES ARE FROM VANCE 1975)

	Full	Assoc	Asst	Lect	Inst	Rich	"Other"	Totals
1971-72								
female %	10.00	15.00	22.00	31.00	32.00	39.00	26.00	18.00
female N	74	99	216	45	49	17	24	524
total N	678	600	942	137	147	56	93	2653
1977-78								
female %	11.17	20.95	33.36	45.99	41.75	36.55	25.91	24.28
female N	117	220	369	63	43	53	100	965
total N	1047	1050	1106	137	103	145	386	3974
change in								
female %	+ 1.17	+ 5.95	+ 11.36	+ 14.99	+ 9.75	- 2.45	- 0.09	+ 6.28

That women are not represented in appropriate proportions at higher ranks is further illustrated in Table 2.3, which shows levels of achievement of rank for groups receiving the PhD at different time periods. These data clearly indicate that women are not moving up the academic ladder or ranks as rapidly or as consistently as their male colleagues. This pattern of lagging promotion rates for women has been persistent for at least the last decade (see earlier _Guide_ reports and Freed et al 1977). Although discriminatory promotion practices are likely to account for at least part of this lag, we lack and badly need systematic information on the promotion process in order to fully explain the causes of this continuing problem.

TABLE 2.3. ACHIEVEMENT OF RANK BY COHORT OF PhD: FOR THOSE HOLDING PhD IN 1977-78, THE NUMBERS OF FEMALES AND MALES AND THE PERCENTAGES WITHIN EACH SEX FOR EACH COHORT WHO HAVE ACHIEVED DIFFERENT RANKS BY 1977-78.

PhD received	Full & Emeritus		Associate		Assistant		"Other"		Totals for Cohorts	
	female	male	female	male	female	male	female	male	female	male
1965 & earlier										
w/i/sex %	56.55	79.87	23.81	13.38	2.98	0.63	16.67	6.11	100.00	100.00
N	95	758	40	127	5	6	28	58	168	949
1971 & earlier										
w/i/sex %	31.48	52.99	42.06	34.31	12.17	5.46	14.29	7.24	100.00	100.00
N	119	922	159	597	46	95	54	126	378	1740
1972 to 1977										
w/i/sex %	0.50	1.30	13.20	20.49	70.81	65.02	15.48	13.19	100.00	100.00
N	2	11	52	174	279	552	61	112	394	849
totals in 1977-78										
at rank %	11.48	88.52	21.49	78.51	33.43	66.57	32.58	67.42	22.97	77.03
N	121	933	211	771	325	647	115	238	772	2589
column #	1	2	3	4	5	6	7	8	9	10

Notes: (a) the 1965 and earlier cohort is completely duplicated within the 1971 and earlier cohort; therefore, it is the numbers for the 1971 and earlier and the 1972-77 cohorts that add to the totals given for 1977-78. (b) within the three cohorts, the percentages given are percentages within sex; e.g., the first figure, 56.55% is produced by dividing the N in column 1 for that cohort, 95, by the N in column 9, for that cohort, 168; for each of the three cohorts, the N's in columns 1, 3, 5, and 7 are divided by the N in column 9 to yield the female percentages achieving rank, and similarly the N's in columns 2, 4, 6, and 8 are divided by N in column 10 for male percentages. Percentages in row of totals in 1977-78 are not within sex, but percentage of each sex at rank.

Women constitute 26.9% of the recipients of PhDs in anthropology for the period 1947 to 1976, and about 32.2% of the PhD recipients for 1970-76.[3] Reference to Tables 1 to 3 shows that only at the lower academic ranks are the percentages of employed women equivalent to (or greater than) the percentages of PhD holders who are women. The increase in proportion of women is greatest at the assistant professor and lecturer ranks (see Table 2.2; chi-square test of change in numbers of females and males at assistant rank between 1971-72 and 1977-78 shows the increase in women significant at P<.001). It is noteworthy that at the assistant rank, which represents the great majority of new hirings, the percentage of women is almost exactly the same as the percentage of recent PhD recipients who are women. Given that new hiring of women at the lower academic ranks seems to be generally equitable at the present, the slower progression of women to higher ranks (discussed above) stands out as the primary current issue in women's occupational status in anthropology.

TABLE 2.4. COMPARISON OF EMPLOYMENT OF FEMALES AND MALES, WITH PhD, BY RANKS, AT 14 MAJOR DEPARTMENTS AND ALL OTHER DEPARTMENTS

	Female				Male				Total at rank			
	Major 14		Others		Major 14		Others		Major 14		Others	
	Row %	Col %	Row %	Col %	Row %	Col %	Row %	Col %	Total %	N	Total %	N
Ranks	N		N		N		N					
Full	7.39	20.24	12.68	14.20	92.61	56.05	87.32	30.21	49.57		26.44	
	17		98		213		675			230		773
Assoc	20.00	19.05	21.48	28.26	80.00	16.84	78.52	31.92	17.24		31.05	
	16		195		64		713			80		908
Asst	35.78	46.43	32.91	41.59	64.22	18.42	67.09	16.19	23.49		29.82	
	39		287		70		585			109		872
Visiting	12.50	1.19	28.36	2.75	87.50	1.84	71.64	2.15	1.72		2.29	
(All ranks)	1		19		7		48			8		67
"Other"	29.73	13.10	29.93	13.19	70.27	6.84	70.07	9.53	7.97		10.40	
	11		91		26		213			37		304
Total % of sex	18.10		23.60		81.90		76.40		100.00		100.00	
Total N	84		690		380		2234			464		2924

Previous *Guide* studies have shown that the more prestigious and important anthropology departments have generally had poor records of employment of women, especially at senior ranks. The 1977-78 data, presented in Table 2.4, show that 14 of the more important departments[4] continue to employ women at senior ranks in very small proportions, although women are well represented at them in lower rank positions. The difference in the proportion of women employed at the major 14 departments and at all others-with the major 14 departments having fewer women on their faculties-is statistically significant (chi-square test of numbers of men and women at the two sets of departments yields P<.01). Within the set of the major 14 departments, the number of women at the full professor level is significantly lower than the number of men (chi-square test yields P<.001).

TABLE 2.5. PERCENTAGES AND NUMBERS OF FEMALES AND MALES WITH PhD IN DIFFERENT
SUBDISCIPLINES, FOR ALL CURRENT PhDs AND FOR THOSE WHO RECEIVED PhD IN PERIOD
1972-77. (NOTE: THE CATEGORY OF ALL PhDs INCLUDES THE SUB-GROUP OF THOSE WHO
RECEIVED PhD IN 1972-77.)

Subdiscipline	Female		Male		Totals	
PhD category	Row %	Col %	Row %	Col %	Row N	Col %
Cultural/Social						
1977-78 all	26.29	65.76	73.71	54.57	1936	57.13
PhD 1972-77	36.21	63.96	63.79	52.30	696	55.99
Archaeology						
1977-78 all	14.01	12.40	85.99	22.52	685	20.21
PhD 1972-77	19.39	12.94	80.61	24.97	263	21.16
Physical						
1977-78 all	21.20	10.47	78.80	11.51	382	11.27
PhD 1972-77	29.75	11.93	70.25	13.07	158	12.71
Linguistic						
1977-78 all	27.48	9.30	72.52	7.27	262	7.73
PhD 1972-77	41.05	9.90	58.95	6.60	95	7.64
"Other"						
1977-78 all	12.90	2.07	87.10	4.13	124	3.66
PhD 1972-77	16.13	1.27	83.87	3.06	31	2.49
Totals						
1977-78 all	22.84	100.00	77.16	100.00	3389	100.00
PhD 1972-77	31.70	100.00	68.30	100.00	1243	100.00

Women are relatively evenly distributed among the cultural/social, physical and linguistic subdisciplines of anthropology, but they remain notably underrepresented in archaeology. Table 2.5
presents a breakdown by sex and sub-discipline for employed anthropologists with PhD degrees.
(The figures in Table 2.5 do not include double counting of individuals who have more than one
sub-discipline listed in the *Guide*; the first named specialty was used in such cases.) Comparative
data for those people who received the PhD in the period 1972-1977 are also presented in Table
2.5 and show some shift in emphasis by women. Greater proportions of women are specializing
in physical and linguistic anthropology and in archaeology in recent years; but archaeology still
remains relatively short of women.

This survey of the 1977-78 *Guide* reveals some, but not a great deal of change in the pattern
of occupation status of women in anthropology that earlier studies have illustrated. Women
continue to gain slowly in numbers and percentage employed. A trend of increase in the
proportion of women employed at lower academic ranks continues. The percentage of women
at assistant professor rank is currently about equal to the percentage of recent PhDs who are
female. There is some indication of an increase in the share of associate professorships held by
women; but overall women are still underrepresented at senior academic ranks, especially among
the more important departments. Women still make up too large a proportion of those
anthropologists employed on a part-time basis and at non-professional ranks. Most notably,
women anthropologists continue to progress less fully and less rapidly than their male colleagues
through the ladder of academic ranks to the associate and full professor levels.

Notes

1. The opinions and assessments expressed in this report are those of the author and are not necessarily those of the AAA or COSWA. The author was a member of COSWA when this report was prepared; term expired July 1978.

2. In each case, chi-square test of numbers of women and men at one rank as against all others was used.

3. These figures are based in part on D'Andrade et al (1975:757) and in part on tabulations I made of the PhD award listings in recent issues of the *Guide*. Because of differences and errors in reporting such figures, they cannot be taken as exact. National statistics give the percentage of women awarded PhDs in anthropology in 1973-74 as 32.8% (Scientific Manpower Commission 1975).

4. The 14 major departments included here are: U of Arizona, U of California Berkeley, U of California Los Angeles, U of Chicago, Columbia U, Harvard U, U of Illinois Urbana, U of Michigan Ann Arbor, U of North Carolina, U of Pennsylvania, Stanford U, U of Washington, U of Wisconsin, Yale U.

References

D'andrade, R. G. et al
   1975 Academic Opportunity in Anthropology, 1974-90. *American Anthropologist* 77(4):753-773.

Forman, Sylvia Helen
   1977 Occupational Status of Women in Anthropology Departments 1976-77. *Anthropology Newsletter* 18(9):10-12.

Freed, Ruth S. et al
   1977 Male and Female Anthropologists. *Annals of the New York Academy of Sciences* 293:25-50.

Scientific Manpower Commission
   1975 Professional Women and Minorities: a Manpower Data Resource Service. Scientific Manpower Commission: Washington, D.C. (prepared by Betty M. Vetter and Eleanor L. Babco).

Vance, Carole
   1975 Sexual Stratification in Academic Anthropology, 1974-75. *Anthropology Newsletter* 16(4):10-13.

Conflict, Coffee,

Cattle and Corn:

Inversion of Gender through

Development in Rural Honduras

Libbet Crandon-Malamud

Libbet, Sylvia Forman's first graduate student, died of cancer during the publication of this volume. She was with us at the initial AAA session from which the volume was developed. She was with us for the last time at the AAA meetings in Atlanta in 1994. As Kay Warren wrote in her obituary which appeared in the *Anthropology newsletter* (Spring 1995): "We will all remember her from the last AAA meetings in Atlanta as she spoke from her wheelchair with great intensity about anthropology and friendship, called on others to savor the past with her, and joked about finally wearing her family pearls with that sexy long black dress." The following is taken from that obituary.

Libbet Crandon-Malamud, 47, Director of the Gender Studies Program and Associate Professor of Anthropology at the University of Arkansas at Little Rock died on Sunday, February 5, after a courageous struggle with cancer. Libbet earned her BA at Elmira College in 1973 and her PhD at the University of Massachusetts, Amherst in 1980. She was Sylvia Forman's first graduate student. Her research centered on medical anthropology, inequality, the social construction of gender, economic development, and Latin America.

Libbet began her career in 1979 as assistant professor of anthropology at the University of Connecticut, Storrs, with a joint appointment in the Department of Community Medicine at the University of Connecticut Health Center, Farmington. She moved to Columbia University in 1983 where she was assistant professor until 1990 and associate professor until 1994, with a joint appointment at the School of Public Health, Division of Sociomedical Sciences from 1985-1994. When Libbet was not granted tenure at Columbia, she faced a dilemma: Would she fight an unfair decision or, given that she was already battling cancer, would she turn to new projects elsewhere? In 1994, Libbet moved to Little Rock as the founding director of the Gender Studies Program and associate professor of anthropology at the University of Arkansas. She brought great energy and dedication to her teaching and program building. At UALR, she worked closely with undergraduates from many different backgrounds, created a new interdisciplinary curriculum on gender issues, brought professors together from public colleges throughout the state to support gender studies, and worked with African-American community organizers to narrow the divide between campus and community.

Libbet's ethnographic research took her to Bolivia, Honduras, Costa Rica, Guatemala, Jamaica, and Brazil with grants from NSF, Rockefeller, Fulbright, the Inter-American Foundation, and OAS. Her work on the politics of medical choice and social change in the Bolivian altiplano was published in a path-breaking book, <u>From the Fat of Our Souls: Social Change, Political Process, and Medical Pluralism in Bolivia</u> (UCal Press, 1991). She edited <u>Beyond the Cure: Anthropological Inquiries in Medical Theories and Epistemologies</u> and published many articles in collections and in journals such as the <u>American Anthropologist</u>, the <u>American Ethnologist</u>, <u>Ethnology</u>, and <u>Social Science and Medicine</u> on the political economy of medical dialogue, international health care planning, and women's involvement in grassroots development initiatives. She was editor-in-chief of the medical anthropology series "Theory and Practice in Medical Anthropology and International Health," Gordon and Breach, Science Publishers.

The ability to convey the intimacy of fieldwork in ethnographic writing of striking theoretical originality was the hallmark of her research. Libbet's early death is a profound loss for the discipline. (Kay B. Warren)

Sylvia was passionate about politics, and particularly incensed about their negative impact on gender. In 1983 she approved when I joined a research/action project in rural Honduras with the Pathfinder Fund. That project gave the women of Linaca an egg production business, making the women owners and managers of their own enterprise. The Pathfinder Fund hoped that such empowerment would curb these women's fertility. Now, 7 years after the project's completion, the enterprise is long dead. To follow the effects of its demise on gender, I returned to Honduras many times, and wrote this (radically condensed) story for Sylvia. It outlines the transformation of the construction of gender within the politics of land reform in rural Honduras. The plot is as old as development, but perhaps Sylvia would have enjoyed the colorful details that give the plot a new twist: to wit, for 400 years in Linaca men fought men over land while women maintained peace, harmony and hearth; development domesticated the men, increased living standards for all, and disempowered the women; in 1992 the advocates of contraception are men while the women reject birth control. *They* focus *their* attention on ensorcellment. I'm only the last of many analysts to blame it all on a misconceived land reform and its fiscal policies.

Linaca is a fertile valley 20 miles from the Nicaraguan border and 15 miles from Danli. To Danli Linacans turn for everything from education, health care, market, and mail to the only outlet for the coffee, corn and beans they produce for the world market. Until 1990 Danli also hosted the largest contra camp in Honduras. Some 700 people from 15 families live in Linaca, many the same families that have lived there for the last 400 years. Every indication confirms that these men and women are God fearing, generous and loving, fiercely loyal husbands and wives (with great family values!) whose warmth and affection for their children radiates with acceptance and humor...and they all hate each other. The homicide rate in Linaca is one of the highest in Central America outside a war zone. Witchcraft accusations are rampant, the business of embrujeria flourishing, and virtually all the participants are women. It was not always thus.

In a country in which less than 20% of all land is agriculturally viable, and 60% of that 20% has been owned by multinational corporations for 100 years, Linaca's fertility is highly visible. People have always flocked to Linaca and fought each other for land. In 1625 when Linaca was public land, the population congregated on the north slope and the men battled each other every season over who got to plant on how much of the valley bottom. In that year one of these men gave the government 600 pieces of silver for 300 manzanas of that land -- a small parcel of the valley -- and to legitimize his power within Linaca he called that parcel Hacienda Santa Elisa.

Over the years the hacienda expanded. In 1971 it enclosed the entire valley. For 350 years, people fought this encroachment while they fought each other, and various arrangements were made. Until 1971 the hacienda ran cattle, raised cane and made liquor out of it, and in the twentieth century replaced cane with coffee. Thus it needed labor. All the other folk in Linaca needed land and resources and traded their labor to the hacienda for usufruct and foraging rights. Linaca was increasingly resource poor and filthy, a result of growing population density, no preventive health resources, and neither education nor alternative sources of income. Infant mortality often exceeded 500 per 1,000. Violent access to land was lubricated with the liquor produced and dispensed at the hacienda, and with arms folks acquired to hunt in the mountains, discourage cattle rustlers and settle disputes.

Under these conditions women sowed corn, harvested cane and cut coffee along with their men, occasionally fought with them, if not against them, and arranged for their own kidnaping, the local means of marriage. In contrast to the men however, the women's control over domestic labor bound them together in mutual concern and action. The women prayed together, collected kindling together, drew water together, made forays into the Danli market together; they served as links between households, channels for inter household exchange, the means of communication and information flow, and the only mechanism for community initiative.

1934 is a case in point. To run the people off all the land, the hacendado burned Linaca down. In response the women sent a delegation to Tegucigalpa to complain to the wife of the Tin Pot Dictator Carias. Carias obliged because his arch enemy was the hacendado's son, and thus he sent soldiers to arrest the hacendado. When the subsequent hacendado enclosed the entire valley in 1971 the government sided with the hacienda, but the *women* confronted the soldiers while the men hid out in the hills *until* the land reform allocated to the 57 heads of household in Linaca 150 manzanas of valley bottom land. In accordance with the reform law, the 57 heads of household formed a new cooperative, and upon those 57 men descended all the obligations and privileges of reform law:

* intensified agriculture
* high yield varieties
* piped water and irrigation
* tractors, herbicides, pesticides
* fertilizers, and a never-ending array of courses.

Overnight these men were transformed from illiterate subsistence peasants to informed farmers, informed mostly about their growing debt.

But the reform law stipulated these benefits could go...

* only to men
* only to one man per family
* and only to landless families at that.

As a few folk like the Brants did own marginal land, coop membership immediately dropped from 57 to 48 and the first structural divisions were sewn in the social fabric of Linaca: between men and women, and between reforms and independents. The Brants became independents while a handful of reform men, like Sam and Carlos, moved their wattle and daub dwellings onto coop land. Thus began a geographic separation between reforms and independents that was concluded in 1990 when the government built housing for all the reforms and clustered them on coop land.

Now the land reform in Honduras has never been known for its successes; so when the men's coop did well, development organizations, international agencies, and land reform institutes invaded Linaca to help the women, dividing them even further with their competition, paltry resources, and attention to only reform women. That story I've told before. It culminated in the egg production project that reunited all the women, cost $240,000, and flourished from 1983 to 1986. Empowered as owners and mangers of their own productive enterprise, the women mobilized to improve the community. They expanded the school, built a health center, brought in an infant feeding center, equipped it with day care and preschool education, bought a corn grinding mill for the community, made plans for a consumo that would undersell the high priced stores around that fleeced the community, installed fish ponds and marched to Tegucigalpa to join the national poultry farmers association to lobby the government to increase egg prices. When the credit association from which the men's coop secured loans collapsed in 1983, and the men faced ruin, the women advanced them loans for two years at 14% interest, both repaid in full. And as an explicit expression of their empowerment, those women married to reform men, saved their egg money and got sterilized. But after the enterprise collapsed, the women refused to speak to each other, except in expletives or to register threats.

The cause of the enterprise's demise can be squarely placed on competitive meddling of local development agencies and land reform institutes. They gave the women conflicting advice and ultimately forced them to restock the barns when the women knew the price of chicks was too high, and the market for eggs too low for them to survive. The cause of this competitive meddling and directives was this organization's own need to compete for a 9 million dollar Economic European Community (EEC) aid package to the Danli area. That aid package was the EEC's contribution to keeping the peace during the contra war in the one place where Honduras's miserable land reform was most vulnerable to the Sandanista's way of looking at things.

The pressure on the women was exacerbated by the fact that they had been working their butts off for $7.50 worth of eggs a month, which required many, like Petrona, to occasionally abandon the enterprise for the hacienda's coffee harvest to cover medical expenses of sick children. This enraged the already overburdened women they left behind. Appearing incompetent because of the enterprise's demise, the agencies and institutes made hay with the women's disgruntlement and blamed the demise on the women's "irresponsibility and mismanagement."

In their competition for the EEC funds, appearance of competency was essential, and these organizations and institutes determined to recuperate the women's losses themselves, give them to the men, and take credit for it.

In 1986, having been bailed out by the women during their worst years of crisis, the men's coop was one of the most successful coops in all Honduras. It met its debt payments, it was still operating after 13 years, and because of the women's coop, the men had received national and international attention. But the men were unable to capitalize. With their productive resources they could not accumulate enough wealth to amortize their loans. The price of corn and beans had decreased throughout the decade (rendered worse now with Bush's Brady plan). The 150 manzanas of corn and beans divided by 48 men could not generate enough income to pay off those loans. What the men needed was more capital assets. And whatever organization could take even partial credit for introducing those assets would have an edge on eligibility for part of that 9 million dollars. Thus the organizations illegally dissolved the women's coop and resolved to give the barns and equipment to the men.

The overwhelming resentment among the women exacerbated conflict already among them. As the rumor spread that it was *some* women's fault, speculation was made as to *which women*. Men of course defended their *own* women and each woman defended herself: thus it was always the other who was at fault.

But of course the men didn't want the bloody barns. They had enough troubles and debts of their own. They knew that if the women couldn't make it go with 3 years of training, they with none wouldn't have better luck. Another loan would burden their credit standing and if they failed to repay, they put their own cooperative at risk. For every coop in operation in Honduras, there are ten other groups waiting for land; and one group waiting for this land in 1986 was the sons of the reforms who by now had come of age and were second class citizens in the coop. The men were acutely aware of this, as was the hacienda which stood to reclaim that land if the men and their sons fought with each other, and were thus found inefficient or unworthy by the land reform institute.

In anticipation of this very issue, and with the history of violence in Linaca, the reform men implemented the law of conflict to cap tensions and prevent open conflict among themselves that could threaten their already fragile cooperative. The law of conflict prohibits sons of coop members to fight each other. Reform men are responsible for any aggressive, obstreperous behavior of themselves and their children toward the children of members, and are sanctioned by expulsion. And an expulsion accrues an advantage to all the rest in a coop in which the productive resources would best serve 25 men, not 48, and whose members in 1991 had three times the number of dependents as in 1973. Thus the men calmly discuss their options and plans among each other at coop meetings, and when Sam's son shot Carlos's son in 1990, Sam was thrown out of the coop. But when Petrona's son killed the Brant boy, nothing was done within the community because the Brants are independents and not subject to coop law. These two factors -- population pressure and the limitations and fragility of the coop -- give the reform men a genuine interest in contraception, and for that very reason they elected one of themselves to be a contraceptive representative who now gives talks and dispenses pills and condoms. But his only audience is reform men. The women of Linaca are united solely in their unanimous rejection of contraception.

Reform women are either already sterilized or beyond childbearing age so contraception itself is a moot point for them though its rejection by independents is not. Independents face entirely different but equally fragile circumstances. From their position, limiting family size makes no sense. Elisa and Lastenia are old women who own their own land; acquired it with their own wits and wiles and rely on their kids for agricultural labor. Like the coop and the hacienda, they risk losing their land altogether if they don't make full use of what Honduran reform law calls its social function. Although both Elisa and Lastenia claim to support education they have discouraged their children from going to school: the school is on coop land and filled with coop kids with whom they get into frays, skirmished and feuds; furthermore excellence in school leads to high school in Danli, too far and too expensive to commute to. Given that employment in Honduras has gone down not up over the last decade, especially with the pull out of American troops, education may well lead to unemployment while depriving the household of needed agricultural labor.

People like Nectalia Brant are more belligerently disposed and aggressively persuade their children to stay at home. In a moment of economic vulnerability, the Brants sold their land to Lastenia and are now landless. Being landless their only source of income and hope of ever acquiring land again and thus a piece of security is saving the pesos earned picking coffee at the hacienda. Though extensively informed by the Pathfinder Fund's project about the blessings of contraception and the evils of too many kids, Nectalia Brant continues to produce children. She is openly embittered and depressed at the failure of the women's coop and the implications that it was her fault. Her opportunities, aspirations and joy have metamorphosed into failure, accusations, and enmity. It is not so much comfort she takes in her children (in a town where there's nothing else to do except play with children) as the restriction of her options to a single viable strategy for security: more kids to pick coffee at the hacienda.

In 1988 evangelism (World Mission) which had been supported in Linaca by a handful of adherents since 1975, suddenly proliferated...among independents. Not one reformer attends. Lastenia's husband, a devout evangelical, says the reason the women's coop failed was because of "maladministration." The Bible says you reap what you sow, he points out, and reasons therefore, that if the women lost all that money, obviously they stole it. God gives us what we deserve, and all the reforms in Linaca are infidels. The Bible also says to go out and proliferate. So much for family planning.

Lastenia makes great use of her 13 children. She must compete with the reforms, and all other women as well, for control over what's left of the infant feeding program, and the mill; and her large family constitutes an imposing opposition.

Today there is no longer any interhousehold exchange, confirming the new ideology perpetrated by development agencies that women can't get along with each other and therefore can't run a business like the egg production enterprise. Within the current labor and production structures, the productive unit is the nuclear household among reforms, and the extended household among independents. Reflecting the coop law, real exchange occurs between parent and child, with all the obligations and privileges attached. The strong fiercely loyal family that has evolved in the last 20 years has done so at the expense of community unity; and women no longer have any need for each other.

But the men -- both reform and independents -- do. Lastenia's husband is very careful in reform company and vice versa: with the rapid turnover of agricultural technology, the constant strain of ever newer plagues and blights that affect the whole valley, and with differential resources, the reform and independent men are forced to rely on each other, and thus to get along. Among each other they never talk about the women. To hang around the men is to sense that nothing every happened in Linaca, that no tension existed, no conflicts nor disputes, nor high anxiety to resolve them. The men can't afford to address them. These now get addressed through the women. Now the women serve as funnels for community conflict and disputes.

This state of affairs eclipses the miserable wages and near extortion of labor by the hacienda; the absolute bankruptcy of the Honduran reform sector and the development community in the Danli area; and the role the Honduran and American governments played in all this with the result that there are virtually NO opportunity structures whatsoever for rural Hondurans, and no government representative that has their interests at heart. Linacans love Americans, they are appreciative of the help the political party offices in Danli provide them -- such as use of a typewriter or referral to a lawyer. They are grateful to the land reform institute and its resources management agency (the current minister of which is -- get this -- the administrator of the hacienda!). And the cost for this was not just the disempowerment of the women of Linaca just when their status in terms of access to education, health, economic resources went up! The real cost was the transformation of women as an interest group into the mechanism for expression of community hostility and conflict.

While Sylvia would have been intrigued by the political dynamics of this story and outraged by the women's disempowerment and transformation, she would also have been bitterly disappointed that this is, after all, another version of an old story we've heard many times before: the costly and destructive transformation of the social construction of gender under the impact of "development."

Planning and Training

to Improve Service Delivery for

Older African-Americans

Sue Perkins Taylor
Howard University

Dr. Taylor is a research and training consultant in applied anthropology, gerontology and geriatric nursing. She combined a career in nursing with anthropology completing her PhD in 1978. She developed and directed the MA Degree Concentration in Applied Medical Anthropology in the department of Anthropology at Wayne State University (1978-1985), as well as the Minority Aging Program for the Institute of Gerontology. Dr. Taylor was a Visiting Professor in the Department of Sociology and Anthropology at Miami University in Oxford, Ohio (1989-1992). Dr. Taylor has served on several local boards and is currently a member of the Board of Directors of the National Caucus and Center on Black Aged in Washington, D.C. She served as a state commissioner on the Michigan Commission for Services to the Aged from 1981-1984. She was appointed an Ohio Department of Mental Health Research Fellow in 1991-1992. She is currently listed in Who's Who in the Midwest, Who's Who Among American Human Service Professionals, and Who's Who in American Nursing. Dr. Taylor maintains her clinical practice as a nursing service administrator and consultant in long-term care nursing facilities. She is currently a member of the faculty in the Department of Sociology and Anthropology at Howard University.

Although the representation of minority elders in the population has increased, participation by minorities in programs and services for older adults has remained low. Strategies for reaching these populations have been outlined in the literature repeatedly since the 1971 White House Conference on Aging (e.g. Bell, Kasschua, and Zellman 1976; Labor 1988; Cuellar and Weeks 1980; Cutler and Harris 1983; George 1988; Kavanagh and Kennedy 1992; Ralston 1984; Richardson 1992; Skinner 1990; Spence 1991; Stanford 1978; Taylor 1980; 1971 White House Conference on Aging 1971). While solutions to the barriers to participation have been offered by researchers, service providers, and consumers of senior programs, the situation has not improved significantly. Two questions are commonly asked regarding the lack of involvement of minority elders in services and programs for older adults. First, "Why don't minorities use services and participate in programs for older Americans?" Second, "How do we target services to potential minority clients?"

This chapter focuses on the steps taken by one agency to address both questions through implementing a one-day training session for service providers. The purpose of the session was to provide cultural sensitivity training to program directors and staff members to help them move beyond simple acknowledgment of low participation by minority elderly persons. The major objective was to aid program staff members in developing action models that work for targeting culturally appropriate and accessible services to low-income, minority clients.

In 1992, I was hired as a consultant to the local Area Agency on Aging[1] to conduct a day-long workshop for directors and staff members of services and programs funded under Title III provisions of the Older Americans Act (OAA) of 1965. The specific goals were to aid program staff members in identifying and removing the barriers that contributed to low attendance in community-based programs.

Focus groups were used to collect qualitative data from the viewpoints of the service providers and minority program participants. Two focus group sessions were held and the findings of these focus groups were incorporated into the training workshop. One group consisted of service providers who were white, younger than their clients, and represented both urban and suburban counties. The second focus group was made up of African American participants in senior programs since they represented the largest minority group in the five county planning and service area and were the minority group being targeted.

The chapter is divided into three sections. First, a brief overview is presented of the Older Americans Act (OAA) of 1965, which outlines the major goals for advocacy, planning and service programs for adults 60 years of age and older in the United States. Second, the findings of the focus groups and the way these data informed the development of the workshop will be discussed. Third, the final section includes a discussion of the role of anthropologists as consultants in developing culturally relevant programs for a diverse aging population.

The Older Americans Act of 1965 and Targeting

The Older American Act (OAA) of 1965 was enacted to provide programs and services to adults sixty years of age and older. The OAA is administered by the Administration on Aging (AoA) within the Department of Health and Human Services (DHHS) at the federal level. AoA disperses funds with the assistance of regional offices and through an aging network comprised of 57 State and Territorial Units on Aging (SUA) and 657 Area Agencies on Aging (AAA). The AAAs contract with local service providers to provide programs and services. Each state is divided into Planning and Service Areas (PSAs) which submit budgets and area plans to the state office on aging. The state submits a budget and plan to AoA for the distribution of funds under Title III-Grants for State and Community Programs on Aging (to be referred to as Title III). As the major system for advocacy, planning and service to older adults, the OAA has been amended and reauthorized by Congress over the past thirty years (for a review of the first 25 years see Binstock 1991; Gelfand and Bechill 1991).

During the 1980's *targeting* was introduced into the OAA with the intent that preference be given to providing services to older individuals with the "greatest economic and social needs." Economic need referred to those with incomes at or below the poverty level. Social need included noneconomic factors (e.g., language barriers, isolation, racial or ethnic status, and disabilities that restricted the ability to perform normal daily activities or threatened independence).

Intrastate Funding Formulas (IFFs) were devised as a method of allocating funds to AAAs. This practice is currently under debate with drafted regulations that direct states to target funds to older adults with the greatest social and economic needs, with particular attention to low income minorities. The manner in which funds are distributed is directly related to the criteria and weighting that is factored into the formula. In the past, states had the autonomy to decide the status differentiation that would classify individuals as being in the greatest social and economic need. These categories varied as did the weight attached to each factor leaving a wide margin of interpretation from one state to another. Regional and local differences led to unequal distribution of service dollars and resulted in unmet service needs in some communities. IFFs have been challenged in the court as discriminatory (see Meeks vs. Martinez) and the debate over the usefulness of funding formulas for targeting continues among advocates for the minority aged (Cutler 1989, Hyde & Torres-Gil 1991; National Caucus and Center on Black Aged 1994).

The 1992 Amendment to the OAA strengthened the mandate for targeting services to those individuals in the greatest social and economic need, with particular attention to low-income, minority individuals. Furthermore, State Units on Aging (SUAs) and Area Agencies on Aging (AAAs) are required to set specific objectives and describe the actions to be taken to increase minority participation (U.S. Department of Health and Human Services 1994). Therefore, the training session discussed in this chapter is in fact, a response to the federal regulations.

Anthropologist as Consultant

As consultants, anthropologists are asked to provide recommendations to practitioners and program directors in the field of aging who are concerned with provision of services to meet the needs of minority elders. The services the anthropologists provide range from designing and providing sensitivity training, to recognizing the pros and cons of designing culturally specific or separate services for the racially and ethnically mixed populations (Taylor 1981). Suggestions for improving programs have included better recruitment of minority board and staff members, locating services in areas of high minority concentrations, improving outreach efforts, and being sensitive to the culture, language, and traditions of the distinctive group (see e.g., American Society on Aging 1992; Committee on Education and Labor 1988; Markides and Mindel 1987; Taylor 1980, 1994).

Anthropologists are in a unique position to be able to incorporate cultural sensitivity training into practice models which can be implemented by service providers. Yet, this is often easier said than done. First, potential clients are often unaware of the skills an anthropologist has to offer.

Second, the anthropologist must compete with colleagues in social work, planning, health and allied professions who feel they were there first.

According to Chambers (1985) the anthropologist in consulting practice is often confronted with one of two models. The first is the administrative model in which the client is the program administrator who has employed the consultant. The second model is the advocacy model in which the consultant is an advocate on behalf of the people or consumers of the services.

The case I am describing here was an example of the administrative model as I was hired as a consultant by the AAA, which was responsible for carrying out the targeting mandate in compliance with federal and state regulations. Two other groups of players had a vested interest in the outcome. The first were the service providers who depended on grants and contracts from the AAA. The remaining group consisted of the targeted consumers who were the intended benefactors of the OAA service dollars. The agenda for all three was essentially the same albeit emerging from diverse directions. The over-all goal focused on the availability, accessibility, and appropriateness of culturally specific services and programs to minority elders in need.

Targeting Services to Minority Older Adults

The Area Agency on Aging served five counties within the metropolitan area with a population of 1,457,220 in 1990. Adults 60 years of age or older numbered 235,473 which was 16.1 percent of the total population of all ages. The total minority aged population was 27,390 or 11.6 percent of the population 60 years of age and older. African Americans constituted the largest minority group with a total of 26,338 persons over the age of 60. Since this represented 96 percent of the minority elderly, the decision was made to focus the targeting workshop on reaching this population. Among the other minority groups represented in the area, American Indians numbered 193 (0.7%). There were 791 (2.9%) Asian elderly persons in the census count. Hispanics, which can be of any race, numbered 591 individuals. Those that could be considered minorities constituted a small segment of the population (U.S. Department of Commerce; personal communication with Ken Wilson, Council on Aging).

Title III-B and Title III-D of the OAA and Ohio state funds provided the following support services: transportation, housekeeping/personal care, home maintenance/repairs, legal counseling, foster care, protective services, medical assessment, socialization/recreation, advocacy, information/referral, and counseling services. Minority elderly persons underutilized all of these support services.

In consultation with the client, it was determined that a one-day training session on targeting services to meet the needs of minority elderly would be provided for directors and staff in the local agencies serving older adults. Two focus groups were used to collect qualitative data to enable us to understand the problem from the viewpoint of the various groups involved. Two focus groups were held prior to planning the workshop. One group consisted of service providers and the other of African-American participants of OAA funded programs. The results of both focus groups were used to develop a training session for service providers.

Focus group research is common in marketing and can work equally well for anthropologists doing management consulting or program evaluation (see Giovannini and Rosanky 1990; Kruger 1988; Morgan 1988). Bryant and Bailey (1991:24) describe a focus group interview as: "...a small group discussion, guided by a trained moderator, to provide insights into participants' attitudes, perceptions, and opinions on a designated topic."

Service Providers Focus Group

Ten Title III service providers representing the urban and suburban counties were selected by the AAA and the consultant to participate in a focus group. Participants were chosen from the Title III-B and Title III-D programs and services. An emphasis was placed on those programs that had experienced some degree of underutilization by minority clients. The group consisted of senior center directors, social workers, and senior advocacy program staff. As service providers they were already acquainted with the targeting mandate and the regulations for compliance. The meeting was held from 9:00 AM to noon in the twelfth floor conference room in the same building as the AAA. The atmosphere was relaxed, the room was comfortable with a marvelous view of the city and refreshments were served. In focus group research, it is extremely important to arrange a setting that is accessible, familiar, and conducive to informal, focused conversation.

In a focus group setting, the moderator is responsible for setting the objectives and formulating the questions to be asked. The following objectives were established:

1. To identify the concerns of service providers inadequately meeting the needs of minority clients.

2. To identify the ways in which the Area Agency on Aging could be of assistance in reaching the minority population.

3. To identify the topics that would be most beneficial in a training session for service providers.

With the emphasis on identifying perceptions, attitudes, and opinions about the problem of underutilization of services by minority elderly clients, six questions were used to generate the data needed.[2]

In response to the first two question all the service providers indicated that minority participation was low and they would like to find ways of increasing involvement. A question was raised regarding what would be considered "adequate" in their attempts to reach the minority population. The group determined that they had no clear concept of the need for services in their areas; or whether or not they were "adequate" in their outreach efforts. Adequacy, they decided depends on the minority census. "If for example," one man explained, " we reach three elderly black families in the service area, is that adequate"? "How do we really know who is in need"?

Others commented that "we can't find the potential minority clients." In rural areas they explained that "minorities are few and frail." "Minorities are hard to reach." One person asked, "Who are the minorities"? "Eligible men (i.e., 60 years of age or older) are a minority." The group discussion revealed that the general consensus was that the minorities in the PSA were mainly African Americans with some Hispanics in one county. A few were from India. The large elderly Jewish population in the area used a center that served the Jewish community and offered a variety of programs and services for elders that are used by non-Jewish members of the community.

When asked about the reasons for low participation by African Americans, the variety of responses about black life and culture were based to some degree on stereotypes and perceived differences in the experiences of blacks and whites. "They participate in meals and transportation services, but they are not interested in other social programs." One individual explained, "Culture is a problem. Our activities don't attract minorities." Another respondent suggested " they grew up in different times -- had different experiences." A senior center director said:

> They have not had time to develop outside interests. At our center there are no blacks dancing, playing bridge, playing pool, or involved in other social activities. They have had to work hard. They haven't had the time or inclination to develop interest. They were too busy trying to make a living.

Along the same line another commented:

> It's a cultural thing -- a life-long thing. Most folks haven't been exposed to going to a place of activity except church. They are close to their church ties and maybe that's enough for them because I don't think they've been exposed as much as whites. I think we (meaning white Americans) are used to mixing more with different kinds of activities, different interest.

Some staff members and directors felt the racial make-up of their staff was a problem. Some felt the need to have racially matched staff and clients. Others asked, "If that's the case, how do we attract minority staff members to rural areas?"

The fourth question asked for their opinion on whether African Americans needed or wanted the services they provided. The group agreed that transportation was a need for most of the older, low-income black population. Respite care (i.e., either in-home or community-based services to provide relief for caregivers of the frail elderly client) was probably a need. However, the service providers had no idea about who might need the service or if it would be used. The discussion that followed revealed their perceptions that black families "take care of their own."

The reasons ranged from a perception of a loving, caring extended family to the notion that "whites are not trusted" and families are "reluctant to take respite care."

The fifth question focused on the role the AAA could play in helping providers to contact hard-to-reach clients. They reported that the primary assistance which could be provided by the AAA would be census data, survey data, and reports of utilization by racial or ethnic classifications for each county.

Finally, the last question was designed to elicit their ideas for what they felt they needed in a training session. They provided a list of thirty items. These included strategies for outreach, information on need, interest and ways of communicating. The group mentioned the separation between the black and white communities. In the larger urban areas, blacks lived in unsafe neighborhoods. "The client is afraid to come out and the social worker is afraid to go in." Finally, much of the information they needed in a training session was related to what they viewed as their own shortcomings and lack of cultural awareness.

Consumers Focus Group

Two men and four women from six different senior centers were selected by the AAA staff and the consultant to take part in the second focus group. They were all African-Americans 60 years of age or older, who had participated in senior programs and were concerned about the low participation of other African Americans. This group met in the same location as the previous group. The following three objectives were outlined for the focus group discussion:

1. To identify the barriers to participation in community-based social support programs sponsored by the AAA.

2. To obtain their suggestions for reaching potential clients.

3. To give them an opportunity for making programmatic suggestions that might improve participation.

They were asked to address the following three questions:

1. Do you feel there is a problem with low participation by African Americans in the centers you represent?

2. What is the reason for low participation?

3. What suggestions do you have for improving participation?

All of the participants in the focus group agreed there was a problem in getting older black Americans to take advantage of the programs sponsored by the agencies. To them the reasons were fairly simple. The barriers to participation were very similar to those found in other studies in the past. One women said, "We know the problem. How we gonna fix it"? The reasons given for low participation included the lack of outreach, demographic factors, attitudes and perception of staff members about the interest of older minority clients, and the age differences rather than the racial differences between provider and client.

One women explained the low participation was directly related to demographics and a lack of knowledge about the center. She said:

> It's the demographics. People move away. Some get frail and move to nursing homes.
> Some die. Others new to the area haven't been told about this organization. Some get the
> senior center confused with the community center about a block down the street.   They
> have to market this organization; they have to advertise.

Others agreed that a major problem is that people just don't know about the services. They suggested that advertising could come through the churches, newsletters of organizations, newspapers and radio. "Barnstorm." "Word-of-mouth." "Put flyers on every door." Beyond the inadequate outreach, this group identified some problems that are difficult to change. " People like to stay to themselves."   Several agreed that some people "don't want to be seniors...don't want to be around old folks; so they say."

The group identified a major problem for all the social programs. They are planned by young, white directors or staff members who cannot relate to people of color. Discussion around this issue revealed that age may be more of a problem than race. "The young see us as old and not able to do anything."   "The activities they offer us are boring."   "They need new programs, movies, something to get people interested." Racial matching was not as much of a problem as the providers thought. "It doesn't matter if they are white, black, purple or green as long as they know what they are doing."

Along the line of staffing the group mentioned that turnover is a problem. "At my center we've come through a lot of directors." They voiced concern that the program directors were "from somewhere else." Directors seldom live in the targeted neighborhood and have little understanding of the day-to-day existence of some older adults. On-the-other-hand one center has a problem that the clients don't live in the neighborhood. "Almost everyone at the center lives outside the area. We can't get people in the neighborhood to come."

Actual programming was a major drawback. Some commented on the lack of choice in activities. "They tell you what you are going to do." There seems to be a tendency for program planners to assume homogeneity of their clients in planning activities. The group identified what they called a "them/us" mentality among service providers. In planning programs for older ethnic minorities, service providers representing the majority or dominant culture often think and speak of their minority clients as "them" and make a clear separation between the client and the provider/ practitioner. "They like soul food." "They like religious music, so for music therapy we'll bring in a Gospel choir." The women in this group said they would have preferred a little jazz instead; the men nodded their approval.

Finally, other barriers to participation included transportation, caregiving responsibilities (caring for grandchildren and/or a spouse or other relative), and the location of the services in hard to reach places. The old standby, "they take care of their own" rings familiar to the clients as well as researchers and practitioners and continues to be a barrier to providing needed services. Where the provider group feels their services are underutilized, the client group feels they are being under served.

The advice of this group was to include the consumers whenever possible in planning whether it is food preferences, music, or outreach. The felt that the program planners had a very limited view of African American life experiences and the rich cultural heritage they shared. Leisure activities they enjoyed in the past could now be pursued in the later years and new experiences were also welcomed.

Designing the Workshop

A workshop was designed and implemented to respond to the Older Americans Act mandate that services shall be directed toward those in the greatest economic and social need, with particular attention to low-income minority elderly persons. The primary focus was directed at identifying the minority elders within each service area and developing strategies for targeting services to those in the greatest need. Fifty eight directors and staff members of Title III social support programs attended. Topics covered in the workshop included cultural diversity and ethnogerontology, recognizing barriers to participation in Title III programs and services, empowering minority elders, and learning from best practice models.

Three major objectives of the workshop were identified. The first was to provide participants with an understanding of the issues and the challenges of targeting services to minority older adults through an understanding of cultural diversity. This could be approached by first presenting a demographic profile of the older minority population in the five county area. More than numbers, the participants need to be cognizant of the meaning of the diversity within their service area.

The second objective was to make providers aware of the kinds of barriers that preclude active participation of minority clients in the programs and services funded under the Older Americans Act. Based on comments from the consumer focus group, it was important that service providers recognize that "them" vs. "us" attitudes may serve as barriers to providing culturally relevant services. The attitudes and perceptions drawn from this line of thinking are enough to account for the continued underutilization of services by minority elders. In order to accomplish this objective, the workshop would provide participants with a way of examining their own perceptions and attempt to dispel the myths and stereotypes about African American life and culture.

Finally, the third objective was to guide participants in identifying problems specific to their own agency with the intent that they would incorporate the various strategies presented as they developed and implemented a plan of action to address low attendance by minorities. Strategic planning guidelines were designed to utilizing marketing techniques, best practice models and incorporate the consumer focus group data.

A day-long workshop was conducted which included a videotape presentation, discussion, and group activities. One of the most enlightening aspects of the day came with the recognition that service providers and consumers may see the problem differently. Service providers and Area Agency staff view low attendance as a problem of lack of interest, inability to adjust to leisure activities (e.g., in a senior center), or engage in community-based or in-home services. From the perspective of the consumer, they may feel their needs are unmet due to services which are either unavailable, inaccessible, or culturally inappropriate.

The following recommendations were made for targeting services to minority elders. First, empower minority elders to become more responsive to ensure that their best interest are considered. Include members of ethnic and minority communities in the total planning, implementation, and evaluation of Title III programs and services.

Second, develop culturally and linguistically appropriate services that are meaningful to the target population and address their needs as they perceive them. This includes hiring minority staff members with bilingual/bicultural capabilities. Among culturally diverse populations, including African Americans, it is not enough to simply know the language, it is imperative that service providers become competent in assessing cultural needs when providing social services, health care, and recreational programming.

Third, a major complaint from the consumer group was the fact that services were sometimes located in hard to reach places. Locate services in ethnic communities. In other words, take the service to the client. Furthermore, potential clients were unaware of the services or programs being offered. Inadequate outreach was a reality. The crux of the problem stemmed from the very limited knowledge providers have about the places different ethnic or minority groups congregate, newspaper, radio or television programs they follow, or ethnically oriented associations to which they belong.

Fourth, a special effort must be made to include minorities on advisory councils, boards of directors and other advocacy roles. Decisions made at these level without minority representation may be part of the problem.

Finally, the service providers were advised to establish both short-term and long-term goals. Set reachable goals with measurable outcomes. The workshop concluded with tips borrowed from marketing and the competitive service industry. Nykiel (1992) offers ten steps to service success in a book entitled *You Can't Lose if the Customer Wins*. These steps include recognition, identification, plans of action, reallocation, prioritization, training, recruiting, communications, follow-up and begin again. Most of the participants represented programs which are at the juncture where they must begin again.

Conclusions

Anthropologists are in a position to offer their ethnographic knowledge and skills to program administrators in order to aid them in developing culturally relevant programs for a diverse aging population. The underutilization of services and programs by minority older adults has been a matter of concern for many Area Agencies on Aging throughout the country. Area plans must include specific service objectives for targeting services to minority elders including training sessions for service providers.

Although further details about the workshop are beyond the scope of this paper, one can assume the impact of any one-day training session is limited. Whether any of the points covered have any lasting effect on the program offerings and outcomes is purely speculative.

It became obvious that when there are racial or ethnic differences between service providers and those they plan to serve, the views of the two groups may be markedly different. The two groups participating in the focus group interviews had different perspectives on the issue of underutilization vs. being under served. The explanations for low participation varied between the two groups. It is essential that service providers reassess current practices when serving diverse populations. The staff must become culturally competent in understanding the life experiences of those they intend to serve. Failure of service providers to achieve cultural competence keeps the barriers in place and further alienates those we hope to serve.

Notes

1. The training session was presented by The Council on Aging of the Cincinnati Area, Inc., the Area Agency on Aging for Planning and Service Area No.1 (PSA 1) sponsored by a Title III Grant under the Older Americans Act administered through the Ohio Department of Aging.

2. These are the six questions which were used to guide the discussion in the service-providers focus group: 1) Do you feel you are adequately reaching minority older adults in your community service area? 2) Is minority participation an issue in your agency? 3) In your opinion, what are the reasons minorities do not participate in your service programs? 4) Do minorities need or want the services you offer? 5) How can the Area Agency on Aging help you fulfill your goals of providing services to minority clients? 6) What kind of information or technical assistance would you like to receive in a one-day training session on "Targeting Services to the Minority, Low-Income Older Population"?

References

1971 White House Conference on Aging
   1971 *Special Concerns Sessions Reports: Asian American Elderly, Aging and the Aged Blacks, The Elderly Indian, Spanish-Speaking Elderly.* Washington, DC: U.S. Government Printing Office.

American Association of Retired Persons
  1990 *Empowerment of Minority Elderly.* Washington, DC: American Association of Retired Persons.

American Association of Retired Persons
  1994 *A Portrait of Older Minorities.* Washington, DC: AARP Minority Affairs, American
    Association of Retired Persons.

American Society on Aging
  1992 *Serving Elders of Color: Challenges to Providers and the Aging Network.* San Francisco:
    American Society on Aging.

Bell, Duran, Patricia Kasschua, Gail Zellman
  1976 *Delivering Services to the Elderly Members of Minority Groups: A Critical Review of the
    Literature.* Santa Monica, CA: Rand Publication.

Binstock, Robert H.
  1991 From the Great Society to the Aging Society--25 Years of the Older Americans Act. *Generations*
    15(3):11-18.

Bryant, Carol A. and Doraine F. Bailey
  1991 The Use of Focus Group Research in Programs Developments. In John Van Willigen and
    Timothy L. Finan, eds. *Soundings: Rapid and Reliable Research Methods for Practicing
    Anthropologist. NAPA Bulletin 10.* Pp. 24-39. Arlington: American Anthropological Association.

Chambers, Erve
  1985 *Applied Anthropology: A Practical Guide.* Prospect Heights, IL. Waveland Press, Inc.

Cuellar, Jose B. and John Weeks
  1980 *Minority Elderly Americans: A Prototype for Area Agencies on Aging: Executive Summary.*
    San Diego: Allied Home Health Association.

Committee on Education and Labor
  1988 *Improving Minority Participation in Older Americans Act Programs.* Committee Publication
    100-89. Washington, DC: U.S. Government Printing Office.

Cutler, Neal E. and C. E. Harris
  1983 *Approaches to Best Practices in the Use of Intrastate Funding Formulas for Targeting
    Services to Older Americans: Final Report.* Washington, DC: Bureau of Social Science Research.
  1989 *Minority Targeting in the Older Americans Act, 1978-1988: From "Greatest Economic or
    Social Need" to Meek vs. Martinez.* San Diego: National Resource Center on Minority Aging
    Populations, University Center on Aging, San Diego State University.

Gelfand, Donald E. and William Bechill
  1991 The Evolution of the Older Americans Act: A 25-Year Review of Legislative Changes.
    Generations 15(3):19-22.

George, Linda K.
1988 Social Participation in Later Life: Black White Differences. In *The Black Elderly: Research on Physical and Psychosocial Health*. James L. Jackson, ed. Pp. 99-128. New York: Springer Publishing Company.

Giovannini, Maureen J. and Lynne M.H. Rosansky
1990 *Anthropology and Management Consulting: Forging a New Alliance*. Napa Bulletin 9. Arlington, VA: National Association for the Practice of Anthropology (NAPA), American Anthropological Association.

Hyde, J. and F. Torres-Gil
1991 Ethnic minority elders and the Older Americans Act: How Have They Fared? *Generations* 25(3): 57-61.

Kavanagh, Kathryn H. and Patricia H. Kennedy
1992 *Promoting Cultural Diversity: Strategies for Health Care Professionals*. Newbury Park, CA: Sage Publications.

Krueger, Richard A.
1988 *Focus Groups: A Practical Guide for Applied Research*. Newbury Park, CA: Sage Publications.

Markides, Kyriakos S. and Charles H. Mindel
1987 *Aging and Ethnicity*. Newbury Park, CA: Sage Publications.

Morgan, David L.
1988 *Focus Groups as Qualitative Research*. Sage University Series on Qualitative Research Methods, vol. 16. Beverly Hills CA: Sage Publications.

National Association of Area Agencies on Aging
1986 *Targeting Resources to the Minority Elderly*. Washington, DC: National Association of Area Agencies on Aging.

National Caucus and Center on Black Aged, Inc.
1994 *A Profile of Elderly Black Americans. Washington, DC: The National Caucus and Center on Black Aged, Inc.*

Nykiel, Ronald A.
1992 *You Can't Lose if the Customer Wins: Ten Steps to Service Success*. Stamford, CT: Longmeadow Press.

Ralston, Penny A.
1984 Senior Center Utilization by Black Elderly Adults: Social Attitudinal and Knowledge Correlates. *Journal of Gerontology* 39:224-29.

Richardson, Virginia
1992 Service Use Among Urban African American Elderly People. *Social Work 37:47-54.*

Skinner, John H.
  1990 Targeting Benefits for the Black Elderly: The Older Americans Act. In *Black Aged:
    Understanding Diversity and Service Needs*. Zev Harel, Edward A. McKinney, and Michael
    Williams, eds. Pp.165-182. Newbury Park, CA: Sage Publications.

Spence, Susie A.
  1991 The Black Elderly and the Social Service Delivery System: A Study of Factors Influencing the
    Use of Community-based Services. *Journal of Gerontological Social Work* 16(2):19-35.

Stanford, E. Percil, ed.
  1978 *Comprehensive Service Delivery Systems for the Minority Aged*. San Diego: Campanile Press.

Taylor, Sue Perkins
  1980 *Cultural and Environmental Influences on Health Screening Programs for Minority Aged.
    Summary Report*. Administration on Aging, Department of Health and Human Services (Contract
    Grant No. 90AR2078). Detroit, MI: Wayne State University, Institute of Gerontology.
  1981 Simple Models of Complexity: Programmatic Considerations in Providing Services. In *Minority
    Aging: Policy Issues for the '80's*. Percil Stanford, ed. Pp. 91-94. San Diego: The Campanile Press.
  1994 Comments and Recommendations. Part II: Synthesis of Applied Research Literature on Health
    and African American Aging: Implications for the Future. John H. Skinner, Comp. In *Health and
    Minority Elders: An Analysis of Applied Literature, 1980- 1990*. Charles M. Barresi, ed. Pp. 70-71.
    Washington, DC: American Association of Retired Persons.

U.S. Department of Commerce
  1991 *Census of Population and Housing 1990. Summary Tape File 1A*. Washington, DC: U.S.
    Government Printing Office.

U.S. Department of Health and Human Services
  1994 Proposed Rules: Part III Department of Health and Human Services, Administration on Aging,
    45CFR Part 1321: Grants for State and Community Programs on Aging: *Federal Register* Volume
    59(52), (17 March 1994).

Support Systems

of Rural Older Women

in Denmark and Minnesota[1]

Dena Shenk
University of North Carolina at Charlotte

I worked with Sylvia Forman beginning in 1976, earning my Ph.D. in 1979. I have been Coordinator of the Gerontology Program and Professor of Anthropology at the University of North Carolina at Charlotte since 1991, where I am currently developing a Master's degree program in Gerontology. Previously I was Director of the Gerontology Program, and Assistant, Associate and then Professor and Chair of the Department of Interdisciplinary Studies at St. Cloud State University, spending 13 winters in Minnesota. I am active in the American Anthropological Association, the Gerontological Society of America, Association for Gerontology in Higher Education and served as President and newsletter editor of the Association for Anthropology and Gerontology. In addition to the research reported on here, I am currently working on in-depth analyses of individual life histories and beginning a project on thriving aging African-American women. I am also actively involved in several community projects and with agencies working with older adults. I love the balance in my work between teaching, administering the Gerontology Program, working in the community and doing research and writing.

There is a major difference in the way the relationship between formal services and informal social supports for the elderly are viewed in various societies. In this chapter, I will explore these differing orientations in relation to the social support systems for the elderly in the United States and Denmark. In Denmark, formal services are viewed as a *right* to be used by any member of that society who is in need of assistance, premised upon a societal model of mutual self-help. In the United States, formal services are generally viewed as an approach to be used when one's informal network is unable to meet one's needs. I will explore the impact of this major distinction on the expectations of a sample of rural older women in each society, and in their use of formal and informal support systems.

The distinction between the basic orientation to the role of informal and formal supports is critical to an understanding of the aging experience in a particular cultural context. Danish service delivery has been built on a strong philosophical belief in meeting the basic rights of every individual.[2] There is also a related Danish belief that survival through hard times depends upon cooperation - not competition (Thomas 1990:45). "For many years, the primary goal of Danish social policies has been social equalization, where few have too much but fewer have too little" (McRae 1975). High priority is placed on providing services that preserve and strengthen the capabilities of the dependent elderly, particularly on services that will enable them to remain in their homes as long as possible (Raffel and Raffel 1987).

The Danish elderly along with other members of Danish society, expect to have their basic needs met through formal services which are seen as the appropriate way to meet individual needs. The effect of these trends is that while Danish older women are comfortable accepting formal services, these services are now less readily available to the extent they have come to expect. At the same time, they are hesitant to ask friends and family for assistance and support. In contrast, elders in the United States, are hesitant to use formal services, especially those which they fear will draw them into a network of formal services over which they will have little control (Shenk 1987). American elders are typically more likely to turn to family and friends to meet increasing needs for assistance.

There is of course, a difference of scale, as Denmark is a small country with 5.1 million people. Fifteen and one-half percent of the Danish population are 65 or older, compared to 12.6% of the U.S. population, but the number of older Danes is much smaller, because Danish society is much smaller.

The system of formal services and programs to meet the basic needs of older adults is one component of the larger Danish system of providing for the basic needs of all citizens. The system of health and welfare services are financed essentially by the income taxes paid by all workers which begin at 51% of earned income. Services are free of charge for all residents, except for certain services provided by nursing homes and social welfare. For these services there are sliding fee scales for those earning more than a basic pension.

The social welfare system in Denmark is based on the concepts of normalization and equalization. The concept of normalization has been described in regard to the mentally retarded as providing the same opportunities and conditions of life to the handicapped as are available to the rest of society and the right to experience and use the environment in a normal way (Bednar 1976:13). "For many years, the primary goal of Danish social policies has been social equalization, where few have too much but fewer have too little" (McRae 1975). High priority is placed on providing services that preserve and strengthen the capabilities of the dependent elderly, particularly on services that will enable them to remain in their homes as long as possible (Raffel and Raffel 1987). The basic orientation of the system of service delivery is towards maintaining the elderly's control over choices, enabling them to lead their lives as independently as possible.

While Denmark developed a comprehensive system of high-quality, government-financed services during the economically strong period prior to 1980, the government is struggling in this new economic climate. Officials are trying to maintain the level of services in spite of budget reductions, increased numbers of older adults, and increased demand for expensive medical technology (Raffel and Raffel 1987). For discussion of the historical development of the system of formal services see Shenk and Christiansen 1993.

The availability of formal services for the elderly since the 1970's in Denmark was summarized in the following fashion by a Social Worker working with the elderly in Aalborg, Denmark (K. Anderson, personal communication, May 13, 1992): The social reforms during the comfortable economic period in the 1970's allowed services to be expanded. Elders received home help daily and the motto was "ask and you will receive." With the 1980's budget problems, there was a need for realism with recognition of the fact that services could not be expanded continually. There was an assessment of what the elderly really needed and a concurrent move from "help" to "self-help." In the 1990's there is a strong move to help elders remain in their own homes as long as possible. She also reported however, some interesting statistics from two recent studies of resource-usage. One study found that clients in their own homes were receiving 4.5 hours/week of service and the other study found 2.5 hours/week. Those in elder housing (eldrebolig) were receiving 19.6 hours or more per week and those in nursing homes (plejehjem) were receiving 30 or more hours per week. The social worker questioned whether this system is really providing a choice for older adults, since they are not likely to receive comparable amounts of service while living in their own homes in the community, as they would in elder housing or nursing homes. These studies made no attempt to determine whether the help being provided was sufficient to meet the needs of the particular elders being served, but the implication of the researchers was that it was not sufficient.

Recent developments in formal services for the aged in Denmark have centered around the theme of "self-help" and have been advanced through the development of experimental projects. The Fynsgade Center in Aalborg, for example has become a model of a multi-service center which also includes sheltered housing. The community center Koltgarden in Arhus is another example of a center that "contains activities aimed at promoting good health, preventing disease and stimulating cultural endeavors" (Wolleson 1989:19).

Changing attitudes are reported in Denmark due to the economic necessity of cutting back on formal services. The elderly still receive formal services because "it is more acceptable. You can receive formal services without losing face" (K. Christiansen, personal communication, May 19, 1992). The current effort is to get people to "care" more, that is, to develop the informal system of care through which people help and support their family and friends.

In the U.S. there is a similar emphasis on encouraging more extensive family care of the elderly. There is a large body of data which suggests that family already provide the bulk of on-going informal care and are in need of greater support from the formal sector. The formal service delivery system is not oriented towards working effectively in cooperation with the informal support system, but rather is seen as a substitute. In regard to our present discussion, a primary question is the culturally-defined relationship between the formal and informal support systems, which frames how the two work together.

Background and Discussion

My discussion is based on the findings of a multi-phase qualitative study of 30 rural older women in Central Minnesota and participant observation and questionnaire data collected from a comparative sample of 30 older women in rural Denmark. The Minnesota research was completed from March 1986 to July 1987 (see Shenk 1987 and 1991). The Danish sample was selected during the summer of 1990 and the interviews were completed by a Danish collaborator. Preliminary research was completed in Denmark from August to December 1981 and a follow-up visit was completed in May 1992 (see Shenk and Christiansen 1992).

The Minnesota Older Womens' Project was completed in several phases which included the collection of: 1) life histories, 2) social network and questionnaire data and 3) photographs of the study participants. The data collection in Denmark was based on a translated and culturally-adapted version of the questionnaire.

The Danish research was completed in Lokken-Vra on the northwest coast of North Jutland, Denmark. The area includes the towns of Lokken, Vrensted and Vittrup. Lokken, a seaside resort town in this century, was initially a seaport and later one of Denmark's larger fishing towns. Vrensted was a larger center and Vittrup a smaller center for the surrounding farming areas. They are both now merely clusters of houses and farms surrounded by open country. A few stores including a grocery are all that remain of each community.

The inhabitants of the area are known as tough and independent people and were predominantly small farmers and fishermen.[3] The Borglum Monastery (Kloster) was active in the community from about 1130 until the sixteenth century and employed many local people. Then as a lay manor house it continued to have a great impact on life in the area until the present. Due to technological advances, it is now run by a few people. A railway line went through the area, but the former Hjorring-Lokken-Aabybro railway was closed in 1963. The former station houses in Vrensted and Vittrup are now private residences.

The American research was conducted in a four-county area of central Minnesota including Stearns, Sherburne, Benton and Wright counties.[4] The American study sample was selected to be similar to the larger regional population in terms of key demographic characteristics, including education and income (see Shenk 1987). The Danish sample was selected based on earlier research with the older residents of the area by my collaborator. The informants were chosen to represent a broad range of patterns in terms of key demographic characteristics.

There are striking differences in the attitudes toward the use of formal services by the informants in Denmark and the U.S. A Danish informant explained that the Danish system of services can be understood in light of the cultural value of privacy. When money was available, formal services were used more because of this pattern of maintaining privacy. Those in need wanted to stay protected and private and would turn to formal services rather than ask friends or even family for help.

The Danish system is designed to assure privacy, by enabling elders to be independent of their family and friends for support and assistance in meeting their basic needs. The American system in comparison, is based on the concept of replacing an unavailable or insufficient informal system of support with formal services. The importance of respecting the elder's needs for privacy and autonomy are not part of the American system of formal service delivery. For example, when I visited an American informants in her home late one morning, I found her dressed in a sleeveless shift. She apologized for not being dressed and explained that the new home health aide who assisted with her bath comes at 1:30. "It's not her; it's what they assigned her. But it's so inconvenient. It's hard for me to get dressed and undressed and dressed again." So she stays in her night clothes until the aide comes. She went on to explain that the agency regularly changes the day and time of her bath, as well as the particular aide, and she has no say in it. "I asked her about coming in the morning and she said that she had to do what the main office told her."

Clearly, each society must develop a framework for effective interaction of the formal and informal systems of care in meeting the basic physical and social needs of the elderly which is based on cultural expectations (see Shenk 1992). The difference between Danish and American opinion on this point is perhaps one of degree, rather than one of kind. The American women generally were wary of using formal services which would draw them into a network of formal services over which they would have little control. Formal services are seen by these rural American women as options to be used sparingly. The American women preferred however, to rely on the formal system for ongoing assistance with personal care rather than seeking help from their informal network. The more personal the assistance needed, the more comfortable they are with a less personal formal service provider (Shenk 1987:17). Assistance can be accepted from a formal service provider without a feeling of loss of independence or becoming a burden as would be the case in depending on a relative or friend.

The Danish system of formal services ideally provides alternatives and choices from which the individual can choose. The goal of the Danish system is clearly to enable the individual to remain in control of the decision-making process and to choose the services which best meet his/her current needs.

The differences between the two samples in their attitudes toward the use of formal and informal supports can be seen in several areas. There are major differences for example, in the primary mode of transportation between the two groups, which reflect cultural differences. The Danes are more likely to use public transportation, walk or use a bicycle, while the Minnesotans more often drive their own cars or get rides from family or friends.

Both groups of respondents were asked a series of questions about both past and future use of formal services. While a similar number had used each of these services, their attitudes toward the possible future use of formal services was clearly different. In general, about half as many informants in Minnesota indicated that they would use formal services, as compared to the Danish sample. In fact, one of the Danish informants got annoyed with these questions, indicating that the services are a "right" and demanding to know: "Why are you even asking about this?"

A similar pattern is evident in the informants' responses to questions about seeking assistance with a range of needs. They were asked for example, whom they would turn to if they needed help when they became sick. More of the Danish women reported that they would seek the assistance of their spouse and slightly fewer would turn to their children or friends and neighbors than in the Minnesota sample. A similar number in each of the two samples reportedly would turn to other relatives for support. While 4 of the Minnesotan women would seek the assistance of a professional, 10 of the Danish women reported that they would seek such assistance.

There was a great deal of variation in the roles professionals played in the lives of the women in the Minnesota sample. While seven had long-term relationships with doctors for example, none were described as friends. In contrast, other types of service providers such as directors of senior centers and volunteer coordinators, were often described as good friends by the American women. These kinds of service providers are of course providing a less personal type of care.

Service providers who came to the American women's own homes were generally essential to their being able to remain in their home. Housekeepers, homemakers and home health aides in particular, were very important to these rural American women and were most often listed as being close to the informant. Some of the women reported close friendships with these service providers, occasionally including them within the first tier of their social network. For example, one informant explained about her home-health aide through county social services: "Marion is good therapy for me. We talk while she works. She tells me her problems and I talk to her. We talk about everything and it never goes any further."

There was clearly a difference in the relationships between those providing household assistance and those providing very personal assistance, like bathing. Those providing personal assistance were very important to the client's social world, but a more distant relationship was generally maintained.

When on-going assistance is needed with intimate personal care, the American women clearly prefer to turn to the formal system, rather than seek help from individuals in their informal support network. They are more comfortable if this personal assistance is received from someone with whom they can maintain a non-personal relationship. Eight of the thirty women for example, reported needing assistance with bathing. All of them are assisted in bathing by home health aides and hired service providers rather than friends or relatives. Even those still living with a spouse, did not receive assistance with bathing from their husband. They consistently reported that they would rather use formal service providers to assist them with personal care than impose on friends or neighbors, or even family. Assistance can be accepted from a formal service provider without a feeling of lose of independence or becoming a burden as would be the case in depending on a relative or friend. At the same time, three of the women assist others with bathing. One assists her husband, while two others are paid for providing personal care.

Relatively few service providers were discussed as part of the social networks of the American informants. These formal providers of care who were part of the informant's personal networks were very important however, in the lives of those study participants. These rural older women use formal service providers to fill gaps in their informal support system. The Danish women in contrast, are more dependent on formal service providers. The nature of their relationships with service providers was not fully explored, but they did not tend to form close social relationships with them.

The women were asked to whom they would turn for assistance if they needed to get somewhere quickly, if they needed money, for help around the house, if they were feeling lonely, needed help with paperwork or help with shopping. While there were variations in the number of women in each case, similar patterns were found. For example, the Danish women were most likely to seek professional help with paperwork or if they needed money, and less likely to turn to children, neighbors and friends. In general, the Danish women were less likely to seek assistance from children, neighbors or friends than were the American women.

Interestingly, the two groups showed less difference when talking about whom they would turn to if they needed help when they were feeling lonely than any of the other areas of need. The responses to this question suggest that the decision about whom to turn to for emotional support, is a very personal decision. There is a great deal of variation in the roles that friends and neighbors play in the lives of the informants, in conjunction with a pattern of strong attachment to family. Some of the American women and all of the Danish women deal with the rural phenomenon of everyone knowing everyone else by maintaining a distance in most of their relationships with neighbors and friends. As one American informant explained:

> "I'm not the kind to put my worries on someone else. I don't usually talk to anyone. I read
> or knit to get over it. If I have a heavy worry, I go to church. I don't talk to anyone."

Or as another American informant explained: "We're not that kind, to watch too close." There was generally a perceived need to maintain emotional distance from neighbors because of the geographical closeness. A few of the American women seemed to thrive on openness and intimacy. An informant who has many close friends and people she talks with intimately explained her view that: "We always need other people....I talk (intimately) with all my friends...I'm sorry for people that can't come out of their shell." It is also worth noting that fewer of the Danish women reported that they never feel lonely and more of them reported not seeking help from anyone other than themselves.

In regard to assistance in each of these areas of need, the Danish women were more likely to turn first to spouses. This is indicative perhaps of the presence of more husbands and in better health than in the Minnesota sample. There is also evidence of a different kind of relationship between spouses in the two countries. For example, the Danish women were more likely to turn to their spouses for help around the house than were the Minnesotans. This seems indicative of a different division of labor between the spouses in Denmark which is less rigidly gender-based than that in the American sample.

Relationships Between the Formal and Informal Systems

In the Danish view, while the necessary **social** support is found among family, friends and neighbors, basic needs are expected to be met somewhere else, i.e., through formal services. Danish older women are comfortable accepting formal services, but not necessarily asking friends and family for assistance. The elderly are willing to use formal services because, as we have already discussed, that is viewed as acceptable and a "right" and you can receive these services without losing face. It is not always easy, however, for elders to request the assistance they need from friends or even family. The current effort at the national level is to get people in the informal sector to "care" more, to develop the informal system of care through which people help and support each other, as the economic situation worsens. It is difficult to imagine these efforts being effective in this cultural context, where there is a clear societal expectation that basic needs be met through formal services. It will be difficult to get the present generations to reorient their expectations towards the use of formal services and to get them to expect more from their informal support systems.

In the U.S. we have the opposite problem of persuading individuals to use formal services effectively in order to reduce the strain on their informal systems of support. The system is not always designed however, so that rural elderly are encouraged to use the services as an aid toward maintaining their independence and autonomy. A powerful example is provided by the American informant who explained that she and her 90 year-old husband were increasingly frail. They still managed alone in their farmhouse. They no longer farmed but had gardened until the previous year. She explained that all she needed was assistance with housecleaning. The dilemma she expressed was based on her perceived inability to pay to hire someone to clean and her unwillingness to turn to social services for assistance. "I'm not going to tell them how much we make. That's nobody's business." In fact, having told me in intimate detail about her life, friends and family, she was unwilling to indicate the range of her income. Her husband has since died and she has moved into a nursing home. The move was difficult for her and she later wrote:

> "I am fairly well and I wouldn't be here, but they say I can't be alone... The nurses and aids are so good to me, but I can't seem to adjust to life here. It is such a lonely and depressing place. My many friends are so good about coming to see me which helps me keep my sanity."

The Danish system of services can be understood in terms of the cultural value of privacy. When money was available, the system of formal services was expanded and a range of home and community-based services were available for the asking. Those in need wanted to stay protected and private and would turn to formal services rather than ask friends or even family for help. It is interesting to note in comparison that in the U.S. also, the most private kinds of care are sought from formal service providers rather than seeking this assistance from friends or even family. In the U.S. it is also recognized that individuals should be able to seek assistance from formal services in order to maintain their independence. The American service delivery system however, is not oriented to maintaining the privacy of those whose needs are met through the formal sector. The "welfare system" mentality in American society continues to label those who need to seek assistance from formal service providers as having failed, as demonstrated by their not being able to meet their needs through informal supports.

Conclusions

In summary, formal services are viewed as a *right* to be used by any member of Danish society who is in need of assistance, premised upon mutual self-help. Having one's basic needs met by formal services allows one to interact with friends and family on a more equal basis. In contrast, in the United States, formal services are more likely to be viewed as an approach to be used when one's informal network is unable to meet one's needs. Rather than functioning to strengthen the informal system of support, formal services in the U.S. generally strain the informal social support network. Formal services are generally seen as a replacement for rather than a supplement to the informal support system.

The realization of the full meaning of this distinction is critical to an understanding of the system of informal and formal services for the elderly in both Denmark and the U.S. The Danish system of services appears to be a response to the societal preference for using formal services to meet basic needs, allowing one to depend on informal supports to meet social needs. The system now clearly perpetuates that preference. In order to keep up the high level of the formal support system during a period of economic regression, more efficient utilization of the available funds will depend on several factors. The focus should be on strengthening the independence of the individual, introduction of a policy of prevention, involvement of each citizen on all levels in these efforts and the sharing of responsibility. Responsibility for meeting the basic needs of the elderly cannot merely be redirected from the formal support system to the informal system of support without regard for cultural expectations.

Notes

1. The research in Minnesota was completed in cooperation with the Central Minnesota Council on Aging. Financial support was provided by the Central Minnesota Council on Aging and St. Cloud State University through a research grant, Extramural Support Grant, Summer Research Stipend, and sabbatical leave and through grants from the St. Cloud State University Foundation, Central Minnesota Initiative Fund and Central Minnesota Arts Council. Research in Denmark was funded by a St. Cloud State University Research Grant and UNCC Summer Research Grant.

2. This philosophical tradition is exemplified by the work of Soren Kierkegard, the Danish philosopher who stated: "If real success is to attend the effort to bring a man to a definite position, He must first of all take pains to find HIM where he is and begin there. This is the secret of the art of helping others. Anyone who has not mastered this is himself deluded when he proposes to help others. In order to help another effectively I must understand more than he-yet first of all surely I must understand what he understands. If I do not know that, my greater understanding will be of no help to him (Bretall 1951, translation of S. Kierekaard, *The Point of View for my Work as an Author*, Part 2, chapter 1, section 2:333).

3. An ethnographic culture change study by Anderson and Anderson (1964; see also Anderson 1990) provides a picture of life in a similar fishing community outside of Copenhagen at the turn of the nineteenth and early twentieth century.

4. The project was completed with the cooperation and support of the Central Minnesota Council on Aging, the regional area agency on aging.

References

Anderson, Robert T. and Barbara Gallatin Anderson
    1964 *The Vanishing Village - A Danish Maritime Community.* Seattle: University of Washington
    Press.

Anderson, Barbara Gallatin
    1990 *First Fieldwork - the misadventures of an anthropologist.* Prospect Heights, Illinois: Waveland
    Press.

Bednar, Michael
    1974 *Architecture for the Handicapped: Denmark, Sweden and Holland.* Ann Arbor: The University
    of Michigan.

Bretall, Robert
    1951 *A Kierkegaard Anthology.* Princeton: Princeton University Press.

Friis, Henning
    1979 The Aged in Denmark: Social Programmes. In M.I. Teicher, D. Thursz and J. Vigilante, eds.
    Reaching the Aged -- Social Services in Forty-Four Countries. Beverly Hills: Sage Publications.

McRae, John
    1975 *Elderly in the Environment - Northern Europe.* Gainesville, Florida: College of Architecture and
    Center for Gerontological Studies and Programs.

Raffel, Norma K. and Marshall W. Raffel
    1987 Elderly Care: similarities and solutions in Denmark and the United States. *Public Health
    Reports.* 102(5):494-500.

Shenk, Dena and Kitter Christiansen
    1993 The Evolution of the System of Care for the Aged in Denmark. *Journal of Aging and Social
    Policy.* Volume 5 (1&2).

Shenk, Dena
    1991 Older Rural Women as Recipients and Providers of Social Support. *Journal of Aging Studies.*
    5(4):347-358.
    1987 *Someone to Lend a Helping Hand - the Lives of Rural Older Women in Central Minnesota.* St.
    Cloud, Minnesota: Central Minnesota Council on Aging.

Thomas, F. Richard
  1990 *Americans in Denmark: Comparisons of the Two Cultures by Writers, Artists and Teachers.*
  Carbondale: Southern Illinois Press.

Wolleson, Anna Marie
  1989 Koltgarden - from Idea to Reality. In *The Elderly in Denmark* Pp.19-22. Copenhagen: The
  Danish Cultural Institute.

Older and Middle-Aged

Puerto Rican Women:

Cultural Components of

Support Networks

Melba Sánchez-Ayéndez
University of Puerto Rico

Melba Sánchez-Ayéndez (Ph.D. 1984) is Coordinator of the Social Sciences Unit and Associate Professor of Social Sciences and Gerontology at the Graduate School of Public Health of the University of Puerto Rico, Medical Sciences Campus in San Juan. For several years, she was Dean of Academic Affairs of the School of Public Health and Chairperson of its Social Sciences Department. From 1991 to 1993 she was a Postdoctoral Fellow in Gerontology at Saint Clares-Riverside Medical Center's International Center on Aging in New Jersey. She has served as Adviser to the Pan American Health Organization on issues related to elderly women, programs for the aged, and middle-aged women. She was a member of the Advisory Committee of the Governor of Puerto Rico's Office for Elderly Affairs. She is currently the Principal Investigator of a national survey on breast cancer beliefs and practices among older women in Puerto Rico that will lead to the establishment of an educational program.

Introduction

This chapter provides an illustration of the cultural context of female support systems, specifically those of older Puerto Rican women and their middle-aged daughters. Gerontological research has demonstrated the cross-cultural prevalence of familial support to older adults in developed and less developed countries despite rapid social change in the last 40 years. Culture plays an important role in the involvement of the family and the community in the care of the elderly. Social networks and the supportive relations that ensue from them have a cultural dimension that embodies a system of shared meanings. These meanings affect interaction, the expectations people have of their relationships with others, and their satisfaction with these relations (Horowitz 1985; Jacobson 1987; McDowell 1981). Gerontological research has demonstrated that who the elderly turn to for assistance and why is related to cultural definitions of male and female roles, notions of family interdependence, filial duty, reciprocity, friendship and neighborliness (Brody 1990; Cameron et al. 1989; Carers National Association 1992; Horowitz 1985; Lewis and Meredith 1989; Rosenberg 1990; Sánchez-Ayéndez 1984, 1992). Those who participate in the provision of assistance also share in this cultural framework to the same or lesser extent depending on factors such as cohort group history, migratory experiences and area of residence.

Caregiver stress is inherent in the process of providing support to the aged, especially to those with frail health and disabilities. Strain is closely related to cultural notions and subjectivity. Research in developed countries, mainly in the United States and Great Britain, has established that the level of dependency of the elderly has something to do with caregiver burden (George 1990; Twigg 1989; Zarit 1990). Yet, the characteristics of the caregiving situation, the meanings that those involved place on the caregiving situation, and the resources and/or support available to the caregiver, also have an impact on the carer. All these are affected by cultural worldviews and values that are seldom considered in quantitative research on caregiver strain.

What elders want and expect of others in terms of care and what principal caregivers provide in terms of support is affected by socially and historically shared meanings (Jacobson 1987; McDowell 1981). The meanings that social relationships have for older persons and principal carers as well as the patterns of interaction and assistance between the aged and those in their supportive networks are influenced by cultural definitions and values. Those involved in the planning and provision of services to the elderly cannot afford to overlook these meanings.

Methodology

The investigation upon which this paper is based is a follow-up to my doctoral dissertation research (Sánchez-Ayéndez 1984) conducted under Sylvia Forman's guidance. I studied the informal networks of support of sixteen low-income, Puerto Rican older women 65 years of age and over residing in an ethnic enclave in Boston from 1981-1983. The follow-up was carried out during the summers of 1988 and 1989.

In-depth formal and informal interviews of 15 of the original older women and the daughter who was the central figure in each supportive network were conducted. A qualitative descriptive approach was used in the analysis. The supportive relationship was explored on two levels. One level examined the types of assistance provided to the older woman by the daughter and to the daughter by the older woman. The second level comprised an analysis of the relationship between cultural meanings shared by the ethnic group which the women identified with and ways in which the networks were utilized.

General Characteristics of the Participants

The median age for the older women was 77 and for their daughters 49. The majority lived in government subsidized housing. Twelve of the aged resided in a different household from that of their offspring. Most of them lived within a two-mile radius of at least one of their children, who generally turned out to be the daughter cited as the principal caregiver. Half of the older women were widows, while two thirds of their adult daughters were married. All of the middle-aged women had offspring who were 10 years of age and older, ranging from 10 to 34.

Types of Support

Daughters constitute a reliable source of support for their elderly mothers even when an older husband is present. The transactional content of the support given to the mothers by the daughters is mostly instrumental and emotional. In terms of the instrumental support, the elders are provided with transportation and escort to places, information, reading and writing of letters for those who are illiterate and/or do not know English, and health assistance. Very few of the older women receive financial help from their families except during emergencies. The emotional support offered to them involves frequent visits and/or telephone calls -- in most cases on a daily basis -- as well as having someone with whom to share worries and problems. The daughters who were interviewed were the principal providers of emotional support to their mothers. Most of them visited their mothers every day or every other day, and spoke to them on the telephone about twice a day. The majority of the elderly women stated that they turn first to a daughter when faced with a problem.

It is generally daughters who are the principal source of assistance during the illness of an elderly mother. The role of sons is more limited. It is generally daughters who more often than their brothers check on the sick mother, provide personal care and perform domestic chores for the aged during times of illness.

The elderly women provide instrumental and emotional support to their daughters and families. The supportive tasks most frequently performed by them include caring for young children after school or when these are sick, cooking and giving advice. Most of the daughters who worked outside their homes stated that their mothers provided childcare and also prepared meals for their households. Grandchildren in elementary and junior high school usually have a snack and supper at their grandmother's house and wait there for their mothers to pick them up after work. It is common for the older woman to prepare and pack a meal for her daughter to take to eat at her home. The older woman's health status plays a determinant role in the provision of these supportive chores.

Cultural Values

Both subsamples of women believe in a double standard of conduct for men and women, the predominance of male authority and greater female emotional strength. Women are conceptualized as patient and forbearing in their relations with men, particularly male family members. The women expressed opinions such as:

If your husband disagrees with you, you may have your way if you work in an indirect manner.   Men should not be challenged straightforward except under certain circumstances. If you are not ill-mannered or overtly aggressive you can live peacefully with any man.

Forbearance and patience should not be confused with passivity or total submissiveness. These women do not perceive themselves or other women as "resigned females" but as dynamic beings who are continually devising strategies for the improvement of everyday situations within and outside the household.   There seems to be a confusion in some of the anthropological literature about Latin American women that seems to be related to a male bias, as well as a tendency to classify value orientations on the basis of rigid dichotomies that leave no room for individual variations or coping mechanisms. The conceptualization of the "resigned female" role in Puerto Rico, and other Latin American countries, derives mainly from male researchers who categorized values according to those of their own sociocultural group, leading to misinterpretation or oversight of significant but subtle differences that exist in the dynamics of female-male relationships. A significant concern in understanding informal caregiving to the aged and also women's issues in Latin America and other technologically less developed countries, is whether models developed in western industrialized societies are culturally sensitive or relevant enough to grasp intricacies pertaining to subjectivity and motivation.   North American and European conceptions of reality have dominated the theoretical perspectives within the social sciences and gerontology.   The standards often used to classify the cultural orientations of different groups around the world have been impacted by the meanings that North American and European societies use in their social constructions of reality. Classifications and evaluations of individuals and/or groups as "passive," "dependent," and "fatalistic" and of societies as "modern" or "underdeveloped," among other terms, have stemmed from schematic analyses of the historical and sociocultural contexts of the societies the researchers come from or where "native" researchers have pursued their formal education, and are not necessarily applicable to the groups and communities that are studied.

Although the women who participated in the study perceive men as authority figures, nevertheless, both age subsamples also describe them as emotionally weaker and not completely reliable. The term _"como niños"_ (like boys) is frequently used when describing grown-up men's actions and emotions. The possibility exists that women, in dealing with their subordinate status, regard men as children who cannot assume the responsibilities or have the emotional endurance of an adult. When men are defined as " grown-up children," it is women who assume the status of the mature persons who can understand men and the child-like demands they make. Under these circumstances the women perceive themselves as assuming the authority role in the "adult-child relationship." However, because these "grown-up male children" are adults with a dominant status women cannot forget their subordinate one. Thus, disappointment, and even bitterness, are expressed when males do not meet what women perceive as the responsibilities of an adult, as in the case of male offspring not participating as much as their sisters in the provision of assistance to their mothers.

The cultural construction of motherhood permeates both elderly and middle-aged women's conceptualization of its centrality in women's lives. The concept of motherhood as expressed by these women stems from their biological capacity for childbearing. Within this framework, motherhood is the woman's main role. It assumes priority over other roles such as wife or laborer. It is through motherhood that a woman realizes herself and derives her biggest satisfactions in life. The respondents all expressed satisfaction or dissatisfaction with their life accomplishments in terms of their offspring. A woman's reproductive role is perceived as enabling her to be more committed to and better understanding of her children than the father. Subjects expressed views such as the following:

> It is easier for a man to leave his children and form a new home with another woman or not to be as forgiving of children as a mother is. They [men] will never know what it is like to carry a child inside, feel it growing and bring that child into the world. This is why a mother is always willing to forgive and make sacrifices; that creature is a part of you. It nourished from you and came from within you. But it is not so with men. To them, a child is a being they receive once it is born. The attachment can never be the same.

Motherhood is also perceived as a link that creates an emotional bond among women. Once a daughter has become a mother a stronger tie with her own mother is expected. The bases for this tie are the suffering experienced in childbirth and the hardships involved in childrearing since childrearing is considered as the main responsibility of the woman. The aged women expressed views such as the following:

> Once a daughter experiences being a mother she understands the hardships you underwent for her. Sons will never be able to fully understand this.

Their middle aged daughters stated, in a similar vein, that:

> It was not until I had my first child that I was able to understand how much a mother can love. Then I felt closer to my mother, even more than before. Then I understood all she had done for me.

Despite the fact that the older respondents and 11 of their daughters had worked or were working outside the home, the women perceive the house as the center around which the female world revolves. The house is viewed as their domain. Decisions regarding household maintenance are generally made by women. Household governance and maintenance are perceived as a female responsibility and co-exist with the breadwinner role of males.

These cultural definitions of the female role affect the types of exchanges that occur within the family networks and are interlinked to the value of family interdependence. Interdependence for these women,

> ... fits an orientation to life that stresses that the individual is not capable of doing everything and doing it well. Therefore, s/he should rely on others for assistance (Bastida 1979: 70-71).

Within this framework, self-reliance and self-esteem are not affected by the provision of family assistance when an adult is undergoing a crisis or has to ask for help. Thus, the older women still expect to be taken care of in old age by their adult children. The notion of filial duty ensues from the value orientation of interdependence. It stems from filial love and reciprocity for the sacrifices that the mother underwent in the upbringing of her children.

Interdependence also means that the elderly mothers will help their adult children to the extent they are able to. Being able to perform supportive tasks for their offspring is a source of emotional satisfaction. Within the interdependence framework, this is viewed from the context of their role as mothers.

Family interdependence is not based upon reciprocal exchange relationships or mutual giving. What is of utmost importance to the older women is that the children visit or call frequently and not that they help all the time. More emphasis is placed on emotional support from offspring than other forms of assistance. This is why frequent interaction with children, whether in the form of visits or telephone calls, is highly valued.

The importance that the Puerto Rican older women attach to the value of family interdependence does not imply that they are constantly requiring instrumental support from children. They try to do by themselves as much as they are able, but when assistance is needed, it is generally a daughter to whom they prefer to turn.

Dynamics of Support and Cultural Values

The difference in conceptualization between males and females affects the dynamics and types of exchanges that occur within the family networks, both in terms of support given and received. In relation to support received from offspring, Puerto Rican older women perceive their daughters as being more understanding and better able to comprehend their problems due to their ascribed qualities as women. Daughters are also considered more reliable. Sons are not expected to help as much as daughters or in the same way. Complaints are more bitter when a daughter does not fulfill expected duties of assistance as an offspring compared to a son, as exemplified in the following quote:

> Men are different, they do not feel as we feel. But she is a woman, she should know better.

Daughters are also expected to visit and/or call more frequently than sons. As women, they are interlinked to the domestic domain and held responsible for the care of family members and the maintenance of family relations.

Two-thirds of the older women who have sons and daughters stated that they confide their problems more often to their daughters, as well as offer advice to daughters on matters related to marriage and children. This does not mean that they do not discuss personal matters with sons or give them advice, but the approach is different. For example, in terms of advice given to adult children by the elderly women, informants stated:

> I never ask my son openly what is wrong with him. I go carefully. I do not want him to think that I believe he cannot solve his problems; he is a man. Yet, as a mother I worry. It is my duty to listen and offer him advice. With my daughter is different; I can be more direct. She doesn't have to prove to me that she is self-sufficient.

> Of course I give advice to my sons! When they have had problems with their wives, their children, even among themselves, I listen to them, and tell them what I think. But with my daughter I am more open. You see, if I ask one of my sons what is wrong and he doesn't want to tell me, I don't insist too much. I'll ask later, maybe in a different way and they will tell me sooner or later. With my daughter, if she doesn't want to tell me, I'll insist. She knows I am her mother and a woman like she and that I can understand.

Sixty percent of the elderly respondents who turn to their children when faced by a problem, said they go first to a daughter when confronted with an emotional problem. Female offspring are perceived as more patient and, being women like their mothers, better able to understand them.

It is generally daughters who provide most of the assistance that the elderly mother needs during an illness. Quite often the daughters take the sick parent into their homes or stay overnight at the parents' home in order to provide better care to the aged parent. Although sons are part of the supportive network that provides health assistance, the general pattern is for the elderly to depend more on their daughters. Sons, as well as daughters, are likely to take the aged parents to the hospital or doctor's offices, buy medicines and contribute financially if needed. However, it is daughters who check more often on their parents, provide personal care and perform household chores during the time the elderly parent is sick. This is also the case when the older adult suffers from a chronic condition or is impaired. The three older respondents who resided with an offspring suffered from a chronic ailment and/or were impaired and all lived in a daughter's household.

Support from the Daughters' Perspective

The daughters who were the main caregivers expressed satisfaction in carrying out what they described as their duty as offspring. They view their supportive behavior in relation to their mothers from the perspective of reciprocity for exchange of the tasks and sacrifices that their mothers performed during their upbringing. All stressed that good offspring ought to help their aged parents according to available resources and capabilities. Filial love was not cited as often as filial duty.

Most of the daughters, particularly those whose mothers required special care, (6 of 15), also expressed that their role as principal caregiver implies stress. Four of the 15 middle-age women reported feeling very stressed, seven stated that they felt stressed often, while four replied feeling little stress. Most of the sources of stress cited had to do with problems with other family members such as conflicting demands from husbands and children, and discrepancies over carer tasks with other siblings who were not assuming as much responsibility in the support of the aged mother. Changes in moods of the older adult and demands for more attention or longer visits from the daughter were reported as a secondary sources of stress. The middle-aged daughters expressed that stress was also caused by their doubts as to whether or not they were fulfilling their role as carers correctly, as well as by guilt feelings as they sometimes feel some resentment towards the aged and their demands for care and more attention.

Daughters who worked outside the home were most likely to state they felt more stressed, but perceived strain is also interlinked to other variables such as support from other family members, other problems in the family unit and health-status and personality traits of the aged. These women seem to be fulfilling all the responsibilities that their roles demand, negotiating flexibility in their everyday chores and duties and sacrificing their free time.

Despite stress being a reality in the lives of most of the middle-aged daughters, only two out of the 15 stated they would institutionalize their mother if they could. These two women were looking after very frail mothers and were faced with other stressful family situations related to substance abuse by their husband and/or children. The majority of the principal caregivers wished they could obtain some help with household chores and receive less interference and criticism from other family members about how assistance was being offered.

Conclusions and Implications

Values related to family interdependence and definitions of female and male roles affect female networks of support within a sample of lower-income middle-aged and older Puerto Rican women in the United States. Although daughters constitute a reliable source of support to their elderly mothers, and in many cases the older adults are not mere recipients but also providers of assistance, satisfaction and stress are built into the dynamics of support. This is what Brody (1985) has termed "normative family stress."

Since Puerto Rican women are traditionally the main providers of assistance in the family, it is more likely that they will experience the stress to a much greater extent than male family members. It is women who must juggle their different roles. Cross-cultural gerontological research indicates that generations of women, like the ones who participated in the investigation upon which this chapter is based, are still enmeshed in each other's lives. Filial responsibility and bonds of affection are strong elements of supportive relationships and are not likely to disappear. Middle-aged daughters who must conduct a balancing act between responsibilities form part of the so-called "sandwich" or "women-in-the middle" generation. The emotional pull that they are confronted with is a stressful reality in their daily lives.

The understanding of the role of women as "caregivers" is intertwined with certain conceptual issues. First of all, carer involvement is something beyond the control of formal agencies. Caregiving responsibilities flow from and are undertaken by the individual (Twigg, 1989). Second, caregiving is an on-going process; it is not static. It occurs through time and its dynamics are influenced by past experiences relating to the relationship between the carer and the care recipient, the health status of the elder and the carer, the length of time that the primary carer has been playing the role, the personalities of the parties involved in the dyadic relationship, and also by structural and demographic variables, as well as cultural meanings.

People's lives are an integrated whole. A person does not cease being a carer to turn into something else. Roles interrelate and overlap and cause tension, stress and conflict. Women who are the main caregivers to an older parent have to make choices due to their multiplicity of roles as social beings. These choices many times are the result of a strenuous decision and can themselves be stressful for both the carer and the recipient of care (Litvin, 1992).

The characteristics of the caregiving situation, the meanings that those involved place on the caregiving situation, and the resources and/or support available to the caregiver, all have an impact on the carer. Strain has situational and subjective dimensions that pertain to cultural worldviews and values. These dimensions are rarely emphasized in quantitative research on caregiver burden. Yet, the carers' definition and evaluation of their situation and its effect on their well-being and the quality of the supportive relationship are affected by their perception of variables such as: role conflict, constriction of social life, mastery of the situation, sense of competence as carer, and definitions of caregiver role as ensuing from cultural notions related to kinship as well as by personal coping strategies and the perception and existence of social support. The impact of culture on caregiver perception and strain and the cultural context of caregiving and caregiver strain need to be emphasized in research as well as in programs including support groups for principal carers.

References

Bastida, Elena
   1979 *Family Integration and Adjustment to Aging Among Hispanic American Elderly.* Ph.D. Dissertation, University of Kansas.

Brody, Elaine M.
   1985 Parent care as a normative family stress. *The Gerontologist* 21:471-478.
   1990 *Women in the Middle: Their Parent-Care Years.* New York: Springer.

Cameron, E., Evers, Helen, Badger, F. and Atkin, K.
   1989 Black, old women, disability and health carers. In *Growing Old in the Twentieth Century.* Margot Jeffreys, ed. London: Routledge.

Carers National Association
   1992 Speak Up, Speak Out. _Listen to Carers_. London: Issue Communications Ltd.

George, Linda K.
   1990 Caregiver stress studies -- There really is more to learn. _The Gerontologist_ 30:580-581.

Horowitz, Amy
   1985 Sons and daughters as caregivers to older parents: Differences in role performance and
       consequences. _The Gerontologist_ 25:612-623.

Jacobson, David
   1987 The cultural context of social support and support networks. _Medical Anthropology Quarterly_
       1:42-67.

Lewis, John and Meredith, Barbara W.
   1989 Contested territory in informal care. In _Growing Old in the Twentieth Century_. Margot Jeffreys,
       ed. London: Routledge.

Litvin, Sandra J.
   1992 Status transitions and future outlook as determinants of conflict: The caregiver's and care
       receiver's perspective. _The Gerontologist_ 32:68-76.

McDowell, Nancy
   1981 It's not who you are but how you give that counts: The role of exchange in Melanesian society.
       American Ethnologist 7:58-70.

Rosenberg, Harriet G.
   1990 Complaint discourse, aging and caregiving among the !Kung San of Botswana. In _The Cultural
       Context of Aging_. J. Sokolovsky, ed. New York: Bergin and Garvey:19-41.

Sánchez-Ayéndez, Melba
   1984 _Puerto Rican Elderly Women: Aging in an Ethnic Minority Group in the United States_. Ph.D.
       Dissertation, University of Massachusetts, Amherst.
   1991 Daughters as Principal Providers of Care to Older Adults in Puerto Rico. Paper presented at the
       IX Brazilian Congress on Geriatrics and Gerontology, I Latin American Congress on Gerontology
       COMLAT and VII Latin American Congress of Geriatrics and Gerontology.
   1992 Puerto Rican elderly women: Shared meanings and informal supportive networks. In _Race,
       Class and Gender_. M.L. Andersen and P.H. Collins, eds. California: Wadsworth:238-252.

Twigg, Julia
   1989 Models of carers: How do social care agencies conceptualize their relationship with informal
       carers? _Journal of Social Policy_ 18:53-66.

Zarit, Steven H.
   1989 Do we need another "stress and caregiving" study? _The Gerontologist_ 29:147-148.

The Politics of Advocacy

In Anthropology:

Organizing the Human Rights

And Environment Study[1]

Barbara Rose Johnston
Center for Political Ecology

I entered the Ph.D. program in anthropology at the University of Massachusetts, Amherst in the fall of 1981, with a previous career in environmental planning and an independent studies "cultural ecology" masters degree from San Jose State University (Geography, Environmental Studies, and Urban Planning). I commuted between UMass and the Virgin Islands from 1981-1983, completing my area studies (Political Ecology, Ethnicity and Ethnic Conflict, and Archaeology) while working in the Virgin Islands as a cultural and environmental resource consultant. From 1984 to 1987 I lived in the islands year round conducting research projects with the territorial government, completing my dissertation, getting married, and birthing two children. Since then I have lived in California, Canada, the Virgin Islands, and again in California working as an environmental studies, anthropology and sociology lecturer and an environmental consultant. Since 1991 I have been a research associate at the Center for Political Ecology (Santa Cruz, Ca.) and a member of their __Capitalism, Nature, Socialism__ editorial board. My work involves the social, cultural, and political economic dimensions of environmental crisis, and is aimed at stimulating social science research and influencing environmental policy. Affiliations include AAA fellow and member of the Environmental Task Force; AFA Executive Board (1989-1992); and Society for Applied Anthropology (SfAA) Fellow, Organizer and Chair of the SfAA Committee on Human Rights and the Environment.

Personal Reflections on the Legacy of Sylvia Helen Forman

Sylvia Helen Forman was as an anthropologist specializing in the politics of our discipline. Forman had little time for written discourse, preferring and seeing greater substantive change coming out of her direct action and activism. She worked within the political structures of academic and disciplinary establishments to direct and affect change, and when she came up against political barriers, she aggressively pushed, restructured, and at times smashed down and built anew. This confrontational and manipulative style was not always easy to take. In the heat of battle Forman typically dismissed the personal politics (ignoring bruised egos) and focused her intense energy on the objective at hand. However, her style -- her commitment and tenacity -- meant that Sylvia Forman got things done.

I was never formally a student of Sylvia Forman's. I was never in her classroom as a student or teaching assistant. She was not my graduate program advisor. Forman did serve as a member of my Ph.D. thesis committee, and in the final stages of my degree program she chaired my dissertation committee. Nevertheless, while I was not technically "Sylvia's student," I will always be Forman's student in the real sense.

We met in the political arena as members of the short-lived U.S.-Grenada Friendship Society. Our relationship was forged during the U.S. invasion crisis where we spent hours in meetings organizing protest action. From the onset we recognized in each other a mutual taste for politics. We had both put in time as students at U.C. Berkeley, and understanding that system, I appreciated her efforts at the University of Massachusetts to structure a student-empowered program, emphasizing the rights and voice of undergraduates as well as graduate students. As a graduate student, and later as an Environmental Studies faculty member at California State University Sacramento, Forman taught me how to chart a course through the political landmines of departmental, campus and disciplinary politics. There were times when she was a sister, an aunt, a mother to me, but first and foremost, we were colleagues.

For me, and perhaps for most of Forman's colleagues, the social and political arenas of the annual American Anthropological Association (AAA) meetings represented the strongest point of intersection in our personal and professional worlds. Sylvia Forman's passions, activism, and life energies revolved around the culture of power. The AAA annual meetings provided her with endless opportunities to study, define, and shape the culture of power in our discipline -- to explore and affect the politics and praxis of anthropology.

Year after year I joined Sylvia Forman in this field to "do" this version of fieldwork. We met in the bar at the Hilton, attended sessions and business meetings together, and talked for endless hours about the history, culture and politics of the institutions and actors that make up our discipline. Forman introduced me to her key informants in the community -- her network of professional colleagues and friends. She provided advice in my nacient efforts at organizing annual meeting sessions, pushed me into political arenas, and once there, supported my endeavors with advice and constructive criticism. As I developed my own agendas and professional networks Forman continued to give: recounting her experiences and insights, providing encouragement, and at times employing her political skills on my behalf. She purposefully taught me how she got things done. Most importantly, Sylvia Helen Forman trusted me to shape my own agendas, employ my own methods and strategies to get things done, and, in her words, "to do it right."

The Politics of Organizing a Disciplinary Voice

In 1991, while compiling material for an environmental quality/social justice textbook, I came across a reference to a United Nations study on Human Rights and the Environment in *Earth Island* (Lowe 1991:8). This article described action taken by the Commission on Human Rights at its 1990 meeting where it endorsed a proposal from the Sub-Commission for the Prevention of Discrimination and Protection of Minorities to explore the relationship between human rights and the environment. The article also summarized the findings from a 1991 preliminary note prepared for the Sub-Commission by the Human Rights and Environment Special Rapporteur, Mdme. Fatma Zohra Ksentini. These findings included an examination of human rights as they apply to four broad areas of potential environmental harm: natural habitats, natural resources, human settlements, and human health. And finally, the *Earth Island* article included a call for contributions, asking individuals, groups and organizations to submit case specific material documenting human environmental rights abuse.

Seeking a collaborative exchange of information, I contacted the Sierra Club Legal Defense Fund (the nongovernmental organization charged with soliciting and compiling material for the United Nations study). I had hoped to exchange case-specific material documenting the social and cultural context of environmental crisis, enhancing their study and my book writing efforts. Case-specific material, it turned out, was lacking. At the time of my contact, participants in the United Nations study were largely human rights lawyers and representatives from interest-specific environmental organizations. Thus, the material basis for the human rights and environment study, at that point, relied upon reviews of national constitutions, legislation and international human rights conventions; a few cases of ecoactivists experiencing human rights abuse; and, descriptions of various sorts of environmental problems. My offer to provide anthropological documentation of community-based experiences of human environmental rights abuse represented the sole offer of social science input.

Realizing the huge need and my limited capabilities, I asked Sylvia Forman for help in organizing some sort of disciplinary input. She had me contact SfAA President Carole Hill and AAA President Jane Buikstra, and together we worked on various strategies to publicize the study and organize broader anthropological involvement. In late October 1991, after numerous phone calls and letters, I drafted proposals to the AAA and the SfAA to form a joint AAA/SfAA Commission on Human Rights and the Environment whose mandate would be to organize, compile and assess case specific material exploring the relationships between human rights abuse and environmental degradation.

Throughout this early organizing period academic and institutional constructs of time were continuously in conflict with timelines established in the political realm. An opportunity existed to strongly assert the anthropological voice in the international policy arena at the crucial formative stage where problems were being defined and policy goals being articulated. We had the opportunity through our ethnographic research to broaden the notion of who is a victim (groups and communities as well as individuals). We had the long term community-based data documenting the role of governments, multinational industry, multilateral institutions, and ideological processes (development, nationalism) in creating situations of human rights abuse. Rising to these challenges meant meeting an externally imposed timeline where, if material was to be included in the Sub-Commission study documents, reports needed to be drafted, reviewed, revised, endorsed, and in the Special Rapporteur's hand by April 1992. Meeting this deadline was by no means easy. All sorts of barriers existed and continuously inhibited our ability to "get things done." The issues which paralyzed efforts to organize and draft contributions included the following questions: Who is to say what version of reality is real? Which anthropologists' work would be included and how would one expert be selected over others? How to achieve formal review and endorsement in this timeline, and who is to review and endorse? What constitutes a disciplinary voice? Who is to fund this endeavor? How would this study conflict and compete for scarce funds with other existing or planned anthropological efforts in the international and environmental policy arenas?

Politely said, in the first four months of the "human rights and environment" project as I struggled to create institutional and disciplinary wide linkages I learned a lot about the culture of politics in anthropology. I certainly came to appreciate the distinct differences in decision making structures of the SfAA and the AAA.

At the November 1991 meeting of the SfAA Executive Committee I received approval to begin forming a committee whose mandate was to study the relationships between human rights and the environment, to submit that material for SfAA review and endorsement, and to submit our work to the United Nations Sub-Commission study. The proposed joint commission did not materialize, though I did find myself inserted at a late date into the AAA Environmental Task Force as a "human rights" representative. Calls for contributions to the "Human Rights and Environment" study were circulated in various sessions and association business meetings at the November 1991 AAA annual meeting (including the Environmental Task Force open forum). I submitted a proposal to the Environmental Task Force in January 1992 to conduct a joint AAA Environmental Task Force and SfAA Committee on Human Rights and the Environment, and this proposal was defeated. Thus, the human rights and environment study proceeded with the institutional review and endorsement of the SfAA, and largely self-funded.

As I struggled to "get things done" I relied a great deal on Sylvia Forman. Following my various interactions with the different arms and legs of our disciplinary institutions, she interpreted actions, or (more importantly) the lack of action. As I drafted statements, proposals and calls for contributions, she provided critical feedback on my organizational and conceptual efforts, helping to articulate the anthropological spin on the human rights and environment problem. And, when I finally got to the point of forming a study group, she provided possible names, addresses, and at times, personal introductions. Sylvia Forman helped lay the ground work for our study. She died a month before our first preliminary report was released.

The Human Rights and Environment Study

Following SfAA Executive Board approval of a Committee on Human Rights and the Environment, this study process began. After meetings with the Sierra Club Legal Defense Fund, numerous phone calls to Carole Hill and Sylvia Forman, and a 10 hour planning session with David Maybury-Lewis and Ted MacDonald of Cultural Survival, and R. Brooke Thomas of the University of Massachusetts, Amherst, a plan emerged for formulating anthropological contributions to the United Nations study process. We decided that our strongest contribution would be in broadening the notion of who are the victims, and in illustrating the processes and mechanisms which initiate, structure, legitimize and reproduce victimization -- essentially providing the descriptive rationale for human environmental rights. Our desire was to present well-documented examples of the relationship between government action (or sanctioned action), environmental degradation, and subsequent human misery. Regional overviews would be followed by a series of cases that described situations of human environmental rights abuse and identified the contexts which predisposed certain groups to victimization. A research and action plan outlining a three-phase study effort (preliminary, final, summary/policy recommendations) was prepared in January 1992, and in February 1992 a committee was formally appointed by SfAA President Carole Hill. I prepared a conceptual overview and case study guidelines, distributing this material to initial committee members, and the 100 or so people who had seen the call for contributions and expressed interest in the study.

In March 1992, the SfAA Executive Board approved and endorsed the draft preliminary report of the committee, authorizing limited financial support to assist preliminary report publication and dissemination. Last minute case studies were added to the draft, and the report was formally released in May 1992. Following the release of the preliminary report, our research plan called for a period of review, revision, and -- through the dissemination of the preliminary report -- broadening the network of contributors and range of cases presented in the "Human Rights and the Environment" study. A final report was prepared in March 1993, reviewed and endorsed by the SfAA Executive Committee, and submitted for consideration and inclusion in the August 1993 Sub-Committee report to the U.N. Commission on Human Rights. Additional copies of this document were distributed to national and international policy and advocacy groups for their use in informing the public and influencing public policy.

The final phase of the SfAA Human Rights and the Environment study process was the preparation and dissemination of a summary overview, aimed at influencing public policy at the national and international levels. This booklet consisted of a conceptual essay, findings from the final report, and several sample case studies. Limited distribution of the final report and production and broad-based distribution of the booklet were achieved thanks to the financial support of the Nathan Cummings Foundation, Human Rights and the Environment fund. In August 1994, Island Press published an expanded version of the SfAA study on human rights and the Environment (Johnston 1994).

Conceptualizing Human Environmental Rights Abuse

In organizing the SfAA study on Human Rights and the Environment and preparing a report, my biggest difficulty was finding a conceptual strategy that links the individual stories from here, there and everywhere into a cohesive fashion. I came up with the notion of "selective victimization" -- an expansion of the environmental racism thesis. Environmental racism, as a term, refers to the relationship between environmental hazards, race and poverty. Simply put, the thesis argues that people of color bear the brunt of the United States pollution problems. Various environmental racism studies demonstrate the role of racial discrimination in environmental policymaking, the enforcement of regulations and laws, the siting of toxic waste disposal faculties, the siting of polluting industries, and the legal sanctioning of minority community exposure to poisons and pollutants.[2]

As a means to contextualize and analyze instances of human environmental rights abuse, the notion of environmental racism allows linkages between histories, cultural notions, political economic conditions, and environmental contexts. Using race and class variables to map out a social demography of environmental hazards has allowed, for example, the recognition that in the United States, poor, black, Latino and Native American communities are consistently hit more severely by pollution and death (c.f. Goldman 1991).

For the purposes of our study -- understanding the ties between human rights abuse and environmental degradation in diverse political, economic and cultural contexts -- the environmental racism thesis provided an effective starting point. The analytical emphasis on examining the social context of environmental degradation allowed us to consider the experience of human environmental rights abuse, as well as various factors that create, legitimize, or transform that experience. However, the focus on race loses its usefulness in many other cultural contexts, especially where other cultural variables (i.e., class, caste, gender, age, ethnicity, religion) structure the differential environmental health experience. In searching for a term broad enough to include diverse variables I developed the notion of "selective victimization."

Selective victimization is a product of cultural notions as well as political economic relationships and histories (of colonialism, imperialism, ethnocide and ecocide.) Victimization occurs and is reproduced via the cultural values and ideals that inform and structure the goals and development agenda of government, national and multinational corporations, as well as local elite. It is these preexisting social conditions which legitimize the loss of critical resources and a healthy environment, resulting in the exposure of certain groups to hazardous environmental conditions while others are free to live, recreate, procreate, and die in a healthy setting.

Study Findings

The various documents produced in this study (preliminary and final reports, booklet, and book) include regional overviews with case-specific examples of human environmental rights abuse (e.g., Latin America and North America), country specific overviews (e.g., Human Rights and Environmental Degradation in China; San Socioeconomic Issues, Environment and the State in Botswana; Resource Development and Indigenous Peoples in Siberia) as well as issue specific-studies (e.g., Nuclear Victimization in the Marshall Islands; Multinational Industry at the United States/Mexico Border; Ok Tedi Mine in Papua New Guinea). Also included are position papers, such as those assessing the role of "resources" in nation and state conflicts in the twentieth century.

Taken together these cases argue that the right to a healthy environment is a basic human right. Across the world and across time some people are more vulnerable than others to experiencing the human consequences of environmental degradation. Their collective experiences represent a form of selective victimization where some people (and their rights to land, resources, health, environmental protection and thus, their future) are expendable in the name of national security, national energy, and national debt. Significant biases exist in the present system of identifying abuse, identifying victims (understanding of environmental risk biased towards male adult Anglo norms), and compensating for loss (biased towards the easily quantifiable, short-term impacts). And finally, that this notion of selective victimization is a significant problematic in structuring resource management, environmental preservation, and sustainable development policy.

The policy implications of these points include:

1. the need to document the immediate as well as long term implications of change;

2. the importance of considering group as well as individual rights; and, recognition that human rights violations occur as a preceding factor, as well as subsequent result of environmental degradation;

3. that processes, as well as individuals and organizations, deny human rights;

4. that the category of "victim" is shaped by preexisting contexts of power and powerlessness: gender, race and ethnic based inequities, as well as occupation, generation, and class are all significant categories of concern;

5. that resource rights (e.g. to land, timber, water), the ability to organize to protect land and resource base, and the ability to transform traditional resource management systems to meet modern needs are crucial factors in ensuring sustainable lifestyles;

6. and finally, that the process of protecting a "healthy environment" may, in some cases, result in human rights abuse.

Applying Anthropology in the Policy Arena

These findings are not startling or new if your perspective is the realm of anthropology. What we were trying to do in this study is to direct our collective research, observations and experiences to the policy arena. This effort was originally designed to submit a report to one person: to the Special Rapporteur whose task was to study the relationship between human rights and the environment and prepare preliminary recommendations for the United Nations Commission on Human Rights. As the SfAA study progressed, we have found our efforts directed towards multiple arenas. The call for contributions prompted many colleagues to reorient the nature of their research, focusing explicitly on the connection between government action or sanctioned action, environmental degradation, and human misery. The resulting preliminary report was submitted to the Special Rapporteur Ksentini, the Sierra Club Legal Defense Fund, the Centre for Human Rights in Geneva, the SfAA Executive Committee, and study contributors and interested colleagues.

This initial circulation prompted requests from numerous quarters. The preliminary report was distributed by the Sierra Club Legal Defense Fund to environmental nongovernmental organizations (NGOs) attending the Earth Summit/ United Nations Conference on Environment and Development meetings in Rio de Janeiro. Our study was written up in an issue of *Race and Poverty* (a news letter for environmental equity/social justice NGOs) which prompted requests from grassroots activist organizations throughout the United States. We also received requests for additional information from interdisciplinary graduate students who used the report to structure their graduate training and thesis writing efforts. The study was written up in an issue of the *Anthropology Newsletter* which resulted in requests for material from colleagues and students as well as additional contributions for the final report. After the November 1992 elections, a summary briefing and preliminary report was submitted to the Clinton transition team with copies delivered to Al Gore, Bruce Babbitt and Timothy Wirth. Portions of the report were distributed with the summary briefing to the incoming congress, thanks to study contributor Greg Button (AAA Congressional Fellow for 1993).

Informal reproduction and circulation of the report resulted in its use as a supplementary text in the classroom, and as background material for the human environmental rights media. Alan Durning, of World Watch, used the report extensively in his 1993 paper on "Guardians of the Land: Indigenous Peoples and the Health of the Earth" (*World Watch* Paper no.112; also, Chapter 5 "Supporting Indigenous Peoples" in *State of the World* 1993). Several study members were able to provide critical comments on his preliminary draft. Informal circulation of the report resulted in a call from a producer of the Public Broadcasting System series "Rights and Wrongs" who requested a copy for background material and to develop possible program themes.

Our final report (May 1993) was distributed to a limited group of contributors, politicians, environmental and human rights organizations, and United Nations Human Rights and the Environment Special Rapporteur Ksentini. This report was twice the length of the preliminary report (197 pages), and included case studies and essays from 17 contributors. The limited nature of our distribution strategy reflected our minimal funds, as well as the recognition of the limits of our target audience (politicians, environmental and human rights advocates, and other members of the international policy community). Recognizing that constraints to applying anthropology in the public arena include issues of "readability" (the language used, the length of the report, the varied nature of cases and essays), we placed greater emphasis on preparing and distributing our booklet.

With the July 1993 release of our booklet *Human Rights and the Environment: Examining the Sociocultural Context of Environmental Crisis*, we entered the final stages of this study process. Some 300 copies were printed and distributed. Over 150 copies of the booklet were mailed to international NGOs, colleagues in the academic community, and to various politicians. Another 150 copies were distributed in person at international conferences and United Nations meetings. Robert Hitchcock, for example, distributed 50 copies at the International Hunter-Gatherer meetings in Moscow in August 1993. I distributed 35 copies at the International Union of Anthropological and Ethnological Sciences Congress in Mexico City in July 1993, and some 20 copies at the Third World Studies Association meetings in Tacoma in October 1993. And Laurie Adams of the Sierra Club Legal Defense Fund (SCLDF) distributed our booklet in Geneva in August 1993. As the SCLDF is an officially recognized NGO by the U.N. Commission on Human Rights (a status which confers the ability to formally present information to the Commission and have it enter the United Nations record), our booklet was presented to the Sub-Commission with their annual contribution to the human rights and environment study. Thus, our study findings and selected cases were formally received by all members of the Sub-Commission, and the Human Rights Commission, as well as entered into U.N. records. The booklet was also distributed to members of the Working Group on Indigenous Populations.

In November 1993 a "Human Rights and the Environment: Discourse, Policy, and Praxis" session at the AAA annual meetings in Washington D.C. generated additional material, which was incorporated into the final study product, a book published by Island Press (Johnston 1994).

Assessing the Efficacy of our Efforts

Letters of support and requests for study documents have been received from all levels of the political arena: state legislators, members of the U.S. Senate, representatives of various arms of the United Nations, social science research directors in private foundations, as well as activists working in all sorts of nongovernmental organizations (everything from Amnesty International to the National Resources Defense Council). I have also had requests to present our ideas and study findings to other disciplines at their annual professional meetings (including the Third World Studies Association and the American Geographers Association).

In regards to our initial objective of influencing a specific United Nations study process, we have had limited direct success. Our material is not quoted or cited in the 1992 or 1993 report from Special Rapporteur Ksentini to the Sub-Commission, or in the Sub-Commission's report to the Commission on Human Rights. At an indirect level, we have played a role in broadening the scope of the U.N. study from its initial focus on individual instances of human rights abuse to its present acknowledgment of the abuse of group rights.

Where we have clearly had the greatest success, is in influencing public awareness of the problems and processes of selective victimization by increasing the accessibility of anthropological research for writers like Alan Durning -- the *State of the World* series is published in 23 languages and distributed across the world. Perhaps more significantly, in the long run, is the way this study is stimulating numerous colleagues across the world and across the applied social science disciplines to reorient their research and writing efforts: linking government action or sanctioned action to environmental degradation and subsequent human misery, and directing their writing efforts to the public and policy arenas.

Retrospect

Looking back over the past four years, my efforts to organize anthropological input and articulate a disciplinary voice in the international environmental policy and human rights arena produced a mixed record of success and failure. Our aim was to assert the anthropological voice in environmental policy arenas, and conversely, emphasize the role environmental conditions and contexts play in human rights abuse. The study achieved some measure of success in that these ideas are reflected in the current language of the "Draft Declaration on Human Rights and the Environment" (adopted by the Sub-Commission on the Prevention of Discrimination and Protection of Minorities in August 1994, and being considered for adoption by the United Nations Commission on Human Rights in March 1995). And, our material has been published in the "environmental media."

On the other hand, success is hard to gauge as the gap between language and action seems almost unbridgeable. Our effort to voice the anthropological perspective was more of a whisper campaign directed towards the ears of a few policy makers, rather than a loud and aggressive voicing of protests on the ground and in concert with members of our "communities." This strategy was consciously employed for political as well as personal reasons. Focusing study efforts on influencing the thought and language of international human rights policy seemed an important, yet (in retrospect) relatively comfortable way of handling our responsibility to the communities studied.

Conclusion

The "Human Rights and Environment" project, like many efforts to apply anthropology, demonstrates our analytical strength and praxis weaknesses. Much of the social science attention to human environmental rights abuse focuses on defining the nature of problems in a descriptive and analytical fashion with the twin goals of understanding the production and reproduction of human rights abuses, and working towards formal acknowledgment of culpability. Relatively little attention is paid to "post-crisis" periods, to the efficacy and long-term implications of response. This is certainly true of my work. We are very good at identifying problems and identifying causal factors. For a number of reasons we are not very good at suggesting ways to resolve problems. When we do recommend strategies to resolve problems, our recommendations are often ineffectively articulated, voiced in the wrong circles, or simply ignored. Our role of advisor rarely carries political authority.

What to do? Some, like Sylvia Forman, direct their energies towards their students and their discipline: encouraging careers in policy arenas and positions with real authority; restructuring training programs and developing retraining programs aimed at delivering the knowledge and tools to effectively work within political institutions. It is these sorts of actions, much more than idealistic statements and rhetoric, which will determine whether we can rise to the continual need to "reinvent" anthropology.

I believe, as did Sylvia Forman, that anthropology has the potential to play a hugely significant role in the unfolding drama that is human life. Today's crises require a recognition that answers are diverse. No single notion, model, or approach is sufficient or capable of handling problems that are synergistic and cumulative. As anthropologists, our analytical capabilities, holistic perspective, and intensive experience with all levels of the sociopolitical web provides us with the tools to make some sense out of chaos. We have the ability to identify and seize significant threads, unravel the tangled complexity of history, culture, political economy, and environmental context, and thus identify where action might be most effective in resolving problems and preventing conflict. But, for our efforts to be heard, we must find ways of understanding the nature of power, and assert ourselves more aggressively into the system of power.

Notes

1. While organizational strategies for the Human Rights and Environment study were strongly influenced by Sylvia Helen Forman, moving the project from idea to reality occurred thanks to the critical input, support and commitment of Society for Applied Anthropology President Carole E. Hill. Following Carole Hill's term as SfAA President, newly elected President J. Anthony Paredes picked up where she left off, providing helpful review of our final report and policy documents, and supporting further endeavors of the Human Rights and Environment Committee.

Portions of this chapter were previously published in the *Anthropology Newsletter* (Human Rights and the environment Study Group, Culture and Agriculture Unit News *Anthropology* Newsletter 33(7):10-11. October 1992) and *Practicing Anthropology*(Human Rights and the Environment: Anthropological Discourse, Policy and Praxis, *Practicing Anthropology* 16(1):8-12. January 1994).

2. See for example, Dana Alston *We Speak for Ourselves: Social Justice, Race and Environment.* Washington DC: The Panos Institute 1990; Bunyan Bryant and Paul Mohai, eds. *Race and the Incidence of Environmental Hazards.* Boulder, CO: Westview Press, 1992; Robert Bullard *Dumping in Dixie: Race, Class and Environmental Quality.* Boulder, CO: Westview Press 1990; Robert Bullard, ed. *Confronting Environmental Racism.* South End Press 1993.

References

Goldman, Benjamin
    1991 *The Truth About Where You Live: An Atlas for Action on Toxins and Mortality.* New York: Times Books.

Johnston, Barbara Rose, ed.
   1992 *Human Rights and the Environment.* Preliminary Report prepared by the Society for Applied
      Anthropology Committee on Human Rights and the Environment, submitted to the United Nations,
      Commission on Human Rights, Sub-Commission on the Prevention of Discrimination and
      Protection of Minorities, May 15.
   1993 *Who Pays the Price? Examining the Sociocultural Context of Environmental Crisis.* Final
      Report prepared by the Society for Applied Anthropology Committee on Human Rights and the
      Environment. San Jose, CA.: Society for Applied Anthropology and the Nathan Cummings
      Foundation.
   1994 *Who Pays the Price? Examining the Sociocultural Context of Environmental Crisis.*
      Washington, D.C.: Island Press.

Lowe, Justin
   1991 Human Rights and the Environment. *Earth Island Journal*: Fall 1991:8.

Bold Enough to Put Pen on Paper:

Collaborative Methodology in an

Ethnographic Life Story

Barbara C. Johnson
Ithaca College

Barbara C. Johnson (Ph.D. 1985) is Assistant Professor of Anthropology at Ithaca College, where she teaches South Asia, Comparative Jewish Cultures, Women and Culture, and Ethnographic Life Stories. Having completed the book with Ruby Daniel described here, she continues to ponder the ethnohistorical relationships between Jewishness, gender, caste and colonialism in South India. She is beginning a new project on text and performance of Cochin Jewish women's folk songs in India and Israel. A member of the Association for Jewish Studies and the American Folklore Society as well as the American Anthropological Association, she has served for several years as an ethnographic consultant for the Israel Museum in Jerusalem. Before teaching at Ithaca College, she spent six years as Director of Multi-Cultural Studies at Goddard College in Vermont, where she was instrumental in establishing a connection between Goddard and Navajo Community College.

Ruby Daniel begins telling her life story with these words:

> It has been suggested that I should write down everything I have heard from my grandparents and from other old people who have heard stories from their own grandparents. So I make myself bold enough to put pen on paper to say what I can remember from what I heard, mostly from my grandmother Rachel (Docho), the daughter of Daniel Haim and the wife of Eliyavu Japheth, both of whom were Rabbanim. They were very orthodox people, but she was a foot above them. The following stories may contain some grains of truth... But there are no records which I can show you."[1]

This chapter is about Ruby Daniel and about the way she and I worked together to produce her life story, once she was bold enough to put pen on paper and write these words. In contrast to traditional life story research, our collaborative process was grounded in Ruby's writing, supplemented by oral material from our tape-recorded conversations and letters. As the subject/author of her own story, she continued to be involved throughout most of the editing process and retains a notable sense of ownership over the final product -- a book entitled *Ruby of Cochin: An Indian Jewish Woman Remembers*.

The following description of our working process raises issues for theory and methodology in life story work, including different types of collaboration, language and voice, form, ownership of the work, audience, interpretation, and power relations between narrator and editor. First let me tell the story of our cooperative story-telling.

"Ruby of Cochin...."

Ruby Daniel lives on a kibbutz in northern Israel, but the stories she tells originate in Kerala, on the Malabar coast of southwest India, where she was born in 1912. She spent the first half of her life there in the ancient Jewish community of Cochin. Her writing conveys the beauty of the Kerala landscape, the tolerance of the Hindu rulers who granted rights and privileges to the Jews, and the kindness of ordinary Hindus, Christians and Muslims who honored and respected their Jewish neighbors. She describes the elaborate Jewish festivals of her childhood, celebrated in a unique Indian style, and she writes about the everyday intimacy of life on the one long street in Cochin called Jew Town, where all the houses were connected and everyone knew everyone's business.

In addition to recounting legends, tales and customs which have never before been written down, Ruby Daniel proudly tells the story of her own family and their ancestors. They were part of one small congregation dominated by the so-called "white" Jews of Cochin. But the Daniel family belonged to the section of that community who were denied equal rights in the synagogue. They were labeled "*mshuchrarim*" or "freed slaves," because their ancestors were said to have been converts to Judaism or the children of white Jewish men and slave or servant women. "*Mshuchrar*" was a label which Ruby's family firmly rejected. Part of her motivation for writing is her desire to set the record straight about her family's origins.

The book is dedicated to Ruby's grandmother Rachel (1864-1944), called "Docho," who was the source of many of her stories. It is also suffused with the courage of Ruby's mother Leah (1892-1982), who fought for her daughter's right to an education. Despite the family's poverty and the opposition of Leah's husband and father, she pawned her gold chain to send Ruby to school in St. Theresa's Convent across the harbor from Cochin. Ruby was the first Jewish girl to study outside Jew Town and the first to finish high school and begin college. In addition to becoming fluent in English, she was one of only a few Kerala Jews who studied literary Malayalam. This combination of skills enables her to translate the Malayalam-language songs which were traditionally sung by Cochin Jewish women, who preserved them in hand-copied notebooks like the one she treasures, passed down from grandmother Docho's great aunt.

Ruby Daniel never married. When her father and grandfather both died in the same year, she left college and took over the support of her extended family, working as a clerk in government offices. She served in the Indian Navy during World War II and emigrated to Israel in 1951. I first met her there about fourteen years ago.

Having first visited Cochin in 1968, I began my extended research on its Jewish community in the early 1970's (Johnson 1975). When I was in Israel collecting material for my PhD. dissertation in 1980, Ruby Daniel helped me a great deal by sharing her recollections and insights about Jewish life in Cochin. I sent her a copy of my completed dissertation (Johnson 1985) and then returned to Israel to ask her and other community members for their reactions. Ruby responded, "I told you more than that!" By this time she had already begun putting on paper many of the stories which she had told me but which had not appeared in my dissertation, as well as translating a number of the Malayalam women's songs.[2]

Almost a year later Ruby wrote to me, less gently, that SHE was going to write more about the history of the so-called "*mshuchrarim*," who had been so misrepresented in some of the sources I had cited. "For your information," she wrote, "a few months ago some of us sat down together and talked and decided that all that you wrote was Bull shit. I am sorry for telling you the truth. But don't be discouraged. Get on..." (letter, 3/3/86).

I was of course intrigued. No one else in the community had been so direct with me about their reactions to my work, and it was clear that Ruby's stories were historically important as well as fascinating. I urged her to write more about her own life, in addition to the stories and song translations. It would make a wonderful book, I said.

She replied: "What interest have people got about my life?... As for publishing all the things I have written I myself don't know what to do with it. If you and Shirley don't do anything about it, it will all go a waste. I cannot write a book" (11/11/86). We began a back and forth process, in which she wrote, I typed and asked questions, and she wrote more. But it was not very efficient working by mail. In 1987 she wrote to me: "I am sorry you have done nothing about the book. Try your best and do something about it. I would like to see it too. I will be 75 in December." "Now I am writing about my life, all the rubbish." she continued. "I shall send it to you one of these days" (letter, 11/21/87).

By this time Ruby had written and I had typed almost 100 pages, including legends, ghost tales, descriptions of Jewish celebrations, song translations and a short personal memoir. The growing manuscript was a collection of fragments, much in need of what Ruby called "arranging." It was clear to me that there were more stories she could tell, especially about her own life, and also that we needed to sit together for an extended time to work on editing them into a book.

Finally in 1990 I received a small grant which enabled me to spend two months in Israel. A friend and I stayed most of that time on Ruby's kibbutz, packing apples in the apple factory to help earn our keep and eating most of our meals in the communal dining hall. The daily life of the kibbutz became much more familiar to me than it had been in my previous short visits. Now I had my own images and experiences of kibbutz life as a context for Ruby's present life, in addition to my personal memories of South India, where I had lived for four years even before I first visited Cochin.

Almost every afternoon Ruby and I sat together in her small apartment, at the low dining table pulled up to the sofa. Here we continued a process which had begun when I first interviewed her. But now, nine years later, these were conversations rather than interviews, though the tape recorder was usually running unless Ruby asked me to shut it off. When she told and re-told stories of long ago in Cochin or remembered her own life in Jew Town, she was filling in the details of a picture which was now very familiar to me. When I asked about times she hadn't discussed much before -- like her work in the Kerala courts and in the Indian Navy -- I was introduced to new characters and situations, personal to Ruby and separate from the life of her family and community, but also familiar to me in the context of my own experience many years ago as a young woman working in India. As Joel Savishinsky noted about conversations in a different research context, "the reminiscing that took place was part of a relationship, then, not a reverie, and this made it a richer and more continuous experience ... [A] common set of interests and a path to the past ... helped to make the process of recollection a dialogue rather than a soliloquy (1991:67).

Each night I transcribed the day's tapes and "arranged" Ruby's words, weaving together written and oral stories. Some nights she would produce a new piece of writing too, inspired by the day's talk. The next day we read through the growing text together, adding and eliminating words, sentences and sections.

Ruby complained and teased about my insatiable desire to know more and more about her life. "Too much engraving makes holes in the pot," she grumbled, quoting one of her many Malayalam proverbs. But she acknowledged, "I wrote such a lot more after you came. When I say one story, then suddenly I think of another story..." When I insisted that she read over the final version of each section and chapter, she sometimes grumbled about that too, but this step remained part of our work together.

Back in the U.S. with a manuscript of about 300 pages, I began seriously searching for a publisher and confronting some of the methodological and ethical issues to be discussed here. Ruby and I continued working together by mail and telephone, and I was able to visit her in Israel two more times before the manuscript was finally completed for The Jewish Publication Society.

Collaboration: Half Rabbit and Half Horse

What is meant by collaborative methodology? In a general sense all life story research which involves a storyteller/ subject and a researcher/editor is implicitly collaborative. In the growing field of life story research and criticism, scholars increasingly demand that the nature of such collaboration be publicly explored. "In any narrated... autobiography there are at least two parties present," states Greg Sarris (1993:91) in his provocative essay on the "Autobiographies" of three elderly Native American women, collected from 1939-1941 by a white female anthropologist (Colson 1974 [1956]) whom he faults for remaining "absent" in her presentation of their "bicultural" project of narrating, interviewing and editing. Colson's work may be seen as typical of "oral histories" traditionally compiled by anthropologists who choose their "informants" and interview them in the "field," then take the raw material back "home" to edit (and often translate) their words alone, sometimes consciously shaping their stories to illuminate anthropological themes -- "absent editors" whose own stories do not appear in the text.

In contrast, writer/editors such as Behar (1993), Brown (1991), Crapanzano (1980), Mbilinyi (1989), Patai (1988, 1991), Shostak (1983, 1989) and Sarris (1992, 1993, 1994) explore in depth the nature of their relationship with their life story subjects, some anguishing over the politics and validity of what they are doing. Still they present themselves as the authors, not co-authors, of their work -- not through lack of awareness, but perhaps because of the nature of their methodology.

Carole Boyce Davies (1992) discusses the "collaborative politics" of writer/editors such as Silvera (1983) and Ford-Smith (editor of Sistren 1986), who have taken a somewhat different approach to their work. They followed up on their initial interactive collection of stories and then took drafts of their written manuscripts back to the life story subjects for further input, incorporating their suggestions into the text at the final stage of editing. This is a method which I suggest to students in my Ethnographic Life Stories class, as did Barbara Myerhoff with her students (Myerhoff and Tuftes 1992 [1975]). But it still involves the writer/editor traveling back and forth between the world of oral conversation with the subject and the private world of her or his own writing.

It's a very different project when the subject -- like Ruby Daniel -- is engaged in writing as well as talking. In reading other life stories, the closest methodological parallel I have found is that of Mamie Garvin Fields and her granddaughter, sociologist Karen Fields, whose writing of *Lemon Swamp and Other Places: A Carolina Memoir* (1983) began with a set of childhood memories written by Mamie Fields to give as a Christmas present -- "an armful of looseleaf pages ... wrapped in a big, red folder marked with the words 'Letters to My Three Granddaughters'." The two women eventually worked out a lengthy process of talking, tape-recording, writing and editing together which sounds familiar to me, as I look back on my own work with Ruby Daniel.

Although Ruby and I are not members of the same family, I have sometimes felt myself sliding into the role of a younger relation of some sort, first as an eager audience for her stories and then gradually as the person responsible for helping her preserve them. I sometimes feel that I myself didn't choose this project, with its intertwined privileges and obligations, as much as Ruby chose me for it. I think that this aspect of our relationship, as well as our collaborative methodology, provides a creative model for life story work in general, though it is not without its complications.

Language and Voice: oral narrative and written text

Transforming a strictly oral narrative into a written text is a perilous venture, almost inevitably creating an imbalance of power between the narrator and the interviewer/researcher. An alienation of ownership is likely to result when the narrator's original words are edited, rearranged and perhaps translated into another language, usually without his or her input (Behar 1993,

Davies 1992, Salazar 1991, Sarris 1993). Fortunately for our project, Ruby Daniel is not only a superb oral storyteller (in Malayalam, English and Hebrew), but also a person who enjoys "putting pen on paper" to re-shape her stories into written form. She has expressed to me a combination of pride and modesty regarding her talents as a writer, as seen in her statement, "It is natural ... I just have an idea, and I just go on writing ... But the English I write, it is a very easy language, very low. I haven't got a high language, only a high school English" (4/90).

The question of her language usage came up at several stages of my work on the manuscript. Ruby originally asked me to "correct" any "mistakes" in her English. In some places I did edit for clarity, and occasionally I added linking words or sentences to connect passages from different written and oral sources. But unlike Colson, who acknowledges having "inverted and knocked whole sentences into a more 'English' [presumably American standard English] shape" (1974:9), I left in Ruby's interjections and repetitions along with idiomatic features of her South Indian English, including the colloquial habit of frequently switching between past and present tenses. Part of the essence of the book is that it preserves the rhythm and flavor of everyday South Indian speech along with the frequent poetic turns of phrase that characterize the style of a particularly gifted storyteller.

Though English is the language in which Ruby writes, and the language in which she and I converse, it is her second language. Her first was Malayalam, the language of Kerala's 29 million people. Like other educated Indians of her generation, she studied in English-medium schools and college. The way Ruby speaks and writes English is very much affected by her rich knowledge of Malayalam. Her everyday speech is peppered with Malayalam sayings and proverbs: "As my grandmother used to say..." She was unique among educated Cochin Jews in choosing Malayalam language and literature as an optional subject in college (equivalent in some ways to an undergraduate minor in the U.S.). This advanced study gave her an acquaintance with classical literary Malayalam, making it possible for her to translate obscure words and phrases in the old Malayalam Jewish songs which are incomprehensible to others who sing them.

Ruby's expertise in writing must be seen as part of a wider cultural pattern, as well as an individual talent. Kerala women have been literate to a much higher degree than women elsewhere in India (Jeffrey 1992). Among the Cochin Jews, some members of Ruby Daniel's family were pioneers in literacy for women, educated as early as the mid-1860's when "the rich girls... in Jew Town did not know how to read or write their names." Ruby inherits her knowledge of the Malayalam Jewish songs from her grandmother Docho -- a knowledge that can be traced back to Docho's great-aunt, who wrote by hand one of the oldest collected notebooks of women's songs. I believe that this intellectual inheritance partially explains why Ruby Daniel is also the first Cochin Jewish woman to write and publish a book.

Form: "The Ordering Imperative"

Another potential pitfall in the collaboration between oral storyteller and writer/editor is the process that Ruby calls "arranging" (a term which seems to me more complex and rich in meaning than "editing"). I appreciate Davies' (1992) identification of this "ordering imperative" as another area of potential exploitation by the writer/editor and alienation on the part of the subject. Certainly it can be just that if the editing and ordering is done without consulting the subject/ author.

In the case of my work with Ruby, there was a great deal of consulting over the editing -- I think more consultation than she really wanted. Her enjoyment of storytelling does not include an enjoyment of editing her stories.

In eliciting and incorporating new material to fill out her life story, I basically followed the chronology and themes she had established in her original 20-page memoir. In contrast, I had a terrific problem deciding what to do with the 23 ghost stories which she had written down in the order in which they occurred to her. For some time we discussed this dilemma every day; then gradually it became clear that the ghosts who lived on her street belonged in the chapter on her childhood, the ghosts who appeared on Yom Kippur belonged with her description of that holiday, and the rest could have a chapter of their own, framed by stories of her grandfather's "scientific attitude" toward the world of the spirits.

Ruby agreed with all these decisions. The only issue of format on which she disagreed came much later, at the stage when I was editing the manuscript for submission to publishers. Over and over I received the response from American readers that the book should begin with Ruby's own story, not (as she argued) with the section on historical tales of her community. On this issue she was overruled, and she is still not happy about it.

Ruby frequently protested at the long sessions on the kibbutz where I cajoled her into re-reading every word of the emerging text, and she continued her teasing complaints by mail. "I have managed to make the corrections as requested... I wonder if all the small details are necessary. Anyway I have done my best to please you... You are insatiable (letter 5/10/90).

But after all, it was the "arranging" which she had originally asked me to do, and in the end she did express her appreciation for my work:

> Because you organized it and turned it into a BOOK. Mine was only a pamphlet. They were things I wrote down. But to turn it into a book, I didn't know... to find out where to put the things I wrote, in different places. How to adjust it. That's what I wanted somebody to help me (taped conversation, 4/ 90).

Whose Book?

After all this conscious collaboration, whose book is it anyway? This was a question my friend Nicky asked both of us in her interview, and this is in part how we replied:

Nicky: So whose book do you think it is now?

Ruby: Half half. (laughter) The notes are mine...Barbara is doing the rest of the work. I wrote down only what I knew ... She added something that I talked... in this thing [the tape recorder]...

Nicky: So Barbara, whose book do you think it is?

Barbara: Oh I think it's definitely Ruby's book, because it's Ruby's story, it's Ruby's words. But then I feel

Ruby: We joined together.

Barbara: Yeah. I feel a sense of accomplishment that I was able also to

Ruby: Yes, she helped me, to make it fifty-fifty. One horse and one rabbit.

Barbara: One horse and one rabbit? (all laugh)

Ruby: Yes, you know, they make sausages, rabbit sausages, and add a little bit of horse meat. So somebody asked, "How much did you add?" "Fifty fifty." "How much is fifty fifty?" "One horse and one rabbit" (taped conversation, 4/90).

Nicky asked who was the horse and who was the rabbit, and Ruby changed the subject. I think rabbits don't need to explain; they can quickly hop under a fence and disappear, while the horse keeps plodding on.

Ownership of the Book

In addition to ownership of the process, there is the very basic question of ownership of the book itself, the final product of all the collaborative work. Here we may consider factors of economics and power, initiation of the project, visibility, and intended audience.

Economics and power

Patai presents a useful model for thinking about power dynamics in life story research:

> Collecting personal narratives, when done with professional and publishing goals in mind, is invariably an economic matter.... An individual telling her own story can be construed to be in possession of raw material... It is the researcher who owns or has access to the means of production that will transform the spoken words into commodities... To a commercial publisher, the existence of a book as a commodity may be its main function. To a professor, the book could be a step toward promotion and salary increases (1991:146).

The researcher can also be seen as a laborer who transforms spoken words into written words, sometimes translates them, edits them, perhaps analyzes their meaning -- and let us not forget the work of peddling the manuscript and seeing it through the press -- illustrations, permissions, copy-editing, proofreading, glossary, index and all.

According to Patai, "The researcher is the person whose time and investment is acknowledged and rewarded. And, as in any asymmetrical exchange, exploitation is always a possibility." (1991:146) In our experience this is not necessarily so. I drew up a preliminary agreement with Ruby about joint control of all the work we do together; we both signed the contract with JPS, sharing the copyright and royalties for the book. Quite literally, the book will be jointly owned, as is true in varied forms with the collaborative work of some other academics (Brown 1991:169, Fields 1983, Mbilinyi 1989:23, Shostak 1989:234).

Does Ruby *feel* the book is hers? Evidence would seem to be that she does. First it is important to remember that she initiated the project herself. Though she credits Shirley Isenberg and me for pushing her to begin the project, my memory is that she began writing down her stories as a direct response to the lack she found in my dissertation and in other written accounts of her community.

Also Ruby has expressed no desire for the privacy or anonymity sought by some life story subjects. Reasons for wanting anonymity vary (Langness and Frank 1981:119-126), with many storytellers being concerned that shame or other harm may come to them if their identities are published (Behar 1993:231-235, Brown 1991:ix, Kendall 1988:126-127).

In contrast, Ruby seems both pleased and relatively secure about her new-found public image as an author. I think that part of this confidence comes from her strong and generally positive sense of the multiple audiences for the book.

Audiences

Perhaps partly because she is herself a reader, Ruby can imagine many different people reading what she has written. When I asked her who she imagined as the audience, she replied: "I thought of everybody, maybe even the Malabar people [non-Jews in South India]. I put in a nice word about them, and I want them also to read it." [3]

What about an audience in Israel, I wondered: "Do you imagine people on the kibbutz reading the book?" This was more complex for her: "They might not like my life story... They might like it, but I don't know." I assume she was unsure because the book criticizes some early kibbutz members from Central Europe for their prejudiced attitude toward Indians, though she also tempers this criticism with an acknowledgment that "We the pampered Jews from India could not understand the behavior of those who had suffered so much in their homeland...I am not going to judge these people whatever they do." But whether criticizing or forgiving them, Ruby seems motivated to enlighten Israelis of European origin about Cochin Jewish history and culture.

Ruby is also aware of a potential audience of scholars and others who want to learn about her community. She is eager to reach readers and researchers who already have an interest in the Cochin Jews and who have read other books or articles or seen films which are inaccurate in their portrayal of her family and relations. She sends out a strong warning to writers who have passed on such misconceptions:

> Those who want to write about the history of the Cochin Jews and their customs beware! Because they would not find an honest commentator, and the result will be a distortion of facts. Most of the stories written by modern writers are the stories told by the so-called white Jews... who felt themselves to be superior to other Jews in Cochin. I am glad to write what I heard from my grandparents and others, to correct some of their distortions. Following is the true story.

Ultimately, I think, the audience which Ruby imagines for the book is her own community of Cochin Jews. As she writes in the introduction, "I thought I shall do something for posterity." Here I assume she is thinking of younger Cochin Jews like her nieces, nephews and second cousins, many of them born in Israel and ignorant of their cultural heritage.

There is however a portion of the Cochin Jewish community whose reactions she worries about. How will the book be received by certain of the so-called "white" Jews from Cochin? Some of her stories are critical of their ancestors, revealing the depth of anger and humiliation felt by Ruby's family for the way the white Jews treated them in the past. While she is eager to confront these community members in writing -- in a way which she does not do in person -- at the same time Ruby is devoted to her community and is on close personal terms with some of the very people whom she fears may be offended by her frankness. "I don't want to embarrass the people," she told me, but she immediately added that she doesn't need approval from them any more, now that she lives in Israel: "I am on the kibbutz, and if I die, [kibbutz members] will bury me somewhere here. In Cochin ... we had to depend on [the white Jews] for everything" (4/90 taped conversation). How can she forget that dependence? When she was young, her family's employment and, indeed, most aspects of their Jewish life were controlled by white Jews, including their right to be buried in the Paradesi cemetery.

If Ruby's economic independence and security as a kibbutz member and an Israeli today are important factors in her attitude toward the white Jews from Cochin, I think that this independence and security may also affect her attitude toward me, a white American professor. If she and I had met in colonial India, the power relations between us would have been very different; but today I think it is clear to both of us that, while she needs my help with the book, I am also dependent on her and her family -- as a visitor in Israel, a non-member of the kibbutz, and a marginal participant in Cochin Jewish life. In more than one way, she is my elder.

In the last few years Ruby has become bolder and less apologetic about what she writes. Final additions to the manuscript show a complex mix of defiance and affectionate respect toward the audience of her own community. First she added: "When what I have written above comes to the notice of the white Jews, there is going to be great controversy. But this is what I have heard from reliable sources." She then included in her carefully worded introduction:

> I thought some day someone will be curious to know where [the Cochin Jews] came from -- some white, some dark, always quarreling about the color but otherwise standing up for one another, following the same customs, praying from the same book to the same God. How we lived in a communal life peacefully, thanks to the regime of the Hindu Rajas.

With or And?

While on the topic of audiences, I must note the various audiences for whom I did my work. The first audience I share with Ruby: the community of Cochin (especially Paradesi) Jews whom I have known for more than 25 years -- especially the "posterity" of their younger generation. The second is a more general readership which I think will be reached by the Jewish Publication Society: Jews in the U.S. and Israel who need to learn more about Jewish cultural diversity. But the third is the audience of my academic peers -- those who are interested in life stories, Jewish culture, the anthropology of India, women's folklore, and so on -- and those who would judge me for my scholarly competence as I search for a secure niche in the world of academia. Back to Daphne Patai's point about economics (to say nothing of self-image).

It is this academic audience who finally influenced a last-minute decision. I had been identifying the authors of our book as "Ruby Daniel *with* Barbara C. Johnson", but my thanks are due to a senior colleague who advised me that this wording would be seriously misunderstood in bibliographies and on my curriculum vitae, as it would under-represent my role in the creation of the book. I explained how important it is that the Cochin Jews realize it is RUBY'S book. "Will *with* or *and* make any difference to them?" my colleague asked.

I phoned Ruby in Israel and tried to explain the ethical dilemma. "What are you asking?" she inquired rather impatiently. "I want to have the authors of the book be written as Ruby Daniel *and* Barbara Johnson." "Isn't that what it says already?" "No, it's Ruby Daniel *with* Barbara Johnson." "What's the difference?" she asked. "With ... and... but... for...? I don't care. I just want to see the book!"

Interpretation I: a New Reading of History

To what extent should an editor/researcher interpret the subject's life? This is an area in which the chance of exploitation and distortion is particularly acute, and I have decisively avoided taking on an interpretive role within the book itself. I was resistant to a suggestion by the editor of another press that I should write a scholarly introduction to the manuscript, telling "what really happened," and pleased when the JPS editor respected my editorial approach.

The question of historical accuracy is bound to arise in regard to any work of this sort, grounded as it is in oral tradition and especially in an elderly person's memory of stories told to her so many years ago.[4] On the one hand, I predict that specialized readers familiar with earlier accounts of Cochin Jewish history will be delighted to learn new information about characters and events with which they are already familiar, as well as hearing stories of which they had not been aware before.[5] They may however be startled at Ruby's statement that there never were any slaves in Cochin. When I first heard her say this, I immediately thought of the written accounts of Kerala slavery which I had read in Indian as well as Western scholarly sources, and of the bills of sale and manumission which had been preserved in Cochin Jewish records. I thought I just couldn't agree with her statement about slavery.

Mbilinyi (1989) and Borland (1991) provide attractive models for how a researcher can discuss differences of opinion with her subject. But neither of their styles would work with Ruby and me. With Ruby I don't argue, I listen. So I bit my tongue and listened as she told these stories over and over, and as I transcribed and arranged them. The listening has been good for me. Like Karen Brown, who learned new things about Haitian kinship by listening to Mama Lola's stories and trying not to impose her own order on them (1991:16-17), I find that my ethnographic and historical perspective is shifting. I am beginning to read earlier accounts of Cochin Jewish history differently (including my own writings) and to raise some new questions about the nature of "slavery" and other forms of servitude in Kerala. It is a complex issue, which cannot be unraveled simply from the standpoint of biblical definitions and laws about slavery and manumission, as many Jewish visitors and scholars have tried to do. Nor can it be understood within the constraints of a western perspective on slavery, as the new generation of "post-colonial" South Asian scholars would undoubtedly agree. I plan to continue my research and thinking on the topic.

But in the meantime I have not argued this point (or any other point about Cochin history) with Ruby. I once asked her how she would feel if I wrote something in which I disagreed with her. "You write what you want elsewhere," she said. "This book is my story." And so it is.

Interpretation II: Inherent in Subject Matter

Though I have tried from the beginning to avoid imposing my interpretation on Ruby's stories, I have come to agree with Karen Fields (1983: xix-xx) and other life story practitioners that the choice of subject matter itself involves interpretation. For example, Ruby and I disagreed at first about how much material to include from her own personal life story, which she felt was less important than stories about her family and community. She indicated several times a feeling of awkwardness about the book's focus on herself; people may think she is trying to make herself important. Certainly the published English-language autobiographies of South Asian women up to now have been written by members of the wealthy cultural elite, not by women from poor families who worked as clerks, see e.g. Rama Rau (1958), Saleri (1987).

I know that until her writing recently began to appear in print, Ruby had not been considered a particularly "important" person in her Cochin Jewish community, nor in the Israeli kibbutz where she lives, where she and her sister are the only Indians. Several kibbutz members reacted in disbelief when I first told them Ruby was writing a book. They hadn't known she could write or even speak in English, they said.[6]

In the face of this relative public invisibility, was it my job to persuade Ruby that her personal story was worth telling? While we were staying on the kibbutz, my friend Nicky, who has taught Women's Writing and Literature, tackled the issue head-on, talking with Ruby enthusiastically about the value of "ordinary" women's stories. In fact Ruby had suggested this perspective herself several years earlier, when she sent me her first autobiographical piece, writing in the accompanying letter, "I just wanted to show the kind of life we led, specially girls at that time" (11/21/87). After talking with Nicky about women writers, something apparently shifted for Ruby, because she began to express this perspective more explicitly. The night after their conversation, she produced a lengthy new piece of writing which began: "People in Cochin seemed to think that women were created to suffer in silence." This piece became the core of an entire chapter in the book, "The Situation of Women in Cochin."

In some ways the presence of two western feminists in Ruby's life could be seen as influencing the content and form of her memoir. It wasn't that we persuaded her that her own story was important in itself, but rather that in the course of conversations with us, she consciously took on the task she had hinted at earlier: representing certain "ordinary" Indian women in her generation through her own story, because, as she says, "it's important for people to know about the lives of ordinary women, people who were not known in the world. Wild flowers who bloom in the forest. Nobody sees them and they fade."

A parallel may be drawn to Rigoberta Menchu's oral memoir -- transcribed, translated and edited by an anthropologist -- which begins with the statement: "It's not my life; it's also the testimony of my people... the story of all poor Guatemalans" (Bergos-Debray, ed. 1984:1). Claudia Salazar calls this statement "a subversion of western individualism" (1991:94).[7] I'm not sure what Ruby would call it. Maybe just common sense?

Why Do You Take So Much Trouble?

I respect Sarris' demand that the anthropologist/editor/ writer be *present* in writing a life story. But I never really considered integrating material about my own life into the book, though other life story writers have done this sort of thing very effectively (Brown 1991, Myerhoff 1978, Narayan 1989, Sarris 1994) and though I have used a reflexive approach in other research (Johnson 1985).

This book is Ruby's story -- incorporating her grandmother's stories -- about her life and her family and her community. I am always learning from her, but I am not her disciple or student (Brown 1991, Narayan 1989). Though she often treats me like a younger relative -- from whom she can expect a South Indian style of respect and the carrying out of varied obligations such as transportation, errands and regular phone calls -- I don't think that Ruby thinks of me as a relative or a substitute relative or a member of her community (Myerhoff 1978, Sarris 1991). I can't imagine her seeing any reason at all to include my story in the book. This may be our book, but it's Ruby's story.

Still I knew that my story belonged in there somewhere. I put it in an entirely separate section -- "Barbara Johnson's Introduction," which follows "Ruby Daniel's Introduction" in the book, and which ends with a reflection on how my life story intersects with hers. The next time I saw Ruby, I asked how she felt about the personal part of what I had written. She said only that she didn't remember my having told her that story about my father. But I do remember our conversation in 1990 -- I can see and feel the way we were sitting on her sofa together, the one light burning, the quiet of a late spring night on the kibbutz.

Earlier that spring Ruby had asked me, "Why do *you* take so much trouble with this work?" My first response was to remind her of complaints from her and from others about my dissertation -- about what I had written and about what I had left out. "I realize that an outsider like me can't tell the story the way a member of the community can. So now you are telling the story in your own words," I said, "and I am glad to help you with that process..."

She snapped back, "So you want *me* to be the *korban* (the sacrificial offering)?" Startled, I laughed: "Yes, I suppose that's right."

This was my first response, but I've been trying to answer her question on many levels ever since. This work is certainly more than a scholarly project for me. I think Ruby was asking quite specifically: Why Cochin? Why her story?

Part of the answer is that I am a Jew -- and as a convert, in some sense a marginal one. When I first went to Cochin for extended visits in the 1970's I was not yet a Jew, so according to Paradesi custom I couldn't sit with the other women in the synagogue, upstairs in the women's section. When I prayed in the Paradesi Synagogue, I sat down in the entrance room where members of Ruby's family used to sit. In some sense my intense personal engagement began then.

It also began further back in my life, during the four years I lived in South India during the 1960's -- first teaching at a women's college and then living closely with a large Indian extended family. The stories Ruby tells of herself as a child, as a student and as a young woman feel familiar to me. I connect them with the lives of my students and close personal friends, and sometimes with my own life. Her South Indian style of conversation and friendship is comfortable too. I feel at ease in Ruby's home.

The particular Jew Town landscape of Ruby's childhood has also become familiar to me. The narrow street with houses all connected, the hanging glass lamps in the synagogue, the swishing sound of coconut palms bending in the wind, the sticky heat and the welcome first drops of monsoon rain -- all these have worked their way into my being.

Familiar also is Ruby's sense of displacement, the loneliness of living among people who have never been in India and who construct it as a fantasy world, or do not acknowledge that such a world exists. In helping her to tell her story, I am in a sense reclaiming a piece of my own, a part that was very formative but that is usually invisible.

And then there are the ghosts. I identify with Ruby and her Grandfather in what she calls their "scientific" attitude toward matters of life and death, but I have never asked her how she reconciles these beliefs with her ghost stories. That 1990 spring night I remember so vividly, just the two of us were talking late in her apartment, without the tape recorder, as we sometimes did. I was feeling very troubled about what to do with the spirits who appeared so frequently in the streets and courtyards and houses of Cochin -- and with people's mysterious dreams which brought messages from the dead. Ruby had written a whole chapter of stories about these Cochin Jewish ghosts and dreams, writing them down in no particular order, just as they occurred to her. At this point they seemed to defy being "arranged," and they were invading my waking and sleeping hours.

"Have you any experiences like these?" Ruby asked. Hesitantly I described sensing my father's presence, a few years after his death, on a dark icy road in Vermont as my car spun out of control and righted itself just in time to avoid a serious crash. She listened attentively.

Then much more hesitantly I recounted a waking dream which had come to me some years earlier, while I was still struggling to write my dissertation. I stood before a whitewashed wall. My eyes were fixed on the outline of an old door, a door which had been plastered over long ago, but I knew it led to the next-door house in Jew Town. A door like the one between her family's two houses, where the ghost of her grandmother's aunt had tried to cross through, as Ruby's mother watched from the veranda. In my dream there was just the outline of a door. I knew I could pass through it, but I stood there, unable to move.

"That's all?" Ruby seemed to ask, though she didn't speak.

"I'm not sure what that dream meant, Ruby."
More silence.

"It could be about this book," she said.

Notes

1. This and all following unattributed quotations are from Daniel and Johnson (1995). Grant support from the American Council of Learned Societies (1990) and Ithaca College (1993) enabled me to spend time in Israel working with Ruby Daniel. I am grateful to Nicky Morris for her thoughtful suggestions on the book manuscript and on this paper.

2. Israeli anthropologist Shirley Isenberg encouraged Ruby to write down her family stories and also organized the song translation project (Isenberg, Daniel and Dekel 1984).

3. Ruby was particularly pleased when the Indian women's journal *Manushi* published an excerpt from the manuscript (Daniel and Johnson 1991).

4. For a thoughtful discussion of this issue in terms of Native American historiography see Wilson 1994.

5. In most cases I decided against overburdening the text with cross-references to other writings, but in a few cases I could not resist documenting some of her stories with footnotes pointing to other historical sources (particularly from the colonial record) which corroborate the involvement of certain foreigners in Cochin Jewish history.

6. Some older kibbutz members did appreciate the value of Ruby's stories about Cochin even before they knew about the book project. In 1987 they celebrated her 75th birthday by translating a few of her stories into Hebrew and putting out a small pamphlet in her honor. As word of her writing has spread through the Cochin community, more and more people are asking her about the book.

7. Also see Sommer (1988) and Beverley (1992) for discussion of the *testimonio* genre of Latin American writers.

References

Behar, Ruth.
  1993 *Translated Woman: Crossing the Border with Esperanza's Story.* Boston: Beacon Press.

Bergos-Debray, Elisabeth, ed.
  1984 *I, Rigoberta Menchu: An Indian Woman in Guatemala.* Trans. Ann Wright. London: Verso.

Beverley, John.
  1992 The Margin at the Center: On *Testimonio* (Testimonial Narrative). In Smith and Watson *op. cit.*
    Pp. 91-114.

Borland, Katherine.
  1991 "That's Not What I Said": Interpretive Conflict in Oral Narrative Research. Gluck and Patai, *op.
    cit.* Pp. 63-75.
Brown, Karen McCarthy.
  1991 *Mama Lola: A Vodou Priestess in Brooklyn.* Berkeley: University of California Press.

Crapanzano, Vincent.
  1980 *Tuhami: Portrait of a Moroccan.* Chicago: University of Chicago Press.

Daniel, Ruby, and Barbara C. Johnson.
  1991 Memories of a Cochin Jewish Woman. *Manushi: A Journal about Women and Society* (New
    Delhi, India) 67:30-37.
  1995. *Ruby of Cochin: An Indian Jewish Woman Remembers.* Philadelphia: The Jewish Publication
    Society.

Davies, Carol Boyce.
  1992 Collaboration and the Ordering Imperative in Life Story Production. In Smith and Watson, *op.
    cit.* Pp. 3-19.

Fields, Mamie Garvin, with Karen Fields.
1983 *Lemon Swamp and Other Places: A Carolina Memoir.* New York: The Free Press.

Gluck, Sherna B. and Daphne Patai, eds.
1991 *Women's Words: The Feminist Practices of Oral History.* New York: Routledge.

Isenberg, Shirley B., Rivkah Daniel and Miriam Dekel.
1984 Nine Jewish Folksongs in Malayalam (Hebrew pamphlet). Jerusalem.

Jeffrey, Robin.
1992 *Politics, Women and Well-Being: How Kerala Became 'a Model.* Houndmills & London: The Macmillan Press.

Johnson, Barbara C.
1975 Shingli or Jewish Cranganore in the Traditions of the Cochin Jews of India, with an Appendix on the Cochin Jewish Chronicles. Unpublished M.A. thesis, Smith College.
1985 "Our Community" in Two Worlds: The Cochin Paradesi Jews in India and Israel. Unpublished Ph.D. dissertation, University of Massachusetts.

Kendall, Laurel.
1988 *The Life and Hard Times of a Korean Shaman: Of Tales and the Telling of Tales.* Honolulu: University of Hawaii Press.

Langness, L.L. and Gelya Frank.
1981 *Lives: An Anthropological Approach to Biography.* Novato, CA: Chandler and Sharp.

Mbilinyi, Marjorie.
1989 "I'd Have Been A Man": Politics and the Labor Process in Producing Personal Narratives. In Personal Narratives Group, eds. *op. cit.* Pp. 204-227.

Myerhoff, Barbara.
1978 *Number Our Days.* New York: Simon and Schuster.

Myerhoff, Barbara and Virginia Tufte.
1992 Life History as Integration: Personal Myth and Aging. (Earlier version in *The Gerontologist,* December 1975). In Barbara Myerhoff, *Remembered Lives: The Work of Ritual, Storytelling, and Growing Older.* Marc Kaminsky, ed. Pp. 249-255. Ann Arbor: University of Michigan Press.

Narayan, Kirin.
1989 *Storytellers, Saints, and Scoundrels: Folk Narratives in Hindu Religious Teaching.* Philadelphia: University of Pennsylvania Press.

Patai, Daphne.
1988 *Brazilian Women Speak: Contemporary Life Stories.* New Brunswick, NJ: Rutgers University Press.
1991 U.S. Academics and Third World Women: Is Ethical Research Possible? In Gluck and Patai *op. cit.* Pp. 137-153.

Personal Narratives Group, eds.
  1989 *Interpreting Women's Lives: Feminist Theory and Personal Narratives*. Bloomington: Indiana
  University Press.

Rama Rau, Santha.
  1958 *Gifts of Passage*. New York: Harper Brothers

Salazar, Claudia.
  1991 A Third World Woman's Text: Between the Politics of Criticism and Cultural Politics. In Gluck
  and Patai *op. cit.* Pp. 93-106.

Saleri, Sara.
  1989 *Meatless Days*. Chicago: University of Chicago Press.

Sarris, Greg.
  1992 "What I'm Talking about When I'm Talking about My Baskets": Conversations with Mabel
  McKay. In Smith and Watson *op. cit.* Pp. 20-33.
  1993 Reading Narrated American Indian Lives: Elizabeth Colson's *Autobiographies of Three Pomo
  Women*. In Greg Sarris, *Keeping Slug Woman Alive: A Holistic Approach to American Indian
  Texts*. Pp. 79-114. Berkeley: University of California Press.
  1994 *Mabel McKay: Weaving the Dream*. Berkeley: University of California Press.

Savishinsky, Joel S.
  1991 *The Ends of Time: Life and Work in a Nursing Home*. New York: Bergin & Garvey.

Shostak, Marjorie.
  1983 *Nisa: The Life and Words of a !Kung Woman*. New York: Vintage, Random House.
  1989 "What the Wind Won't Take Away": The Genesis of *Nisa: The Life and Words of a !Kung
  Women*". In Personal Narratives Group, *op. cit.* Pp. 228-240.

Silvera, Makeda, ed.
  1983 *Silenced*. Toronto: Williams-Wallace.

Sistren.
  1986 *Lionheart Gal: Life Stories of Jamaican Women*. Honor Ford-Smith, ed. London: Women's
  Press.

Smith, Sidonie and Julia Watson, eds.
  1992 *De/Colonizing the Subject: The Politics of Gender in Women's Autobiography*. Minneapolis:
  University of Minnesota Press.

Sommer, Doris.
  1988 "Not Just a Personal Story": Women's *Testimonios* and the Plural Self. In Bella Brodzki and
  Celeste Schenck, eds. *Life/Lines: Theorizing Women's Autobiographies*. Pp. 107-130. Ithaca:
  Cornell University Press.

Wilson, Angela Cavender.
    1994 Native American Oral History and Academia: Reconciling Two Views of Historical Tradition.
    Paper delivered at conference on Native Women Historians: Challenges and Issues, Southwest State
    University, Minnesota.

Gender and Resource Management

in an Andean Agropastoral

System[1]

Lisa Markowitz
University of Kentucky

Since 1992, Lisa Markowitz has been involved with the Small Ruminant CRSP, a USAID supported university consortium, on a research project based in Bolivian agro-pastoral communities. As Resident Scientist for the University of Missouri's Rural Sociology Program and as a member of an interdisciplinary team, she worked within the Livestock and Forages section of the Bolivian Institute of Agricultural Technology. At present, she is integrating and interrogating the Bolivia materials toward development of systems methodologies for use in fragile lands. Her next project involves a return to Peru, where she conducted her dissertation fieldwork, to explore the relationships between grassroots herders' organizations, NGOs, and state policy. She currently teaches anthropology at the University of Kentucky.

Introduction

Newcomers to San José Llanga remark on the absence of people in the town's center. Indeed on most days the central plaza of this Bolivian village is deserted save for a few scampering dogs and pre-schoolers. The children's older siblings, parents and grandparents are scattered over some 7,000 hectares of community land, engaged mostly in tasks of cultivation and livestock husbandry, and the reproduction of community and household. The technical demands and ecological constraints of agropastoral production at over 12,000 feet above sea level require physical dispersion of people and animals and the coordination of these movements in careful syncopation with the needs of family and community life. This social choreography is largely orchestrated by women heads of households, who define themselves variously as cooks, weavers, housewives, spinners, ranchers, cowherders and, mostly as shepherds, but do not call themselves farm managers. Although few men in the community would use that term for self reference either, their authority over the allocation of farm resources is assumed by outsiders. Male bias (Elson 1991) endemic among local institutions proffering technical extension renders the managerial role of women invisible and their roles as active and knowledgeable farmers and stock-raisers shadowy.

This limited vision reflects the assumptions and institutional structures of western agricultural science (Elson 1991; Ferguson 1994) and discourses about the beneficiaries of Third World development projects (Escobar 1988; Parpart 1993). These factors, which have led to an emphasis on women's domestic activities and consequent neglect of their roles in agricultural production (Buvinic and Mehra 1990:301), are reinforced by proximate material conditions. Agricultural and resource management programs world over tend to suffer from over-loaded, women-poor staffs, unable or unlikely to disseminate technical information in ways that will reach women (Jiggins 1986; Mehra 1993). These and even more basic constraints like the lack of gasoline to fill institutional vehicles impede livestock extension in the central *altiplano*. Existing projects oriented toward women in Bolivia often contend with uninterested or antagonistic state officials, who perhaps feel daunted by the particular efforts effective with women farmers: the recruitment of Aymara or Quechua speaking technicians, literacy training, "unorthodox" meeting times and so forth. At another level, groups interested in working with rural women find their organizing hampered by a lack of understanding of the specific pressures and workloads confronting potential female participants, and have little idea how to integrate such information into the planning and execution of their projects (Gisbert and Quitón 1994).

The institutional neglect of women agro-pastoralists in the south-central Andean *cordillera* and *altiplano* deserves attention because of the very visibility of their daily participation in simple commodity and subsistence production. Campillo (1993:28) reports high female involvement in livestock husbandry throughout Latin America, and in the Andean region, where women participate in agriculture at higher rates than elsewhere on the continent (Deere 1987), women and children are primary caretakers of small ruminants -- sheep, goats, llamas and alpacas (Caro 1992; Fernández 1989; Harris 1978). Despite rich ethnographic accounts of both high Andean pastoral and agro-pastoral communities, relatively little work in the literature addresses the ways in which women coordinate the system of production, especially in the Aymara central *altiplano*. The intent here is to use the San José case study to portray the full range of womens' activities in agro-pastoral production, and, especially, to highlight their managerial responsibilities. Such depictions can counter the biases and tendencies described above by informing the design of programs that recognize and respond to women's roles beyond those of farm wife and farm worker.

San José Llanga

The community lies some 130 km south-southwest of La Paz, in the drainage system of the Desaguadero River. A fair dirt road constructed in the late 1980's links San José with the town of Patacamaya, a truck-stop midpoint on the La Paz-Oruro highway. The climate is semi-arid with average annual precipitation at 406 mm. and some 150 nights of frost occurring throughout the year. In contrast to *cordillera* agro-pastoral communities where production is organized around compressed ecological zonation (Brush 1979:10-11) the rolling altiplano lands grade by only 60 meters. *Comunarios* distinguish between the low lying pasture zone, *la parte baja*, and the slight uplands, *la parte de arriba*, where most cropping occurs. Overall, some 30% of land within community boundaries is used for regular cultivation. Much of this land is in fallow at any given time, a critical grazing resource. Another 6.5% is dedicated to forage crops, while 48% is natural pasture (Massy 1994:46).

The village itself consists of around 100 families distributed through more than six zones, each originally the settlement or *estancia* of an extended kin group. Each zone is comprised of between nine and twenty families, many of whom share the same last names, reflecting consanguineal ties, and a tendency toward patrilocal residence. Three zones lie close to the nucleated 'center' of town, which contains the plaza, central church (there are four in total, including the Adventist meeting house), school, four tiny shops, and a milk delivery center. The three other zones, strung along a usually drivable dirt road, are as far as a fifty minute walk or fifteen minute bike ride from the center. According to community elders, the nucleation has occurred gradually over the past few decades, and is related to greater market participation and road construction. Community documents from the 1970's record remarks encouraging "urbanization" as a way of facilitating requests for basic services to state and non-governmental institutions. The increasing orientation toward this center space parallels tendencies elsewhere in the altiplano to use space to symbolically affirm community status (Carter & Albó 1988:462).

Local livelihood rests on multiple productive sectors, and recent research (Jetté 1993; Medinacelli 1993) shows that these have shifted in emphasis and location over the years as people respond to national and regional economic and institutional change. Today, most residents combine raising sheep, cattle and a few donkeys with temporary off-farm employment and cropping. People grow several varieties of potatoes, quiñua, barley, and to a lesser extent, faba beans, and dedicate sizable parcels of land to forage cultivation, principally barley, alfalfa and oats. In recent years, food cultivation has been oriented toward auto-consumption and most people eat what they grow.

Each of the livestock species provides different kinds of non-monetary resources: from donkeys, portage; from cattle, milk, traction and dung as fertilizer and fuel; from sheep, mutton, blood and various viscera, wool, hides, dung as fertilizer, and seasonal cheese. All three animals, through defecation, recycle nutrients back into both grazing and agricultural lands. Household controlled flocks number on average 43, and a few families manage more than 100 sheep. Over a third of the sheep in the community are managed by a non-owner, usually through an *al partir* arrangement. Most San José families raise a few cattle; holdings range between one and ten with an average of six head. In late 1989 through the intervention of a Bolivian organization, Fomento Lechero, a milk delivery center and daily collection system were established. This program has spurred rapid growth of a community dairy sector, involving investment in improved (Holstein and Brown Swiss crosses) cows and the allocation of land to forage crops, especially alfalfa, making cows the "privileged" animals in San José.

Both grazing and agricultural lands belonging to households in a given zone tend to be clustered together, although not necessarily near the houses. People typically reside some distance from both their pastures and grazing land -- a 45 minute walk to pasture sheep or dig potatoes is common, although the distance varies by season with ground and forage conditions. Unlike many Andean villages, very little grazing land is held communally, nor does a communally managed system of sectoral fallowing exist. All parcels in the cultivated area belong to individuals or families, and the tiny area of community pasture is of the lowest quality, practically devoid of vegetation. Households control on average just under 39 hectares of cultivable and grazing lands combined, with total holdings ranging between 5 and 76 hectares. With partible inheritance, considerable fragmentation of land has occurred over the years so fields are small and dispersed throughout different productive areas. Families typically control 23 to 30 parcels, with better off households holding larger rather than more lands (Cala 1994). Areas with productive potential are used in the following way: about 5 hectares are cropped for food and another 5 for forages, 16 hectares lie in fallow, and about 10 hectares comprise rangeland (Cala and Jetté 1994).

Just over 400 people currently live in San José, a fluctuating figure in light of high temporary and permanent migration rates. Like other *altiplano* towns, San José is characterized by fluid population dynamics which both reflect the vagaries of the high mountain production system and ameliorated some of its difficulties by increasing the amount of land available for those who remain. The out-migration rate among the parental generation is nearly one half.[2] Families who have migrated return for planting, and then again at harvest; occasionally families whose migration was unsatisfactory come back; and several elderly single residents tend to rove between San José and other settlements. However, unlike other highland communities, prolonged absence of male household heads is not the norm. Rather men may be involved in wage work during the winter months when agricultural demands have subsided or work sporadically throughout the year. Young males are the most common migrants; women between 14 and 25 outnumber males in the same age group by nearly 2 to 1. In this regard, San José follows both the broader highland pattern of economically driven male migration to eastern lowlands (Webb 1989:17), and that of pastoral societies generally (Dahl 1987:272-73).

The Household Labor Force

Today, with private ownership of lands[3] and livestock, households are the nexus of production and consumption in the community. Household here refers to the co-resident nuclear family: parents and unmarried children who share a house, cook together and identify the same animals and lands as their own. This residential group may temporally include elderly parents, visiting siblings, nieces and nephews, grandchildren (by migrant sons and daughters) and sons and daughters in-law. However, it is far from an independent entity. Like smallholders throughout the Andes (Orlove and Custred 1980) families in San José cooperate with neighbors and relatives in numerous economic and social undertakings. Families count on extra-household assistance to carry out agro-pastoral tasks, especially during harvest and planting. As Collins (1986) has pointed out, the important linkages that generate support grow out of agnatic, affinal and fictive kin-relationships between individuals. For example, the constant demands of herding are alleviated by mother-daughter or sister-sister household heads trading off their flocks on alternating days. The ability of an aging couple to "borrow" their 15 year old god-child for a week through *prestado de hijo* to mind cows and sheep frees them for other activities. In San José the importance of extra-familial resources extends from labor to land and livestock, as families increase their holdings with land loaned by emigre siblings (who may expect to be feted with its products -- roast lamb and sacks of potatoes -- when they visit) and care for the cattle of absent adult children.

Gender and Work

Newly established couples in San José set up their own household as soon as their resources permit. The pattern of bequeathing lands to sons, while giving daughters only livestock encourages patrilocal residence, with brides moving to San José or to the zone of their husband's family.[4] The regional pattern of women and men sharing or coordinating virtually all tasks of agro-pastoral production contrasts with tendencies in peasant systems of sub-Saharan Africa toward formal maintenance of gender specific farming sectors. The need for both male and female participation in production and household reproduction reflects and sustains notions of complementarity, that a conjugal pairing is better and more complete. This view is manifest symbolically in ceremonies honoring local deities, when small candies are carefully laid out in twin envelopes carried to the ritual site as the offering of couples.

Women and men do work together in agricultural and ruminant production, either sharing in immediate tasks, or taking on different activities within the production cycle. Overall, household distribution of labor is flexible within San José, with few tasks performed exclusively by males or females. In San José both women and men perform the exhausting work of cutting and stacking forages. The cultivation of potatoes, the most important food crop, requires several steps and males and females share in the various phases of planting, mounding dirt around the plants, applying fertilizers and pesticides, and harvest. Ground breaking is done by tractor, driven by a hired male specialist. At planting men do consistently drive a *yunta*, yoked cattle, while their wives or daughters scatter seeds but women asserted that they could also mange a *yunta* if necessary, although none actually had.

Nonetheless strong gender differences in orientation and responsibilities are evident especially in domestic, commercial and political, and finally, livestock management realms. Although men will assist in cooking, clothes washing and child care, women bear primary responsibility for the reproduction of labor. They deal most with the rearing and nurturing of children, and those tasks that ensure the physical well-being of household members. (Reproduction of the labor force is subsumed under the much broader concept of social reproduction which includes maintenance of those cultural conditions that permit continued participation in the labor force.) In twenty-four hour recalls, women mentioned cooking, washing clothes, housecleaning and childcare 63 times to 11 similar responses by males. Women manage the family larder, using their income streams to purchase food (Valdivia et al 1993), monitoring supplies, and planning menus. As primary caretakers of babies and toddlers, they weave nursing, changing, cuddling, and playing into all other activities. Fathers, on the other hand, are rarely seen in community or productive endeavors with a young child in tow.

About 85% of male household heads engage in cash generating activities compared to a rate of 25% for their female counterparts. Men's seasonal or intermittent employment includes construction, tailoring, weaving, mechanics, and petty commerce. Women sew, knit, weave and spin items to sell or trade in their spare moments, or regularly attend the Patacamaya Sunday market, a forty minute bus ride or five hour walk away to vend homemade cheeses or purchased sundries. Men are much more likely to represent their families in community, zone or producers association meetings and projects. Community membership obligates each family to send a representative to monthly or bi-monthly *asambleas*, and give about 10 person days annually to community projects, e.g., repairing the church school or roads. Sub-community dairy and irrigation organizations also require time and labor commitments. Since the early 1990's, new school construction and installation of a potable water system has placed additional demand on people times. Men usually represent their families in these undertakings. When women do participate, they are more likely to assume the "support" tasks of hauling water for adobe making or preparing lunch for carpenters. (It is not unusual to see women or their teen-age daughter fill-in performing heavy labor -- digging out the foundation for a water tank or rebanking the river -- but men are present in much higher numbers). Finally, it is men who take on the ten or so rotating positions of community authority and exercise public leadership in community meetings, local planning, and relationships with external institutions.[5] The following descriptions illustrate some of the gendered differences in the ways household heads use their time.

> On a Monday in late October, Irma Huanca rose at 6 A.M., and helped by her twelve year old son prepared breakfast for her family of nine. After straightening up the kitchen, she organized herself for a day of sheep herding by packing up her year old baby, spinning materials, a cold lunch and loading up the donkey. Around 9:00 accompanied by her 4 year old daughter she headed out to spend the day tending and watering sheep and spinning, and was joined by her 9 year old daughter in early afternoon. They returned after 6:00, to a dinner the older children had prepared. Through the evening she darned thick woven blankets. Although Irma's husband, Victor, sewed in the evening too, repairing clothing, his day passed quite differently. He also rose at 6 and by 7:00 was waiting at the milk delivery center for the arrival of the milk pick-up truck. As a member of the community dairy association, he was on duty for the month as an *acopiador*, recording the amount of milk delivered by other *comunarios* and checking for purity. At 9:00 he attended a long community meeting which lasted until early afternoon. He then went to check on and give forage to the cows his 14 year old son had staked out in the morning. He returned home before supper and helped the children with their homework before sewing.

On a Wednesday, during the school vacation in February, Tomasina Mamani and her 18 year old daughter prepared breakfast for the family of seven. After the daughter milked the family cows, the two walked to the family's alfalfa plot about 25 minutes away and cut forage all day long. At midday they were joined by Daniel Mamani who had spent his morning first in the office of the dairy group with whom he works performing artificial insemination, earning about (US) $1.25 for each injection. After delivering the household's milk, he attended a community meeting that continued until late morning. The couple returned home for the evening meal prepared by their 15 year old daughter, rested and listened to news on the radio. The girl, who had been herding sheep all day, was relieved of the flock in mid-afternoon by her 13 year old brother after he and his 6 and 2 year old brothers brought the cows in early from pasturing.

Agro-Pastoral Rhythms

These sketches also point up the coordination required between multiple production sectors and the essential contributions of the juvenile work-force to the household choreography of production and reproduction. It is important to keep in mind that although the agricultural workload is great, there is never a break from animal care; pasturing, feeding, watering and protecting animals cannot be put off. As one elderly women responded when I asked if she was going to a fair, "And who will take care of my sheep"? Under the privatized San José land tenure system small ruminants need continuous attention. Cattle, on the other hand, are often led out with the sheep between 9 and 10 in the morning but then pegged-out apart, and moved from pasture to pasture just ahead of the flocks. Or the cows may be pegged out for several hours at a time, then shifted after they consume the surrounding vegetation. This may involve leaving the cows in nearby (20 minute walk) pasture, and returning once or twice to move them.

Sheep and cow shuttling fall within the greater seasonal rhythms of agricultural production and the availability of pasture. When women talk about their busyness from season to season, they refer to the demands of agricultural tasks, while with one exception, herding and childcare are regarded as constants to be negotiated. In the beginning of the agricultural year and end of the dry-season, herders must lead sheep the longest distances through the low-lying native pastures in search of remaining vegetation, averaging a walk of 8.4 km a day in September and 7.7 km. in October (Roció Victoria 1994:66). Moreover in the planting season, October through mid-December, the community enjoins pasturing animals in fallow fields of the *parte de arriba* to give grasses a chance to sprout. Herding and planting therefore must be conducted far apart. In mid-December the community officially prohibits grazing in large sections of the pasture zone to allow forage species their time to recuperate. January, February, and March are the peak labor demand times for grazing both sheep and cattle in the agricultural areas. Even though this pattern reduces traveling distance (e.g 5.8 km. for the sheep in February [Roció Victoria 1994:66]), women say that the rainy season is the most difficult time to herd. The muddy ground makes walking more difficult and the herding day lasts longer with livestock grazing an average of 8 hours compared to 6 hours and 40 minutes during the dry months (Roció Victoria 1994:71). Also during this period, it takes two shepherds (usually a mother and school age child) to keep sheep out of cultivated fields (once sheep get into potatoes they are impossible to get out). They also must protect first and second year quinua fallows, since these produce a pioneer species, valued for human consumption. A further complication comes from the conditions in the riverine alfalfa plots below. This high protein staple for cattle and supplement for sheep, if ingested while still green can causing fatal bloating (*timpanismo*). Herders need to know exactly how long a given animal can be permitted to graze, and must have the strength to yank a hungry cow to safety.

As the rains cease in March, herding becomes technically easier but the demands on women increase. The school summer vacation has ended reducing the household labor force, and harvest season begins. Women consistently say that after Easter comes one of the busiest periods, with potatoes, beans and quiñua ready to harvest, and forage crops to cut. In early winter the frigid nights allow *chuño* processing (freeze dried potatoes) and hay-making on dry days. Both sheep and cattle are grazed in crop residues from the recent harvest. As the post-harvest processing comes to an end in July, women enjoy their easiest season. During this time they "only" have to care for livestock and the home. Sheep are grazed in the natural pastures but long searches for forage are not yet necessary. And, without agricultural chores, those men present also have more free time and assume a larger part of animal care.

Dispatching the Troops

Over the course of the year women not only perform nearly all types of productive tasks but also direct the work activities of their children. From the age of 4, children contribute to the family labor force. Small children run errands, feed chickens, wash dishes, peel potatoes, look after toddlers and assist their parents and older siblings. By 4 or 5, children regularly accompany their mothers and big sisters tending sheep, and assist them by chasing after strays. The allocation of cattle and sheep care tasks to youngsters over 6 must be organized around the school schedule since the primary grades meet from 8:00 AM until noon, and the junior high grades from 1:00 to 5:00 PM. Hence, quite a lot of shepherd switching goes on as older children stake out cattle or lead out sheep in the morning and younger ones spell or assist older family members in the afternoon. (It should be remembered that some of these children have an hour to walk each way to school). By the age of 8 or 9 a child can help a lot in nearly all cropping and animal care activities. As one mother explains, it doesn't matter if they are girls or boys. It depends on the child; some just don't like to work. The 24 hour recalls completed by 65 school children show younger children active in herding cattle and sheep and assisting in food preparation. Notably, after the age of 12 not one boy mentions kitchen work, while the girl's involvement increases. Young women who have finished with school (none have attended more than 8th grade)[6] report their primary occupations as herding sheep, spinning or cooking. Depending on the needs of their particular households, they may become the primary sheep or cattle caretakers, or take on many domestic duties freeing their parents' time for agro-pastoral production and community commitments. Observation, and household-based family recalls in which boys speak of playing ball and visiting friends in the afternoon suggest that young adolescent males have more free time than their sisters.[7]

The importance of children as small ruminant shepherds has been noted in pastoral (Browman 1990) as well as agro-pastoral systems (McCorkle 1992). In San José a child of 9 is considered capable of herding on her/his own although often two young children are dispatched together. Women explain that by the age of 13 their daughters can herd well, but an adult may still come to take over when cows and sheep are permitted to graze in alfalfa fields when *timpanismo* poses a danger. Mothers say younger children need instructions:

"I tell the 10 year old not to go through other people's pastures so there won't be problems. I also tell her to water the sheep twice if there's no well, if there is, then make them drink as many times as they want. When you don't make them drink, they don't want to graze and they just stop. Also I tell her the places where she has to take them, what time she has to come back because sometimes she comes home too early. She already knows how to herd and how to lead the flock (Paredes ms)."

The reliance on older daughters explains in part the asymmetry in the community age/sex structure. Young women are as eager as their brother to migrate, at least for a few years. Their mothers, however, reliant on their help both in domestic chores and animal husbandry, often refuse to allow them to leave.

Sheep, Cattle and Women

Although men are certainly aware of flock and range conditions, women in San José are the ones who monitor pastures and decide each morning, given the caliber of the available shepherd(s) where to take the flock. They also have firm views on the art and science of herding, as demonstrated in the following excerpts (Paredes ms). A 65 year old women asserts "the growth and reproduction of the sheep depends on the shepherd (*pastora*). If she gets up early, and herds from early until late the sheep will grow rapidly and multiply." Another woman says "you can satisfy the animals by taking them to different types of grasses or to alfalfa plots. If you lead them to just one spot, they won't want to graze and will get tired and won't gain weight, but herding them in different grasses will fatten them up. That's why I take them to the *ch'iji*, the alfalfa, the fallow fields, and the wheat and barley stubble." A 41 year old woman explains her technique:

"You make them eat a type of grass bit by bit until they're satisfied, then take them to another area. Then you get them to drink water every little while on their own. We haul water out of the well for them 6 times a day, me alone or with my daughters. If it's the rainy season they can drink out of ponds. I lead them up high to graze too, where they eat *ajara, pasto bandera*, and other grasses. If not, I give them some green alfalfa."

Herders frequently mention the importance of watering animals. A woman in her twenties says "You have to give them water 3 or 4 times a day since drinking increases the quantity of milk, the quality will be just as good, and the lambs will grow rapidly."

Not only are women the shepherds and overseers of the flocks but they are also the managers, making most of the decisions about the timing of activities and the allocation of significant ovine products[8]. Performing, along with their daughters, most of the daily -- herding, watering -- and seasonal work -- shearing, cheesemaking, medicating -- associated with sheep, female household heads also determine when and how to proceed with these activities. They also independently decide when to sell animals, how to dispose of the income, and predominate in making decisions about such by-products as wool, hides and dung. Their husbands are most likely to have a voice in the decision to sell the last of these to truckers who carry the manure to eastern *cordillera* valleys. Men also play a role in culinary matters, sometimes initiating the butchering of a sheep for household consumption or suggesting a particular dish. Sales of live animals, wool, hides and cheese are usually carried out by women who use the revenues to purchase family food.

In contrast, care and management of cattle tends to be much more the purview of men. Despite the involvement of women in milking and herding, men play the major role in management and marketing. Women are in charge of cheese-making but say their husbands are the ones who determine the allocation of milk revenues. This money is usually reinvested into the dairy sector to buy feed supplements for cattle and forage seed. While couples discuss whether to sell a whole cow, this major transaction is physically handled by the man who takes the animal to market and uses the proceeds for savings, to invest in off-farm activities, and in over half the cases, to cover production costs, either new cattle, or other inputs for the livestock sector (Espejo 1994). Further, men wear the public face of commercial dairying through their membership in the dairy association to which over half the community families formally belong. Early in 1994 I took ID card photos of the association's 30 most active members and only a single woman was among the group (The full organization roster listed only three other women out of 63 members.) Thus far all officers of the group have been male. While meetings and talks by the regional extension agent are open to women, they are overwhelmingly attended by men.

Gundren Dahl (1987) notes that in extensive stockraising systems men dominate in management of large ruminants for reasons having to do with defense of the herd and the limitations that childcare places on women's mobility. Happily for *comunarios* rustling has not posed a menace, and women manage to care for children and pasture animals simultaneously. When asked why they care for sheep and men for cattle, women laugh and say it's because men are lazy, and don't like having to chase after the animals. One man, grinning, told me, that sheep keep the young girls too busy to get into trouble. Other men say that women haven't participated much in the dairy group activities because most have had little education and cannot understand the Spanish language materials, an explanation that captures a local dimension of the dairy extension program.

The nation-wide Fomento was conceived without consideration of gender roles, nor the specific constraints on women's time imposed by their multiple productive and domestic responsibilities (Mihotek 1993). Although women are nominally welcome to participate, awkward morning meeting times, the necessity for occasional travel to Patacamaya and nearby communities, the Spanish training booklets, and the male technical staff all mitigate against their involvement and acquisition of the knowledge and skills important for raising improved cattle.[9] Severe logistical constraints face the extension staff themselves, with a single individual responsible for dealing with dairy groups in 25 communities of the Patacamaya region. In sum, the design and implementation of the program echo the tendencies of extension programs summarized in the introduction, which lead to the exclusion of women.

Discussion and Conclusions

The question can be fairly raised that given the already high workload of women, is one less responsibility really such a liability? Is it necessary for women to enter the management of all farm sectors? Negative responses assume that joint decision-making based on pooled information occurs, and that men are regularly present to share in the labor of husbandry and forage production. That men dominate in determining the allocation of cattle resources is clear (although not necessarily at the level of should push-come-to-shove). In agropastoral systems like San José, each productive sector is integrated into the next, both physically and in terms of resource trade-offs. Expansion or reduction of one sector affects the availability of resources -- land, forage, labor, cash -- available for others. For example, increasing alfalfa and other forage production in recent years represents a growing demand on household labor, which recent data collection suggests, falls heavily on women who complain that new technologies have increased their workload. Dairy cattle also embody a major family financial investment, and extensionist comments as well as frequent deliveries of substandard milk and disease outbreaks indicate that producers need further training in the care of these valuable beasts. Studies of agriculture technology transfer programs do not support the assumption that information men receive in the course of extension programs "trickles across" to women (Jiggins 1986:37). This set of conditions leaves families vulnerable to the advent of greater male absence, not an unlikely prospect given regional trends, both because of their labor contribution and the greater husbandry knowledge, however imperfect, they bear.

Dissemination of information directly to women increases the flexibility of rural households to cope with a wider range of circumstances, a critical ability in fragile environments like the central *altiplano* where people continually contend with climactic and socio-economic uncertainly and risk. The flip side of information flow is the knowledge that women farmers have to offer agricultural scientists, especially those concerned with increasing food production in marginal areas. Recent recognition of the limits and increasing degradation of highly productive agricultural regions has drawn attention to semi-arid and high mountain lands in attaining global food security (Glantz 1994; Scherr and Hazell 1993). Designing and implementing projects that increase yields without adverse environmental or social consequences requires input from farmers of all sorts.

Downtown San José appears not at all prepossessing, but the basis of local livelihood, the agropastoral system of production is deceptively complex, a social choreography that encompasses the seasonal patterns of livestock and agricultural activities, the daily coordination of people, sheep and cattle, and the demands of labor reproduction over a broad spatial field. Women here, as in other rural communities (Benería and Sen 1982:167) assume the roles of producer, caretaker, and manager and their ability to juggle numerous demands underscores the high value of their time, and managerial ability (Cloud 1985). No one benefits from the omission of these household heads (or their daughters) from agricultural research or extension programs, and the potential pay-offs of their inclusion are high.

Notes

1. This research was carried out as a part of the United States Agency for International Development Title XII Small Ruminant Collaborative Research Support Program under Grants No. DAN-1328-G-00-0046-00. Additional support was provided by the Social Science Unit, College of Agriculture at the University of Missouri. I thank Christian Jetté, Magali Caceres, Edgar Cala, Rigoberto Espejo, Juana Huanca, Valeria Paredes and Rosa Lizarraga for their assistance. Thanks also to Corinne Valdivia and Dena Shenk for their comments and suggestions.

2. Of the group represented by adult household heads in a sample of 30 homes, out of a total of 174 siblings interviewed and reported, 83 or 47.7% live outside of San José. The siblings of those 83 migrants gave drought (20), search for work (19), and marriage (14) as the most important reason for moving, mentioning as well, business pursuits, kinship, and simply "being used to the place" as motivations. In a number of cases when drought was not given as the proximate cause for their departure, it was a factor. For example, people responded "my parents left here after the drought (1983) and they (my brothers) grew up there and got used to it." And even when drought was not explicitly mentioned, people cite poor agricultural production and lack of land as the reasons their siblings sought other employment. Education is another pull. Members of the current generation of migrants in progress would often explain that giving their children a good education (widely considered unavailable in San José) motivated their move.

3. Early in this century all grazing lands were held communally. The process of privatizing pastures was completed in 1965 (Jetté 1993).

4. People in San José say that it makes more sense to give land to sons since the daughters get married anyway and leave. The contemporary preference of bequeathing land to sons reflects a Spanish influence that has, in some places, superseded indigenous patterns of bilateral- mother/daughter, father/son inheritance (Carter and Albó, 1988). It may also have to do with 1952 Agrarian Reform legislation which awards land to single males over 18, married males over 14, and to widows with children (Jemio cited in Deere 1987:172). In contrast, at marriage young men and women receive approximately equal numbers of sheep, 9 and 10 respectively and one cow apiece from their parents (Espejo 1994:104)

5. Although communities in the Province of Aroma have a history of leadership positions held by a couple, with the man and woman, known as *mama t'alla*, (Alavi 1993) having distinct duties, none of the elders in San José who were interviewed recalled this practice.

6. Survey data confirms this in practice, showing that out of 30 households, eight men but no women had attended high school (*medio*). While figures for junior high attendance were similar, 39 females gave elementary school (*basico*) as their highest level of education, compared to 19 males.

7. Recent SR-CRSP sponsored thesis research indicates that notions of appropriate male and female tasks seem most pronounced during adolescence, and recede after marriage. While little boys accompany their mothers and sisters to herd sheep, as a boy approaches adolescence this takes on the stigma of "girls' work" to be avoided (Paredes ms).

8. Intra-household decision-making can be difficult to study but in this case triangulated research methods: case studies (Paredes ms); a 45 household economic survey (Valdivia et al. 1993), and participatory group meetings led to similar conclusions. The gatherings were held with small groups (4-7) of women household heads to discuss management and control of animal resources and decision making. We found the use of ECO-GEN (Ecology, Community and Organization, and Gender) methodologies developed by researchers affiliated with Clark University to be effective, and adapted techniques originally applied in the Philippines. For example an exercise that pictures a banana palm tree and then a series of question about the ways leaves, flowers, fruits, etc. are used, became the template for a similar exercise with pictures of sheep and cows.

9. Instructive contrast may be drawn from a UNIFEM sponsored dairying project in the northern *altiplano* in which extension work was explicitly directed to women producers. Conceived with both practical and strategic gender needs (Moser 1994), the project not only improved household income but heightened women's leadership and organizational capabilities (Flora 1992).

References

Benería, Lourdes and Gita Sen
1982 Class and Gender Inequalities and Women's Role in Economic Development - Theoretical and Practical Implications. *Feminist Studies* 8:1.

Browman, David
1990 High Altitude Camelid Pastoralism of the Andes. In *The World of Pastoralism: Herding Strategies in Comparative Perspective.* J. Galaty and D. Johnson, eds. Pp. 323-352. N.Y: Guilford Press.

Brush, Stephen B.
1977 *Mountain Field and Family.* Philadelphia: University of Pennsylvania.

Buvinic, Mayra and Rekha Mehra
1990 Women and Agricultural Development. In *Agricultural Development in the Third World.* C. Eicher and J. Staatz, eds. Pp. 290-308. Baltimore: Johns Hopkins University Press.

Cala, Edgar
1994 *Sistema de Tenencia de Tierras,* BA Thesis, Sociology, UMSA, La Paz.

Cala, Edgar and Christian Jetté
1994 Posesión y Control de Tierras en una Comunidad del Altiplano Central. IBTA 138/Boletín Técnico 07/SR-CRSP. La Paz, Bolivia.

Campillo, Fabiola
1993 Género y desarrollo: Las mujeres del campo y la producción agricola. *Ruralter* No. 11/12:19-46.

Caro, Deborah
1992 The Socioeconomic and Cultural Context of Andean Pastoralism." In *Sustainable Crop-Livestock Systems for the Bolivian Highlands.* C. Valdivia, ed. Pp.71-92. Columbia, MO: University of Missouri.

Carter, William and Xavier Albó
1988 La comunidad Aymara: un Mini-Estado en Conflicto. In *Raices de América: El Mundo Aymara*, X. Albó, ed. Pp.451-492. Madrid: Alianza América.

Cloud, Kathleen
1985 Women's Productivity in Agricultural Systems: Considerations for Project Design. In Gender Roles in Development Projects. Overholt et al, eds. Pp.17-56. West Hartford, CT:Kumarian.

Collins, Jane
1986 The Household and Relations of Production in Southern Peru. *Comparative Studies in Society and History.* 28(4):651-671.

Dahl, Gundrun
  1987 Women in Pastoral Production: Some Theoretical Notes on Roles and Resources. In *Women in Pastoral Production*. Stockholm: Etnografiska Museet, 1-2, Pp.246-274.

Deere, Carmen Diana
  1987 The Latin American Agrarian Reform Experience. In *Rural Women and State Policy*. C.D.Deere and M. León, eds. Pp.165-187. Boulder: Westview. 1987.

Elson, Diane
  1991 Male Bias in the Development Process: An Overview. In *Male Bias in the Development Process*.D. Elson, ed. Pp. 1-28. New York: Manchester University Press.

Escobar, Arturo
  1988 Power and Visibility: Development and the Invention and Management of the Third World. *Cultural Anthropology* 3(4):428-443.

Espejo U., Rigoberto
  1994 *Prácticas Socioeconómicas de Tenencia y Adquisición de Ganado, Estudio de Caso: Comunidad San José Llanga*. BA Thesis. Sociology, UMSA. La Paz, Bolivia.

Ferguson, Anne E.
  1994 Gendered Science: A Critique of Agricultural Development. *American Anthropologist* (96)3:540-52.

Fernández, María
  1989 El Dominio Tecnológico de la Mujer en la Ganadéria. In *El Trabajo Familiar y el Rol de la Mujer en la Ganadéria en Comunidades Alto-Andinas de Producción Mixta*. M. Fernandez, ed. Serie Comunidades Informe Técnico #101. Huancayo, Peru: INIPA.

Flora, Cornelia.
  UNIFEM Women's Milk Project. Unpublished manuscript.

Gisbert, Maria Elena and Mery Quitón
  1994 Gender Issues Associated with Labor Migration and Dependence on Off-Farm Income in Rural Bolivia. *Human Organization* (53)2:110-122.

Glantz, Michael H.
  1994 Drought, Desertification and Food Production. In *Drought Follows the Plow: Cultivating Marginal Areas*. M. Glantz,ed. Pp.9-30. New York: Cambridge University Press.
  Harris, Olivia
  1978 Complementarity and Conflict: An Andean View of Women and Men. In *Sex and Age as Principles of Social Differentiation*. J.S. La Fontaine, ed. Pp.21-40. ASA Monograph #17. Academic Press.

Jetté, Christian
  1993 A Diachronic Analysis of Changing Resource Use Patterns on the Central Bolivian Highlands. Small Ruminant Workshop. San Juan, PR. September.

Jiggins, Janice
 1986 Gender Related Impacts and the Work of the International Agricultural Research Centers. CGIAR Study Paper #17. Washington, DC: The World Bank.

Massy Quiroga, Nelson
 1994 *Mapeo y Caracterización de Campos Nativos de Pastoreo del Cantón San José Llanga*. BS Thesis, College of Agriculture, Universidad Tecnica de Oruro.

Medinaceli, Ximena, Ramiro Jiménez, and Mery Quitón
 1993 Historia Demográfica de Aroma-Umala-San José. SR-CRSP Final Report. La Paz, Bolivia.

Mehra, Rekha
 1993 Gender in Community Development and Resource Management: An Overview. Collaborative Research Report. Washington, DC: International Center for Research on Women, World Wildlife Fund.

Mihotek, Kathy B.
 1993 Evaluación de la Participación de la Mujer en los Módulos Lecheros Creados por el Programs de Fomento Lechero. La Paz: World Food Program. 1993.

Moser, Carolyn
 1993 *Gender Planning and Development: Theory, Practice and Training*. NY: Routledge.

McCorkle, Constance M.
 1992 The Agropastoral Dialectic and the Organization of Labor in a Quechua Community. In *Plants, Animals and People*. C.McCorkle,ed. Pp.77-97. Boulder: Westview.

Orlove, Benjamin and Custred Glynn
 1980 The Alternative Model of Agrarian Society in the Andes: Households, Networks and Corporate Groups. In *Land and Power in Latin America*. B.Orlove and G.Custred,eds Pp 31-54. NY: Holmes and Meier.

Parpart, Jane
 1993. Who is the `Other'?: A Postmodern Feminist Critique of Women and Development Theory and Practice. *Development and Change*. (24):439-464.

Paredes, Valeria
 Género y Participación de la Mujer dentro de un Sistema Agropastoril. Unpublished manuscript. La Paz, Bolivia.

Roció Victoria, Zulma
 1994 *Distribución y Comportamiento en Pastoreo del Ganado Doméstico en el Altiplano Central de Bolivia*. BS Thesis. Facultad de Ciencias Agricolas y Pecuarias. Universidad Autonoma "Tomas Frias". Potosi, Boliva.

Scherr, S. and P. Hazell
 1993 Sustainable Agricultural Development Strategies in Fragile Lands. AAEA International pre-Conference on Post-Green Revolution Development Strategies in the Third World. Orlando. July.

Valdivia, C., E. G. Dunn, J. Sherbourne, J. Céspedes and L. Markowitz
  1993 The Economics of Gender and Livestock: Dairy Expansion and Agropastoral Systems in the
  Bolivian Altiplano." Assoc. for Women in Development. Washington D.C., October.

Webb, Anna Kathryne
  1989 The Social and Economic Situation of Poor Women in Bolivia. AID Division Working Paper,
  Washington, D.C.: Latin America and Caribbean Region.

Zacarias, Alavi
  1994 Personal Communication.

Women's Groups in Belize,

Central America:

the Quest for Female Autonomy

Irma McClaurin
University of Florida, Gainesville[1]

Irma McClaurin is an Assistant Professor in the Department of Anthropology at the University of Florida, Gainesville. She was Assistant Professor at Grinnell College from 1993-1995. Her areal focus is the Caribbean and Latin America. Before returning to Grinnell, where she completed her B.A., she worked for 18 years as an academic administrator. She has an M.F.A. in English and has published 3 books of poetry. Her current research is on women's groups, part of her forthcoming book from Rutgers University Press on women and gender in Belize. She is also working on a biography that analyzes the intersection of race/class/gender as sociocultural variables that help explain the suicide of a contemporary successful, black middle class journalist. Future research interests include the effects of tourism in developing countries, as well as ethnicity and national identity.

They come, old and young, with a host of children straggling behind them. They are married, common-law, divorced, widowed, and single. They arrive from places with names like Guinea Grass, Chan Pine Ridge, Barranco, Mango Creek, Crooked Tree, San Antonio, or Big Falls. Some of the women must rise before 5:00 AM to catch the only bus that passes through their village or town at that unseemly hour. Others have been up early to cook rice or bake fresh tortillas for husbands who will not tolerate leftovers. They wash, cook, and clean house at the approach of dawn so that there can be no excuses to be detained.

They come, wrapping a few tortillas or pieces of Creole bread in a towel to snack along the way, knowing that a free lunch will be served. Some have never heard of a "workshop." Most are shy; they stick together and speak in Mopan, Ketchi, Creole, or Spanish. A few come because they want to share their knowledge and experiences. They are women who have earned the right to speak, who can now say they have *trained* their husbands to eat leftover rice; trained their men to accept the fact that once every three months they will attend this meeting for women. They ignore the male comments that imply when a bunch of women get together no good can come of it; they refute the male belief that women only come together to gossip; and they tolerate the male fear that women coming together means that soon the woman will try to wear the pants -- "She de get upstart now."[2]

These women, Creole, Mestizo, Maya, Garifuna, East Indian, or mixed, lead themselves in games designed by the facilitator to "break the ice" and get them to learn something about one another. When lunch comes they organize themselves to serve food so that everyone gets a plate and some can take home leftovers. They listen eagerly to the workshop presenter, who is a younger, single woman, educated in the States. After listening for a while, they think maybe she is not so different. She tells them how she too was trained to cook and wash clothes by hand, even if you have a washing machine. And she encourages them to participate with this simple statement: "every idea is a good idea." She lets them know that she really believes women have valuable contributions to make.

In every district, they meet in schools, in rooms over bars, in community centers, wherever space is made available. They travel far because they believe in this thing called a women's group. They are members of organizations like The Belize Rural Women's Association (BRWA), Belize Women Against Violence (WAV), Belize Family Life Association (BFLA), Breast is Best (BIB) -- national organizations, with local chapters, that have sprung up over the last twenty years, partly in response to specific community needs, or perhaps as a result of the momentum generated by the United Nation's Decade for Women.

And for years they have formed their own community or village groups with names like Lufuliria Women's Group, The Sandy Beach Women's Cooperative Society, Ltd., The Maura Lopez Designer Group, Orange Walk Rotary Ann, and the Xunantunich Cultural Committee.

The catalysts that brought these groups into existence are often obscure. It may have been the vision of an individual woman, who has long since left the group but whose spirit remains; it may have been the persistence of domestic violence in the community and a few women brave enough to speak out against it; or it may have been a desire to change their economic status. I am told, however, that many came in the beginning because they felt the need to come together with other women, just to talk, to learn -- there seems to be security in numbers.

Though the reasons for the formation of these women's groups in Belize, Central America are varied and their origins often obscured, what is evident is that throughout the country women are engaging in collective action. They come together not just to share stories, however, but also to act together toward specific social goals like increasing women's representation in the labor force, strengthening legislation that requires men to financially maintain children born outside of marriage, better housing, job training, and workshops on assertiveness that better prepare women for employment outside the home. Under the auspices of these forums where they meet to discuss a diversity of issues that range from domestic violence to child care to teenage pregnancy, women's groups create the structures and emotional support to foster each member's journey toward female autonomy.

Background

There are several key features in the composition and scope of women's groups in Belize, Central America that may seem unique to the country's sociocultural development. Some of these include the diversity among groups' participants, the existence of social and cultural barriers that impede some women's membership, and the personal importance of these groups in the lives of individual women. Yet the writings of feminists in the Caribbean, Latin America and the United States (Bolles 1991; Ellis 1986; Jelin 1990; Kaplan 1982; Mohammed 1991) provide ample proof that such features are not unique to Belize, but may be viewed as generic to grassroots women's groups in a wide range of geopolitical and sociocultural contexts.

While it is impossible to give a complete description or analysis in this short space of the structural and social components of a given society that conspire to impede the development and progress of women's groups, or may even facilitate them, the following theoretical propositions help me to establish the boundaries of this chapter by focusing on the structural, symbolic, and political value of women's groups. The first proposition is that women's groups serve important social functions for their members; they build new linkages for women in the area of social relations, provide additional networks of support, and build women's self esteem. The second proposition is that women's groups are not simply the outgrowth of spontaneous eruptions by women in reaction to specific issues or events but should be viewed as a particular phase in the development of female agency, often along an historic continuum of women's collective action. The third proposition is that implicitly and explicitly women's groups challenge the gender conventions of a community or society by providing women with a forum within which they may critically examine and develop strategies to alter social norms. Thus, activities and programs that increase women's economic autonomy, build leadership skills, teach them to value existing household skills and pursue a course that will benefit them as an individual actually highlight the inherent cultural contradictions that women face between their fulfillment of social roles as wives and mothers and their personal fulfillment of goals and dreams as individuals.

The aim of this chapter then is to explore the meaning of these facets of women's groups for individual women and as members of a politically and economically disenfranchised segment of Belizean society. Such groups must always be examined within a country's specific geographic, historical, sociocultural and economic contexts.

Formerly the British Honduras, Belize gained independence from Britain in 1981 and sits as "a virtual English-speaking island in a sea of Spanish language and culture"(McClaurin, 1995). Shared borders with Mexico and Guatemala have had implications for the country's population which has grown almost twenty percent to 204,000 in 1991 due to an increasing influx of Central American refugees (Central Statistical Office 1990). The resulting numerical domination of Mestizos threatens to upset the delicate ethnic balance that Belize has maintained since colonial times.

The country has a foot in both the Caribbean and Latin America and is unique to both regions because of the obvious absence of serious ethnic conflict. While prestige and privilege related to ethnic groups affiliation prevails, acts of violence against any particular ethnic group are individual rather than institutional. Fredrik Barth (1969) has argued that where there is no competition for strategic resources, ethnic conflicts are minimal. This would seem to hold true in Belize where spatial arrangements create ethnic niches. There are six districts with their own ethnic integrity that allow groups like the Mestizo, Maya, Garinagu (Garifuna) and Creole a certain degree of linguistic and cultural autonomy in those regions of the country where they dominate. Other groups present in the country, whose influence is less evident, are Mennonites, East Indians, Syrians, Lebanese, Chinese, and ex-patriate Americans, Canadians and Britains. Despite such heterogeneity, all Belizeans participate in a national culture that has been largely shaped by a melange of African and British cultural traits in contrast to the rest of the Central American region with its obvious Spanish linguistic and cultural core (Stone 1994).

Interestingly, these ethnic group affiliations seem to have had very little impact on how women's groups organize. This is largely because grassroots organizations tend to mobilize along the prevailing ethnic composition of their region, local communities or neighborhoods. On the other hand, membership in non-governmental organizations (NGOs), which are primarily funded by external foreign agencies, extend their memberships across ethnic boundaries, often bringing together town and village women for workshops and activities. Under this national aegis, inter-cultural collaboration is encouraged. Whether NGOs have been successful or not is a question beyond the scope of this chapter, but one that needs further analysis. Despite language and cultural differences among Belizean women, they are bound together by their limited access to economic, educational and political resources, lending to their experiences a high degree of commonalty.

The Situation of Women In Belize

As is true globally, women in Belize comprise one-half of the population and most of them recognize that they occupy a marginal and devalued position in their society.[3] Studies by Kerns (1983), Stavrakis and Marshall (1980) and others (Development 1984; Mehra and Buvinic 1989; Ministry of Labor and Social Services 1988; UNICEF 1991) on Belize show that women's position is tenuous at best. As a social group, women are impeded by their lack of financial autonomy, making them economically dependent upon men, a situation discussed briefly below. The predicament of women in Belize can best be characterized as one marked by under employment, low wages, limited access to job training, and limited access to necessary resources that would enable them to create viable economic alternatives.

The Political Economy of Sex

A crucial dimension of some women's lives in Belize is the prevalence of domestic violence in the form of physical and emotional abuse and the perpetuation of what I call an "economic-sexual" cycle (cf. McClaurin 1995 and McClaurin 1993). One Belizean woman, Mary, describes the characteristics of this cycle:

...More often than not when a woman, a young teenager gets pregnant she drops out of school. She's dependent on her family. The male may stay in school, so the impact, [the] economic impact hits the female more because she is the one left with the children, and she is the one not getting the training and the additional skills in order to improve her situation; so she finds herself doing mainly domestic tasks in homes.

Belize's inability to provide adequate employment and livable wages, along with unwritten school policies that penalize pregnant girls so that they lose any opportunity to acquire skills and training all feed into and create a set of social practices that perpetuate and maintain women's subordinate status in the society.

Women in Belize tend to articulate their concerns in economic and survival terms directly related to their social roles and the obligations they incur as mothers and wives, or under the aegis of what Sylvia Walby calls "gender politics" (1986:3). They do not, in contrast to their American and European counterparts, describe their situation in our feminist terms of equality and equity, though there is no doubt in my mind such matters are at the source of their discontent. Belizean women's attitude and language are consistent with what Pat Ellis sees as characteristic of women in the Caribbean. She says:

...Many Caribbean women perceive themselves and their status more in terms of education and work opportunities and the effects of adverse social and economic conditions than in terms of inequality (Ellis 1986:1).

It is women's adverse condition as a social and politically marginalized group that highlights their lack of control over the strategic resources and political capital needed to alter their situation. Nor can they depend upon traditional political parties, whose male-centered agendas fail to respond to women's needs (Palacio 1990).[4] Moreover, often national women's organizations are preoccupied with the larger picture of long-range development planning. As a result, they sometimes fail to create programs that have an immediate effect on women's everyday lives and in those areas where women need them (Alvarez 1990). It is not surprising then that some women organize or become members of these women-centered grassroots organizations to address the practical matters of daily life, which are also matters of their very survival.

A Tale of One Local Women's Group

This activism is more discernible in local women's groups, which have been fashioned into instruments of women's agency and within which they are able to operate without the constraints imposed by political parties or those imposed by external foreign funding agencies. Where such local (grassroots) groups are most effective is in their impact on the behaviors and attitudes of the communities where members live. I present one women's group as a case study to assess its impact on both the community and individual members' lives as well as its effect on policies and processes at the national level that determine women's position and status in Belizean society.

The Orange Walk Community Group

Orange Walk is one of the fastest growing towns located in the north of Belize. Culturally and linguistically it is homogeneous, with Spanish-speaking Mestizos comprising well over half of the town's population, which stood at 11,014 in 1991.

The Orange Walk Community Group (OWCG) lists its membership at thirty women, but has a working core of ten women.[5] In addition, some of the women have persuaded their husbands to participate, although the organization is still a women-centered group. The group meets on a fairly regular basis in the bottom of Maria Rodriguez' home. It is these features that Rodriguez recognizes as essential to the "success" of her group:

> ...You have to have a core to be able to function . . . [My] house is very central to members. This is a secret to groups. You have to have a central location to meet, and have to know each other.

Consistent with Caldeira's (1990) theory, Rodriguez says she formed the group in 1985 initially to "socialize." She was able to bring women together primarily because of the stable character of her community. In answer to my question about why the group has persisted for almost seven years, she responded:

> This community is stable. Change is minimum. People own their own homes. . . .All our members are in the neighborhood. The group has expanded a bit, but this has worked perfectly. It is perfect for getting information out.

Since its inception, the group has broadened beyond its initial goal of socializing, which entailed planning trips to different parts of Belize for members and their friends and relatives and putting on a cultural show for the community.

Now, according to Rodriguez, the group's central aim is to develop women's leadership skills and community awareness. She is careful to distinguish her group and their objectives from the many women's groups throughout most of Belize. She says:

> My group has never been to teach [women] arts and crafts. Our goal was to become community-minded. Women can do arts and crafts if they want. Our goal is to educate women to become leaders in the community, give them basic training; nothing to frighten anyone [meaning men]. . . .We educated women in speech training, encouraged them to get out of their shells, that they are leaders, that they have power.

Here Rodriguez touches upon a crucial characteristic of a large number of women's groups in Belize. Many tend to emphasize traditional domestic skills such as sewing, cooking, and child-rearing as the primary aim of skill development. In doing so, they lock women into employment opportunities, such as domestic work, waitressing, or store clerk, that are historically undervalued, underpaid, and limited in their opportunity for future job mobility. This is one of the contradictions of designing development projects based on what women already know. Because women are often performing these tasks as part of their responsibilities in social reproduction, such projects do not distract them away from their daily chores and, thus, are the least disruptive to their lives. However, those activities that use homemaking skills may also be considered a form of subterfuge, under the guise of which women are able to escape the confines of their homes with the least amount of repercussion or reprisals.

"Success" for a women's group must be internally defined. In this instance, Mrs. Rodriguez uses fairly traditional criteria. She interprets the group's persistence, the regularity of meetings, and the relevance of their activities to the needs of the community as indicators of their success. But she also incorporates some of the standards of the new politics in making her assessment. In her mind, the group is successful because her members are more involved in other organizations as leaders, and some have even become more active in traditional party politics and the community's Village Council, though the OWCG intentionally divorces itself from any political party affiliation. Rodriguez sees the main agenda for the group as one of creating leaders -- real *women* leaders. She says:

> . . . Most women's groups are these that do things with their hands, but this group isn't. Our women have become leaders in other women's groups. They were trained that they are leaders.

In this respect, OWCG has successfully negotiated the difficult boundaries between women's groups and local political processes. Her members train themselves in how to make their issues the concern of the larger community. Mrs. Rodriguez might argue that because they have selected issues that affect all members of the community, they are able to be heard. In doing so they diminish the boundaries between the social spheres of the household, which women dominate, and the public, which men are thought to dominate (cf. Rosaldo 1974).

Beyond this successful broadening of the group's concern into community concerns, one other indicator of a group's success is the degree to which it influences individual members' lives. Marta, a long-term member of OWCG talks about how she has personally gained from her participation:

> I have changed; I gained more friends and can talk more freely. It is nice to be among people and see what you have in common. I've learned to share and cooperate. . . .[I have] worked as secretary and treasurer in the group [and I like] to "put up" [save] money. When I say I will do things I will do them. [In my] other women's group, The Homemakers, [I have] been president and treasurer. [My] skills in [OWCG] helped [me] with The Homemakers. . . . In [OWCG] we try to understanding each other's problems. I like . . . [OWCG] more [than The Homemakers] because we help others -- I like that. The money we make is not for us but for others.

The history of OWCG and Marta's personal testimony both seem to validate Caldeira's thesis that women's groups facilitate change in interpersonal relations, within individuals, and in gender roles. This group has also challenged the culture of gender in Belize by inviting men to participate alongside of them. In doing so, they seek to alter the typical male attitudes and behaviors that are automatically suspicious of and hostile toward women's groups and those activities where women come together.

Rodriguez displays a specific strategy to break through this attitude. She says that by having couples socialize with each other, the group has managed to diffuse the typical male attitude of suspicion that surrounds women who do not stay at home in isolation. The result is a bond of common interests between the couples (husbands and wives) who often find themselves in opposition to each other in other aspects of their lives. In the context of these groups, men and women now work toward common goals that benefit their community.

In order to understand the group's impact in the community, I asked: "Do you think your group has changed what people think about women?" Rodriguez responded:

> Definitely! You used to have problems where husband and wives never go anywhere together. Now they go as couples. The macho thing is not as strong. [We] have had problems when women talk about meetings with men in it, but we have managed to overcome that. . . . Through joking [in the meetings] women have their own way of getting across [their point] and they have straightened some lives. [Also] meeting with other couples and seeing how they live, and [we] have learned for women to talk to men and know nothing going on. People can see that now.

The group's activities center around issues that relate to women's everyday lives and that enhance the collective of the community. Not all women's groups in Belize are so successful. Many are short-lived, emerging out of a single issue and disappearing when that issue has been resolved.

One of the most crucial dimensions of OWCG is its emphasis on self-reliance. The group insists on fiscal autonomy and has not sought funding from Belize's national women's organizations. In fact, the OWCG is vocal in its criticism of those larger organizations who they perceive as spendthrift. The group does not totally reject financial assistance, but they are eager to avoid relying on outside "handouts" to solve the community's needs.

The group is adamant in its rejection of the dependency syndrome for itself. Therefore, even when they get external assistance, as was the case in a garden project funded by a Canadian organization, the group insists that those who participate in this activity also make a contribution, no matter how small. Thus, people had to pay a few dollars for the soil and seeds they received as part of the garden project, a feature Rodriguez firmly believes fosters self-respect and nurtures independence.

The Semiotics of Women's Groups

The above case study illustrates both the functional and symbolic significance of women's groups. Functionally, these groups form a structural base from which women are able to mount specific strategies (i.e. practical solutions) to address some of the problems they face in their daily lives. The result is the emergence of what Caldeira defines as "new forms of politics."

Not only do women's groups enable women to gain "access to institutionalized political decision-making channels or . . . [access to] . . . policy reform . . . " legislation (Bush 1992), but they also function to strengthen existing social bonds among the members (generally based upon friendship, kinship, ethnicity, or community interests), create supportive environments, and provide the needed resources for women to develop economic and leadership skills that sometimes motivate them to change in such a way that they challenge the behavior, attitudes, and social policies that structure gender relations in their home, their communities and in the larger society. Further, Caldeira asserts that these "new forms of socializing" are in fact the most significant aspect of women's groups. Beyond their obvious functional importance, women's groups in Belize also have a symbolic dimension. They are often the necessary catalysts that some women require to gain an understanding of their position as victims or marginalized citizens in their society.

This awareness develops primarily as an outgrowth of the social support women receive. As members of a group with a coherent vision, women come to view their personal circumstances as part of a collective experience structured by gender, and work together to develop new strategies for coping. A major objective of such groups is to coerce women in a positive way to challenge how they are perceived by their male partners, to question the roles prescribed by the community and to learn to value their contributions to their households. In effect, women are encouraged and nurtured to become active agents in their own lives.

At a more personal level, the meaning or "value" of women's groups can ultimately be measured by the benefits women say they derive from their participation, rather than by some external criteria. For example, one woman explained: ". . . [I feel] that women are no longer in the background; that I am not the only one with a particular problem." Another stated: "I feel very confident that what we're doing is not in vain; [we] help ourselves, children and the community. I learn a lot about people, their behavior -- that teach me and I learn from that." All the women I interviewed who participated in women's groups generally agreed that ". . . [It] helps you have a strong self-esteem to [talk] to women like yourself. When you talk to other women you get courage to solve your problem." These comments affirm the far-reaching impact of women's groups on individual lives. It is an impact that transcends the sometimes temporary organizational existence of such groups.

Conclusion: With An Eye Toward Tomorrow

Women's groups in Belize cannot be dismissed, as some Belizean men would have us do, as the result of spontaneous outbursts of emotions by frustrated women. Rather, these groups must be viewed, and valued, as local responses to what women feel are intolerable conditions of social and economic inequities. Moreover, their responses are not just "accidental," (cf. Brenner 1991; Hyatt 1991) but emanate from Caribbean and Latin American traditions of women's groups strongly rooted in volunteer service and church organizations, nationalist politics, and in the last two decades, the globalization of women's issues (cf. Pietila 1990 and Edgell 1991).

While the voices and experiences of Belizean women presented thus far affirm the efficacy of women's groups at the individual level, their impact at the state and national level are less clearly observable. Further, Diane Bush warns that there is a danger in interpreting success as only the "enactment of state reforms or [the] institutionalization of movement organizations" (Bush 1992:603). Rather, as I pointed out earlier, the value of a group is best determined by the degree to which it supports women in their efforts to change their personal lives, as in the case of Marta, or encourages them to challenge institutional arrangements like marriage, motherhood, and their shared fragile economic position, features in Belizean society that perpetuate and maintain its problematic and oppressive culture of gender. Ideally then, the value of grassroots women's groups like the OWCG are to be found not in their ability to get formal legislation passed or in their ongoing organizational structures but rather in their development of women's self-esteem, leadership skills, and their existence as safe forums within which women may freely verbalize their concerns.

However, the ability of women's groups to impact public policy cannot be minimized. Where it does occur, it has the possibility of improving women's economic situation and their overall quality of life. This is especially evident in those arenas in Belize where women have established a voice in the public sphere. For example, in the area of child support, women's demands for men to be accountable for the children they have fathered outside of the legal arrangement of marriage put enough pressure on the state to lead to changes in national laws on child support and the creation of a Family Court system and procedure. Collectively women, via such organizations like Women Against Violence (WAV), have waged a systematic campaign against the cultural legitimatization of domestic violence as a private matter and an acceptable dimension of heterosexual relationships. As a result of their efforts, the Domestic Violence Bill was passed by the Belizean Government in March 1993. Its implementation marked a new phase for Belizean women's rights and certainly confirms the ability of women's groups to move beyond the community boundaries of their organizational goals and reach the ears of the state.[6] Such examples clearly prove that women's agency at the personal and community level, spearheaded by women's groups, have broader social implications, and can challenge, modify, and even alter the culture of gender operating in their society.[7]

At the onset of this chapter, I proposed that women's groups had multiple significance at the levels of the individual, the community, and the larger society in the arena of gender politics. While many of the groups I encountered in Belize lacked the formal organizational structures which are often a necessary criterion for the acquisition of foreign funding, they have nonetheless amassed indigenous (community) resources to build a new base of support for women. Whether the structures are informal or formal, whether the activities are practical or ideological, women's groups have assisted women in their quest for female autonomy, and have been the major catalyst behind changes in the rules of the culture of gender in the homes, communities and nation -- the major arenas of Belizean women's lives. Indeed, women in Belize "de get upstart now," and none too soon.

Notes

1. This essay is derived from a chapter of the same title in *Women in Belize*, copyright 1995/1996 and is reprinted by permission of Rutgers University Press. An earlier version of this essay also appears in *Women and the Culture of Gender in Belize, Central America*, Ph.D. Dissertation, 1993, University of Massachusetts at Amherst. The main ideas of this chapter were tested out in the following papers: "Women's Spaces, Women's Places, Women's Groups in Belize, Central America," delivered at the Annual Meeting of the American Anthropological Association, December 5, 1992 and "Toward the 'New Politics': Women's Groups in Belize, Central America, delivered at the Fifth International Interdisciplinary Congress on Women, Universidad de Costa Rica, San Jose, February, 1993. In the course of revising this I appreciate the suggestions made by Dr. Nina Glick Schiller, who made insightful comments on one of the earlier versions of this work. However, I take full responsibility for the final results presented here.

2. To "get upstart" is a Creole phrase used to refer to children who attempt to act like an adult. When applied to women, the phrase is meant to admonish them for acting assertive, independent and beyond the boundaries of what men believe to be their proper role -- submissive and subordinate.

3. Reports by UNICEF-Belize (1992-1996) and the International Center for Research on Women on the situation of women in Belize, reach similar conclusions. They observe that: 1) both men and women have high literacy levels, however, men have greater access to higher education than women; 2) women between the ages of 15 and 44 are generally involved in some form of conjugal relations -- either in consensual unions or married and "79 percent of women between the ages of 15 and 19 years do not have permanent partners" (Mehra and Buvinic 1989, p. i); and 3) the fertility rate of 5.2 among Belizean women is three times higher than other Caribbean nations and higher than some of the surrounding Central American countries (UNICEF 1991, p. 1).

4. For a history of the development of Belize's political party, see Shoman, Assad. (1987). *Party Politics in Belize*. Belize: Cubola Productions. His political genealogy is, unfortunately, primarily androcentric and ignores the contributions women have made to Belize's nationalist and independence political movements.

5. While the location is real, the names of groups and members are pseudonyms.

6. The efficacy of the implementation of the Domestic Violence bill must be monitored over the next few years to see if it can deliver on its inherent promise of eradicating the institutionalization of domestic violence as a legitimate practice in Belize's culture of gender. On the horizon is a bill against Sexual Assault.

7. Another example of collective agency is the Women's Worker's Union formed in May 1992 to protest wage and work conditions in the garment industry. Their efforts publicized the problem of minimum wage levels which were increased in fall 1992 for manual (male) workers. This initial wage increase, however, excluded domestic workers and shop assistants, occupations usually held by women, until the Belize Organization of Women and Development (BOWAND) waged a public campaign to rectify the matter. In 1993, after BOWAND's efforts, the government increased the minimum wage level for these latter occupations. (For more information, see Bowand's *Minimum Wage Campaign* , Presentation for SPEAR's Studies on Belize, October 21, 1993.)

References

Alvarez, Sonia
1990 *Engendering Democracy in Brazil*. Princeton University Press.

Barth, Fredrik, ed.
  1969 *Ethnic Groups and Boundaries: The Social Organization of Culture Difference*. Boston: Little,
  Brown and Company.

Bolles, A. Lynn
  1991 Doing It For Themselves: Women's Research and Action in the Commonwealth Caribbean. In
  *Perspectives and Resources: Integrating Latin American and Carribean Women into the Curriculum
  and Research*. Edna Acosta-Belén and Christine E. Bose, eds. Albany: Center for Latin America and
  the Carribean (CELAC) and Institute for Research on Women (IROW).

Brenner, Johanna, and Barbara Laslett
  1991 Gender, Social Reproduction, and Women's Self-Organization: Considering the U.S. Welfare State.
  Gender & Society 5(3):311-333.

Bush, Diana Mitsch
  1992 Women's Movements and State Policy Reform Aimed At Domestic Violence Against Women: A
  Comparison of the Consequences of Movement Mobilization in the U.S. and India. *Gender & Society*
  6(4): 587-608.

Caldeira, Teresa Pires de Rio
  1990 Women, Daily Life and Politics. In *Women and Social Change in Latin America*. E. Jelin, ed.
  London: Zed Books.

Central Statistical Office
  1990 *Belize Population at 1980* (Census) *and at 1990* (Quick Count Exercise). Belmopan: Government
  of Belize.

Edgell, Zee
  1991 *In Times Like These*. London: Heinneman.

Ellis, Pat, ed.
  1986 *Women of the Caribbean*. London: Zed Books, Inc.

Hyatt, Susan
  1991 Accidental Activists: Women and Politics on a Council Estate. Annual Meeting of the American
  Anthropological Association, Chicago, Illinois.

Jelin, Elizabeth, ed.
  1990 *Women and Social Change in Latin America*. London: Zed Books, Inc.

Kaplan, Temma.
  1982 Female Consciousness and Collective Action: The Case of Barcelona. *Signs* 7(3):545-566.

Kerns, Virginia
  1983 *Women and the Ancestors: Black Carib Kinship and Ritual*. Urbana: University of Illinois Press.

McClaurin, Irma
    1993 Women and the Culture of Gender in Belize, Central America. Ph.D Dissertation, University of
    Massachusetts, Amherst.
    1995/1996 *Women Setting Limits: The Power of Gender in Belize*. New Brunswick: Rutgers University
    Press.

Mehra, Rekha and Mayra Buvinic
    1989 *Women and Development in Belize*. International Center for Research on Women.

Ministry of Economic Development
    1984 *Belize Labour Force Survey*. Central Statistical Office.

Ministry of Labour and Social Services
    1988 *Policy Statement on Women Belize*. Government of Belize.

Mohammed, Patricia
    1991 Reflections on the Women's Movement in Trinidad: Calypsos, Changes and Sexual Violence.
    Feminist Review No. 38 (Summer):33-47.

Palacio, Myrtle
    1990 Elections in Belize City -- Who is Participating? A Critique of Our Voting System. SPEAR's Fourth
    Annual Studies on Belize.

Pietila, Hilkka and Jeanne Vickers
    1990 *Making Women Matter: the Role of the United Nations*. London: Zed Books.

Rosaldo, Michelle Zimbalist
    1974 Woman, Culture, and Society: A Theoretical Overview. In *Woman, Culture & Society*. Stanford:
    Stanford University Press.

Stavrakis, Olga and Marion Louise Marshall
    1980 Women, Agriculture and Development in the Maya Lowlands: Profit or Progress? *Belizean Studies*
    8(5): 20-28.

Stone, Michael Cutler
    1994 Caribbean Nation, Central American State: Ethnicity, Race, and National Formation in Belize,
    1798-1990. Ph.D Dissertation, University of Texas at Austin.

UNICEF
    1991 *Children First: A Situational Analysis of Women and Children*. UNICEF Belize.

Walby, Sylvia
    1986 Gender, Class and Stratification. In *Gender and Stratification*. Rosemary Crompton and Michael
    Mann, eds. Cambridge: Polity Press.

Hear You Tell It:

Teaching Anthropology in Prison[1]

David Glyn Nixon
National Park Service
Annapolis, Maryland

David Glyn Nixon took his first anthropology class in high school and decided on the spot to adopt anthropology as his life's work. He completed his undergraduate degree at the University of Maryland in cultural anthropology, and went on to graduate school at the University of Massachusetts, Amherst where he met Sylvia Forman. After completing his Masters fieldwork in the Isle of Man, he became her student. Under her guidance, he developed his interests in North American peoples, agriculture, and along with Oriol Pi-Sunyer, further developed his interests in political anthropology. Sylvia also introduced him to education, and as her teaching assistant, he learned the fundamentals of effective teaching. Sylvia helped direct his dissertation research in Massachusetts politics, and although she did not live to see it completed, her influence is plainly there. Nixon is currently employed with the National Park Service as a cultural anthropologist.

Introduction

I think that the core contribution of anthropologists in our world is to teach in one way or another. Whether we conduct field research, engage in community development, participate in activism and advocacy, or lead classes in college, we have always placed learning about others and communicating that knowledge at the center of our profession. In this chapter, I illustrate my experiences teaching in unusual and difficult circumstances in prisons. I started teaching college-level courses in prison in 1992. What began as a brief summer job pursued out of curiosity, quickly developed into a major area of professional interest. I show the strategies I followed in order to manage dangerous field circumstances (cf. Sluka 1990), but more importantly I wish to demonstrate lessons about education I gained through my experiences. Being teacher of prisoners led me to explore the dynamics between education and experience, to develop my skills in presenting education as a tool claimed by the user. Finally, I wish to point out the roles anthropologists can play in prison education as well as research in corrections.

"Nowhere": Now-Here or No-Where?

Prisoners secretly write and publish inspirational literature in order to instruct each other about how to survive their incarceration. Correction administrators and officers consider such writings to be contraband, to be confiscated whenever they are discovered. One example of such inspirational literature is the story of _Nowhere_ (Anonymous n.d.).

In this allegorical tale, a man by the name of John suddenly finds himself in a dismal, smelly, muddy wasteland called Nowhere. The morass is divided into quarters and bounded all around by a towering wall. Overhead an inaccessible bridge spans the sky from horizon to horizon.

John immediately loses his name and is called New Guy. He is told, "here, what you become is what you are, and what you are is what [you're] called" (Anonymous n.d.:1). New Guy spends years wading around, encountering various Nowhere inhabitants who require him to conform to their expectations. New Guy spends time with "Wall Runners," "Throwers," "Handstanders," "Teacher/Guardians," and "Stargazers" but rejects each in turn. They either attempt to victimize New Guy, or they entice him to victimize others. Half way through the tale, New Guy has yet to find his place in Nowhere.

The tale of _Nowhere_ is richly interwoven with complex images and metaphors, and we, living on the other side of the wall, can scarcely grasp all the shades of meaning encapsulated within each symbol. But the central point of _Nowhere_ concerns recovery of identity. New Guy, like every one entering the penal system, loses his identity, for it is his very essence which has been tried, convicted, and sentenced. Each prisoner has been judged guilty of a specific criminal action, but as Foucault points out, "...judgement is...passed on the passions, instincts, anomalies, infirmities, maladjustments, [and] effects of environment or heredity...." (1979:17; see also Gould 1981:122-145). Individual behavior which has been criminalized is the focus of legal conviction, but the qualities of the person are also criminalized, and subject to corrections systems. Convictions impose a new identity, and prison administrators and guards affirm the prisoner's defective identity on a daily basis (c.f. Jones 1992).

Jails are not only designed to deny individual freedom because of past transgressions, but are also arenas for treating the prisoner for present disorders. One branch of treatment programs is that of education and training. Educational programs are available for a small minority of prisoners, and through them the body of the prisoner is subjected to close scrutiny by educators, trainers, and other pedagogical specialists.

According to official penal literature, treatment reflects the authorities' commitment to reintegrate the prisoner into society. Rehabilitation is weighted equally with the custodial, security, and control functions of correction institutions. In reality, attention paid to prisoner education often falls far short of the ideal. Prison administrators assign education low priority in systems which are short of funds.

In addition, education programs are resented by guards, who tend to see them as undeserved gratuities. "I guess I should commit a murder, and then I'll get a free education," commented a guard, not for the first time. Guards could even disrupt my classes. On several occasions, a guard entered my classroom, yanked a student by the collar out of his seat, and marched him out the door. No explanation or apology was ever given. In another case, a guard got tired of keeping a building open for my class, so he entered my room and informed me that class was over. I had no one to whom I could appeal his decision.

Some prisoners who wish to become students have made highly personal ethical decisions to transform themselves. In one prisoners's words, they are trying to "better themselves." It is this ethical choice which informs their behavior within the classroom and shapes their approach to their own intellectual development. Choosing to become a student then is a method or expression of their new chosen identity. On the other hand, prison students are aware that education and educators can be tools used against them. Corrections treatment practices often rely on "confession" (as articulated by Foucault 1979) or "banker education" (as articulated by Freire 1970) through which prisoners learn to observe authority, hierarchy, and conformity, while still reinforcing stigmatic social labels which greatly affect prisoners' lives outside of penal institutions.

A Glimpse into the Classroom

The process of labeling and dominating people is hardly one-sided in prison, that is originating with the guards and terminating with inmates. Prisoners themselves create and maintain their own systems of social stratification, which adds to the teacher's challenge. Prisoners' social labeling operates along dimensions of sexuality, crime, age, gender, race, religion, conduct, and other social statuses. Prisoners strive to achieve respect or insignificance; either condition contributes to their survival. A prisoner who is respected by other prisoners can do time more easily. Failing that, a prisoner who is seen as inconsequential is less likely to be hassled. A disrespected prisoner, however, attracts abuse (Davidson 1983). The most respected inmates are professional killers serving life terms, while among the least respected are sex offenders. In addition, personal conduct within prison can greatly affect the degree of respect paid to prisoners by other inmates. Tough guys who confront authority gain respect, while those who steal or inform lose it (c.f., Earley 1993).

Here are a few examples from my notebooks on students' behavior while in class. These example serve to illustrate the complexity of prisoner realities and how they influence classroom behavior. I learned these peoples' stories over several months, and since I was not given any access to my students' court files, it made the task of teaching effectively that much harder.

Alan[2] was a police officer who had been caught dealing drugs. In prison, Alan became a predator of smaller and weaker men and had a reputation for coercing sexual favors from them. Because he was a cop and an open homosexual, he was despised by the other prisoners. Alan was also my teaching assistant, and in this position held considerable influence over the other students' ability to complete their course work.

Another student, Tina, had been convicted of conspiring to kill her husband and was serving a lengthy sentence. She was appealing for commutation on the grounds that she had acted in self-defense against her abusive husband who had intended to kill her first. As one of the few female prisoners in my classes, she had to be careful about her behavior with her classmates as well as with the prison guards; both parties might interpret any cordial gesture as a sexual invitation.

Sean was convicted of a sexual offense and occupied one of the lowest statuses in prison life. He gained respect by performing services that other prisoners could not do for themselves. Usually, Sean helped illiterate prisoners read and write letters. By making himself invaluable to some, he developed a small circle of protectors and allies. In the protected atmosphere of the classroom, Sean often tried to dominate the conversation in order to make his voice count among his peers.

Finally, Juan, a powerful man with an intense personality, was respected and feared by the other prisoners. Although his former role as a drug dealer was not especially meaningful in prisoner rankings, he had "faced down" or defeated enough opponents to mark him as an important man. An African-American with connections among Hispanic inmates, Juan maintained a strong influence over many others. His cooperation was essential in order for me to conduct any kind of class, for if he chose to dismiss me, then the others would follow his lead.

These were people who had killed, raped, stolen, and dealt drugs. These were also my students, and their realities from the prison yard crowded into the classroom, filling it with competing systems of social control and dominance. In order to teach I had to learn and account for their realities. The first thing I had to do was to reinvent the relationship between student and teacher in this environment.

The contrasts between student and professor are striking. For one thing, in order to qualify to teach inmates, one must have very little in common with them. That is, one's record has to be clean. The ideal prison educator is expected to set up a classroom where education is a one-way street. The student learns from the instructor and uses that imparted knowledge for self-reform. The professor, on the other hand, is not to learn anything from the students. For they, being criminals, are not supposed to have anything worth offering to the law-abiding instructor (except for playing their role as subjects in criminology studies). The challenge for the teacher in the face of enormous obstacles is to impart to prisoners tools for implementing their appropriate moral decisions affecting their own lives. In the classroom, the most noticeable obstacles are the students' sometimes cynical attitudes toward education as effective rehabilitation.

Some inmates state emphatically that prison is not a place where rehabilitation takes place. Their folk analysis is quite close to Michel Foucault's (1979, 1980) in that for them, prisons are loci for a number of fields of power relations based on class, gender, race, ethnicity, community, and other social identities. Prison is a place designed to break one's spirit and sometimes the body. As one of my students put it, "To work for a prison, one belongs to a tradition dedicated to protecting the public by abusing anyone under your charge; male, female, or anything in between." Hence, prisoners resent free people because they often perceive the public's attitude as being "we don't care what you do to them as long as you keep them off the streets." In our current political climate where politicians are willing to build more prisons but not expand rehabilitation programs at comparable rates, prisoners often feel that they are locked in a struggle with the public as well as with their jailers. It heightens the antagonism between prisoners and anyone from the outside proposing to teach them.

One of my students once told me,

> "Anyone who makes any attempt to help inmates must have a family member in prison, or have no self-worth themselves....Christian charity notwithstanding, there are very few who will enter a prison other than clergy, family, and those blasted, good-hearted liberals. Fact is, I'm not too sure if I can trust you myself. You look too Republican, yet...there might still be some hope for you, we'll see."

Given this mixture of hope and caution, students and teachers experience a tenuous relationship at first, each side suspecting the motives of the other. My second day of teaching illustrates my students' concerns. I taught cultural anthropology in several Massachusetts prisons. These ranged from men's minimum security prisons with occasional female prisoners bussed in from a nearby correctional institution, to men's medium security prisons. My courses were administered through the Prison Education Program, Division of Continuing Education at the University of Massachusetts at Amherst. At the appointed time, the guards unlocked the school building, and my students filed into the classroom. I was trying to get an antiquated VCR set up, when one of my students said:

"You know that reading you gave us?"

"Yeah," I replied.

"Well, that was some [frigging] hard reading, you know," he bellowed. The class leaned forward to see my reaction.

Someone hooted, "Hard words!"

"Damn hard words!" another chorused.

Now, I was shocked, as you might imagine. They had actually done the readings. In the immediate give and take which followed, it became apparent that everyone had done the readings three times. Everyone had come to class prepared as best they could. Balanced against their desire to master sophisticated reading was their fear that I had set the course up to put them down, to intentionally fail them and thus justify my superiority. In order to resolve the tension, I could not respond in the same currency of violence and brutality which characterizes prison life. I had to acknowledge the student's concern without validating the way he had acted. I encouraged him to articulate what precisely was giving him trouble, while reminding him that as a group we would explore the materials together.

I encourage personal expression and differing points of view in the classroom, but our diversity of feelings, insights, and perceptions have to be negotiated with the realities of prison life and the larger social context in which prisons are situated. Claiming a new identity requires asserting distinctiveness in some way. New identities strain against imposed ones. Take the example of the ex-police officer serving time for dealing drugs. He might make an excellent point in class discussion. To even acknowledge his comment places one at odds with established order. This is the dilemma any one teaching in prison faces. One is caught between the requirement to go along to get along, but at the same time needing to introduce problems, issues, and challenges. Unlike in traditional college campuses, in a prison classroom, a debate can lead to a knife fight, and the teacher must make careful choices in how any particular issue is explored.

I learned from my students the expression "hear you tell it" as a respectful way of entertaining a diversity of opinions and statements. "I hear you tell it," means that I agree with you, or alternately, that I acknowledge your opinion but I might have another way of looking at the topic. My students include members of the Nation of Islam, atheists, and fundamentalist Christians, most of whom find it very difficult to accept anthropological treatment of topics including evolutionary theory, human origins in Africa, and the social construction of race and gender. I bring these topics up by first making sure that we have made the classroom a safe, although not always comfortable, place where perspectives and voices can be expressed and shared. In my teaching, I invite students to hear anyone tell it, recasting prison discourse into a technique for building a community of learners, a community which includes both the teacher and the students. Since neither of us, the teacher nor the inmates, could effectively operate in each others' social setting, we had to create an environment where we could share our experiences, to develop different social relations.

I attempt to create alternative learning environments which allow prisoners to explore and internalize anthropological lessons on their own terms and for their own purposes. Regardless of the type of anthropological course I teach (e.g., cultural or physical anthropology), I endeavor to select course materials which allow discussion and call for decisions from students. For example, if I am teaching a course on physical anthropology, I have the students first read Stephen Jay Gould's book, *Mismeasure of Man*. The students are invariably enraged by the history of scientific racism and its legacy in current debates about the human condition (vis *The Bell Curve*, Herrnstein and Murray 1994). By introducing material which points out how evolutionary science has been used inappropriately in the past, we as a community of learners must decide how to examine and interpret the rest of the standard course materials concerning human evolution and biological diversity. If I am teaching a course in cultural anthropology, I have the students watch Akira Kurasawa's film, *Rashamon*. I ask questions about who killed whom, and the students take great delight in playing detective and trying to arrive at a definitive answer of what really happened in the film. Both materials activate critical judgement and more importantly allow inmate-students to use their own experiences as integral components of the class. Letting students voice their experiences and viewpoints allows them to evaluate standard introductory materials and to accept them and use them on their own terms. My job as part of a community of learners is to help them acquire the means to articulate some of their experiences in ways which invite growth in themselves and among their classmates.

Why Student-Inmates Take Courses

Student-inmates take classes for different reasons. All inmates agree that the worst effect in prison is the stress that boredom produces. Hence, many prisoners seek out programs of all kinds to find company and simply to do something different. Educational programs such as courses leading toward a General Education Diploma and college-level courses can offer prisoners an escape from the concerns of the prison and a chance to talk about things other than past exploits on the street. One of my students said, "if you're doing time, then use it to your advantage, use your time positive-like."

Not all prisoners are taking classes to relieve their boredom, however. Some of them have made an ethical choice to conduct their lives differently. Education for such students is the way to set their choices in operation. As one of them put it, "I take classes to better myself." One of my students said,

> "If you're doing time, then use it to your advantage, use your time positive-like. Go to the weight room and get yourself in shape, take some classes and learn something. Become a better person. Most of these [friggers] in here don't do that. They just talk all day about what they used to do, and they rot in here. They're not going to be better people when they get out."

Denied active participation in the economy and society, prisoners often feel that the only permitted work they can contribute is to work on themselves.

Conclusion

Michel Foucault depicted the modern penal system as a place where delinquency is produced partly through the social labeling of infirmities. The history of modern prison rehabilitation he contends, is not a history where inmates were provided with instruction but that through instruction they were taught nothing. The tradition of rehabilitation in this country was started by the Quakers and quickly became perverted to manufacture not functional citizens from criminals but more criminals. The advantage of maintaining such a system was that criminality was used (intentionally or not) to dilute the collective potential of workers, to divide them against themselves and to make them fearful.

As a counter argument, there are those who, while recognizing the enormous weight of power exercised against inmates and the preponderance of ill will toward rehabilitation, maintain that rehabilitation is not entirely a fool's errand. For some, prisoner rehabilitation, no matter how well-intentioned and effectively carried out, cannot achieve its potential without fundamental reordering of the entire penal system and the cultural contexts by which crime is perceived and acted upon (e.g., Jones 1993). For others, however, education if conducted in certain ways, can be a means for achieving the ethical goals some prisoners choose to accomplish (e.g., Boudin 1993). The teacher does not transform the individual, since that is not true education, but creates the experience and provides the tools whereby the students work to solve problems for themselves.

Anthropology has been well-received by my students. First, the topic matter is always interesting, and the students generally enjoy any attempt I make to bring the outside world to them. But beyond the immediate exposure to other ways of life, anthropology also provides an avenue towards grasping different patterns of meaning and perceiving. In particular, cultural construction of knowledge and identity allows students to explore and express their ethical choices.

Of course, a single class in anthropology is not going to save these people. It would be naive in the extreme to take this position. However, the teacher does have a role to play in developing and strengthening students' commitment to their ethical decisions. Anthropologists are well-suited to the task because as the students start shaping and defining their new identities, the class discourse becomes more multivocal and contextualized in personal experience.

Returning to the tale of _Nowhere_, in the end New Guy encounters the last inhabitant of his nightmarish landscape, an Old Person. The Old Person asks New Guy his name, and it takes a few moments to recall that he is John. In affirming his name and identity, John then transcends Nowhere, but not without some practical effort. John achieves the bridge over Nowhere's morass and finds that it is in actuality a rainbow. The tale ends there, but like any good story, the end is only a fresh beginning. John's efforts are directed toward uncertain conclusions.

Although many of my inmate-students are still serving time, Tina (the woman serving time for conspiring to have her abusive husband killed) was eventually able to get parole and early release. She started lecturing on college campuses around Massachusetts about domestic violence against women. She visited my university recently, and my conventional students and I attended her presentation. She was articulate and clearly reached her audience, and we spent a very productive evening in an engaging dialogue about issues of gender politics, violence, family, and kinship. Tina was able to relate her experiences to my free students who were then able to examine their own experiences at home, school, and work.

When I first entered prison classrooms, I was already a seasoned teacher, but in prison I learned a lot about teaching. Core concepts I developed in traditional classrooms were often inappropriate in prison classrooms. For example, the concepts of "the problem student" and how to deal with misbehavior were completely inapplicable in such a setting. I had to rethink many of my standard pedagogical techniques and approaches, and when I returned to traditional college classrooms, I brought many new lessons and ideas to my educational approach. In many ways, my experience in prison improved my teaching in general.

Leading classes in prison can be a teacher's dream come true, if you can stand it. All the students come prepared and willing to learn, and hence discussions can be a refreshing change from other experiences I have had in classrooms. But the potential for helping students make major changes in their lives can also be rewarding. If a student chooses to reform his/her live, then the teacher helps to direct and channel that student through enormous distances of changing identity.

Finally, I have made the case that anthropologists have a lot to contribute through prison education. Corrections facilities are arguably one of the largest and fastest growing businesses in the United States. Anthropologists should find them rich sites for study and employment, but also important in the direct and residual effects corrections have in the lives of people all over the country. As anthropologists are increasingly drawn to work and research among North American peoples, prisons and other systems of incarceration deserve greater scrutiny and involvement.

Notes

1. I gratefully acknowledge the contributions of those who have helped me compose this chapter. First, I could not have survived long in prison without the support of corrections officers and inmates. My classes proceeded only with their cooperation. My special thanks go to Laurence and Anne Mitchell for technical support, Helen Wüscher for comments, and Dr. Dena Shenk for her patience and editorial advice. All errors, however, are mine.

2. The names have been changed for the usual reasons.

References

Anonymous
    n.d. *Nowhere*. manuscript available in personal files.

Boudin, Kathy
    1993 Participatory Literacy Education Behind Bars: AIDS Opens the Door. *Harvard Educational Review* 63(2):207-232.

Davidson, R. Theodore
    1983 *Chicano Prisoners: The Key to San Quentin*. Prospect Heights, IL: Waveland Press.

Earley, P.
    1993 *Hot House*. New York: Bantam Books.

Foucault, Michel
    1979 *Discipline and Punish: The Birth of the Prison*. Alan Sheridan, trans., New York: Vintage Books.
    1980 *Power-Knowledge: Selected Interviews and Other Writings, 1972-1977*. New York: Pantheon.

Freire, Paulo
    1970 *Pedagogy of the Oppressed*. Myra B. Ramos, trans., New York: Continuum Press.

Gould, Jay
    1981 *The Mismeasure of Man*. New York: W.W. Norton.

Hernnstein, R. and Charles Murray
  1994 *The Bell Curve: Intelligence and Class Structure in American Life*. New York: The Free Press.

Jones, Ray
  1993 Prison Higher Education in Massachusetts: An Exploratory Cultural Analysis. Unpublished Ph.D.
    Dissertation, Department of Education, University of Massachusetts, Amherst.

Sluka, Jeffery A.
  1990 Participant Observation in Violent Social Contexts. *Human Organization* 49(2):114-126.

Poverty and Difference:

Ethnographic Representations of

"Race" and the Crisis

of "the Social"[1]

Susan Brin Hyatt
University of Massachusetts, Amherst

Susan Brin Hyatt began work toward her Ph.D. at the University of Massachusetts in 1989. She had completed her M.A. in anthropology at the University of Michigan in 1980. During the intervening years, she was employed as a community organizer based in the multiethnic parishes of southwest Chicago, where she worked alongside neighborhood residents to tackle such issues as disinvestment, affordable housing and school reform. Convinced that grassroots activism was a phenomenon deserving of greater attention from cultural anthropologists, and that its impact on the lives of poor and working-class women was particularly significant, she entered the department of anthropology at UMass hoping to carry out such a study. That dissertation, entitled, "From Government Of the Poor to Government By the Poor: Women and Community in Northern England," has been very much influenced by Sylvia Forman's own commitment to using anthropology in the service of social justice, and is now reaching its completion.

Introduction: White Ethnographers, Black Subjects [2]

"Celebrating differences" has become one of the slogans of the so-called "new multiculturalism." Despite the luster of egalitarianism which envelops this expression, its invention has taken place within a force-field of power relations, a fact which its very sound serves to obscure rather than to illuminate (see also Gupta and Ferguson 1992). As such, although it purports to serve as a means of culture-critique for students, its ostensible neutrality actually upholds the hegemony of the unmarked norm, rather than acting to challenge it.

This notion was made abundantly clear to me in a writing class I taught in 1991. An earnest and well-intentioned young man, who was white and presented himself as heterosexual, explained seriously to a racially mixed class that he was writing an essay on his diverse range of friendships, a fact of which he was very proud.

"I have friends who are Black and gay and handicapped," he said, "And, I'm writing about how I accept them even though they are different."

In a sudden flash of insight, I asked him why he didn't turn around that idea in his writing; that is, why didn't he write about how his friends accepted him even though he was different from them?

"But, he objected, looking genuinely perplexed, "*I'm* <u>not</u> the one who's different -- *they* are.

This exchange prompted me to consider the ways in which we all absorb an understanding of hierarchies of "difference" and how we, as teachers, may unwittingly continue to reproduce those hierarchies in our classrooms. As an anthropologist and prospective teacher of anthropology, I recognized that the notion of difference, as it is deployed through ethnography, complicates our attempts to show students that such "differences," be they defined along the lines of race, gender, ethnicity, class, sexuality or a host of other possible means of discriminating among people, are "made up" categories, generated out of inherent and too-often unspoken assumptions about the embeddedness of inequality.

I began to think back on my own undergraduate training and to examine what I "knew" about one community which had been identified as "different": that of impoverished urban Blacks. As a white American born at the dawn of the Civil Rights movement, I, like many of my peers, grew up inspired by that struggle and by its protagonists (though, it must be noted, with very little experience of personal contact with the Black community). I was an avid consumer of Black popular culture, including the music of Motown and the "Blaxploitation" films of the 1970's.

When I entered college in 1972, I enrolled in a course in urban anthropology, and read numerous ethnographies about Black "ghetto life." At that time, when I imagined Black people in the abstract, my first thoughts were, on one hand, of heroic figures like Rosa Parks and Martin Luther King, of epic marches and moving speeches delivered in front of the Lincoln Memorial -- and, on the other hand of the riots which were decimating the inner cities. Whatever I thought about Black Americans, whether I valorized the heroism of civil rights activists, or despaired of the violence and destructiveness of the rioters, in either case, all of my own images differed markedly from those Black men and women whom I encountered in the pages of the "ghetto ethnographies." This was a contradiction I never thought to examine. Nor did I ever question the fact that the most widely-read texts of that time were those studies of Black communities which had been conducted and written by whites.[3]

In that body of "ghetto ethnographies," produced in the late 1960's and early 1970's, Black men hovered on the margins of society, relegated to the terrain of streetcorners, where they were completely alienated from the "normalized" worlds of family and work. Black women, on the other hand, were matriarchs, always firmly situated within the home, where they offered succor to members of their complex and extended families.

My project in this chapter is *not* one of rehabilitation which would seek to counter such characterizations of Blacks and of poor Blacks in particular by combing the ethnographic literature of that period for alternative portrayals (cf. Terry 1991:36); it is, rather, to examine these ethnographies as a discursive field within which the poor, and the Black poor in particular, were constructed as particular kinds of subjects under the scrutiny of the white anthropological gaze, and to understand how those constructions reflected and upheld the hegemony of that domain which Foucault (1980:117, 1984:88) and others have named "the social." In this chapter, I attempt to deconstruct some of the assumptions which guided white ethnographers in their studies of the Black poor, and to explore some of the reasons why such representations have endured and, indeed, flourished, into the present moment.[4]

Poverty and the Rise of "the Social"

During the nineteenth century, there was a decisive shift in the dominant view of people and their environments. Where prior conceptualizations had explained differences of position, role, and general well-being among individuals as a function of a divine order and as a consequence of their own moral worth and personal conduct (Horn 1988:395), new "modern" notions decreed that the social order, with all of its variation, was neither natural nor inevitable. Rather than being seen as an immutable phenomenon, society was now viewed more like a laboratory, where experiments could be conducted toward the goal of creating new and superior formations. "Life" was divided up into separate nexuses of activities and relationships, like "the community" and "the family," which were identified as strategic sites for the interventions of new technologies such as public health, education, hygiene, urban planning and social work (Horn 1988, 1991; Rabinow 1989). This re-classification of life as consisting of separate and distinct arenas, in which professional knowledge could be deployed in the service of engineering a "better" society, led to the rise of the idea of "the social" as a domain which could be governed through purposive planning and regulation, rather than by force (Horn 1988,1991; Rabinow 1989).

The turn toward an ethnography of poverty was conditioned by the nineteenth-century recognition that the existence of poverty posed perhaps the single greatest threat to the overall equilibrium of the social order (see Himmelfarb 1991; Procacci 1991). Beginning in that period, the poor were regarded not merely as "unfortunates," but as a genus of human being possessed of a fundamentally different character, resulting in a deficient sense of self and society which condemned them to a faulty and blighted existence (Himmelfarb 1991; Procacci 1991; Horn 1988,1991). Preventing such an outcome therefore required that professionals intervene in the practices of everyday life and in the spaces where everyday life was lived (Horn 1988:395). After all,

> If an individual's action was a function not of his moral character, as liberals believed, but rather of his place within a social whole, then it made little sense to try to reform the individual separate from the social milieu in which his actions were formed and normed (Rabinow 1989:11).

Explanations of the persistence of Black poverty in the American cities of the mid-twentieth century harkened back to this idea of "social milieux." In order to transform the lot of the Black poor, it was deemed necessary to first document and understand more fully the lifeways of that particular milieu.[5]

This agenda, which called for in-depth studies into the nature of Black communities, was furthered by Oscar Lewis' work on "the culture of poverty" (1959;1966). Although the impoverished families about whom Lewis was writing were not Black, but were, rather, Mexican, his writings found resonance with the social scientists and policy-makers of the 1960's, whose greatest preoccupation was with the threat of violence and social disruption they perceived as emanating from urban ghettos.

In a 1966 article, Lewis stated that through his studies of poor families, he was able to identify, "some 70 traits that characterize the culture of poverty" (Lewis 1966:21). People living in the culture of poverty were said to exhibit "a low level of organization" (Lewis 1966:23). Furthermore,

> The individual who grows up in this culture has a strong feeling of fatalism, helplessness, dependence and inferiority... Other traits include a high incidence of weak ego structure, orality and confusion of sexual identification, all reflecting maternal deprivation; a strong present-time orientation with relatively little disposition to defer gratification... and a widespread belief in male superiority...(Lewis 1966:23).[6]

Such pseudo-scientific exercises, which called for the enumeration and classification of various "traits," were intrinsic to the practices of modernity and to the rise of the social. It was through this process that some groups were established as "normal," and others, like the poor, were rendered "deviant" (Foucault 1979:182-184; Hacking 1982; Urla 1993).

Belief in the notion of a "culture of poverty" suggested that those populations who had suffered the most direct and deleterious consequences of inequality, the poor and the Black poor in particular, could not be helped primarily through the adoption of extensive measures which endeavored to redress the unequal distribution of resources. Rather, they would be better served by strategies which would encourage them to eliminate those particular traits which had been "scientifically" identified as dysfunctional, and which therefore prevented them from achieving upward mobility in the first place. It was the acceptance of this notion which guided the decisions regarding which communities the urban ethnographers of the later twentieth century chose to study, and which questions they subsequently sought to answer.

"Missing the Civil Rights Movement": Anthropologists and the American Ghetto Ethnography of the 1960's

In a perceptive article entitled, "Missing the Revolution," Orin Starn (1991) addresses the question of how so many anthropologists working in the Peruvian Andes could have failed to note or to document the particular social conditions which would ultimately give rise to the revolutionary movement, "Shining Path." A similar argument might be used with respect to the number of anthropologists working in the American ghettos of the 1960's, who declined to examine, and in some cases even to mention, the emergence of the Civil Rights Movement and its significance for the communities in which they were located.

Starn (1991:66) uses the term "Andeanism" to describe the romanticized and exoticized representations of the inhabitants of the Peruvian highlands promulgated by ethnographers. He argues that because ethnographers studying Andean life focused on "discrete villages with fixed traditions" instead of on "syncretism and shifting identities" (Starn 1991:65), they simply did not "see" the circumstances which would give rise to a social movement of astounding power and violence. Anthropologists had overlooked the crucial links which connected rural and urban communities (Starn 1991:64) and had neglected to recognize the significance of the particular social institutions which "integrated" seemingly disparate communities and interests (1991:70).

In a parallel manner, anthropologists working in the Black slums of the United States throughout the 1960's and 1970's also practiced a kind of "ghettoism," portraying these communities as discrete and bounded cultural entities, created by a particular system of socio-economic relations, but isolated both from this larger context and, perhaps even more importantly, *from one another.* Regardless of whether the Civil Rights Movement actually "happened" in particular communities when ethnographers were present (and, in many cases, significant events did occur either concurrently with or in close proximity to the research being undertaken), the impact of events such as riots at one end of the continuum, and marches and other non-violent demonstrations at the other, is almost wholly absent from this literature. [7]

Revelations of alternative forms of sociability, particularly apparent in studies of male "street corner societies," constructed "difference" while simultaneously denying that such differences might serve as a catalyst to meaningful social change. Informed by ecological models and by concepts of territoriality and adaptation, these ethnographies portrayed ghetto communities as occupying a unique niche within the larger well-balanced "ecosystem" of the social order.

The studies of male "street-corner societies" which dominated the ethnographic literature of the 1960's and 1970's on Black communities traced their lineages back to the original work of that name written by William Foote Whyte in 1943. Whyte's work, conducted in an Italian district in an eastern city, followed an earlier tradition of ethnographies of poor communities, which centered primarily on documenting the emergence and lifeways of European immigrant settlements (e.g. Riis 1902, Wirth 1928; Zorbaugh 1929). During the latter part of the nineteenth century and for the first half of the twentieth, such communities were a cause of great concern as they were regarded as potential breeding grounds for all manner of ills, ranging from disease and epidemics to criminality. According to Zorbaugh's description,

> the slum is a bleak area of segregation of the sediment of society; an area of extreme poverty, tenements, ramshackle buildings, of evictions and evaded rents; an area of working mothers and children, of high rates of birth, infant mortality, illegitimacy and death...
> The slum harbors many sorts of people: the criminal, the radical, the bohemian, the migratory worker, the immigrant, the unsuccessful, the queer and unadjusted (Zorbaugh 1929:9,11).

These slums of the early part of the century were, to use Zorbaugh's term, "highly cosmopolitan": "Foreign colonies, urban, rural and alien cultures, diverse tongues and creeds exist side-by-side, mingle and interpenetrate" (Zorbaugh 1929:151). Jacob Riis (1902), the social reformer, journalist and photographer, also documented the multifarious spectrum of individuals who inhabited the tenements of New York in settlements which were either ethnically mixed or which were immediately contiguous to one another.

During this earlier period of urban ethnography, "Negroes" are mentioned simply as one community amidst many others. During the first World War and particularly following World War II, however, massive migrations of Blacks from the South to the industrial centers of the north transformed the topography of these urban landscapes. What had once been a tolerable "Black belt" of African American settlement now became "the ghetto" (see Drake and Cayton 1945:58-74). As the public perception of the locus of social danger shifted from concern about immigrant settlements to anxiety centered on "Black ghettos," social scientists in search of urban neighborhoods to study also turned their attention toward those communities.

From the crusader Jacob Riis to William Foote Whyte to the ghetto ethnographers of the sixties and seventies, all of these observers were certainly motivated by a concern for social justice and reform. Elliot Liebow, author of the ethnography, *Tally's Corner* (1966) is no exception and his is one of the most widely read of the "ghetto ethnographies." Liebow did not live in the community where he conducted his study, but commuted on a daily basis to "hang out" with the denizens of a particular streetcorner in Washington, D.C. He saw his own work as an important corrective to other studies of the poor which simply enumerated their deficiencies (1966:4). In addition, he argued that his focus on men complemented studies of Black communities to date which had focused too exclusively on women and children (Liebow 1966:5). Clearly, Liebow was referring here to work undertaken by sociologists and social psychologists, as the vast body of ethnographic work on Black communities conducted by anthropologists was, and has remained, largely androcentric (see B. Williams 1992:169).

Liebow (1966: 219-221) refuted the notion that ghetto-dwellers were culturally distinctive, and argued, instead, that the particular configurations of life within the ghetto resulted from the ways in which these men had been disabled by structural inequalities. "It is, rather, the cultural model of the larger society as seen through the prism of repeated failure," he wrote (Liebow 1966:221).

These points offered a not insignificant critique of mainstream views, particularly within the historical context of the time when Liebow was writing.[8] Nonetheless, it is telling that he does not even note the occurrence of either the riots or the Civil Rights Movement *until the last two pages of the book*. Evaluating the prospects for social change, Liebow (1966:230) writes:

> In a sense, we have already forfeited the power to initiate action in this area. The moral initiative has long passed over to Negroes and political initiative seems to be moving in that direction, too. This may be a disquieting, even fearful development to some segments of our society. In the long run, however, the sooner and the more effectively Negroes organize to promote their own self-interests... the sooner and more effectively we can get on to other problems standing in the way of building a democratic society.

The "we" in that paragraph is defined explicitly a page earlier as "white middle-class persons" of "good will" (Liebow 1966:229). How are any of "us," however, able to see the two dozen men who are the subjects of *Tally's Corner* as capable of organizing anything more ambitious than a Saturday night "bender," when they have been described in the previous pages with sentences like, "Lovemaking, mate seeking, gambling and drinking are important foci of adult life" (Liebow 1966:16)? Liebow acknowledged that the streetcorner men were victimized by broader economic and social conditions beyond their control (like job discrimination). Nonetheless, his representation of their lives is ultimately dis-empowering. These men may no longer have been the frightening criminally-inclined demons who haunted the white imagination; but, neither were they visible as members of a community which would ultimately create one of the defining social movements of twentieth century American life.

To be sure, not all individual African Americans did participate in any direct way in either the Civil Rights Movement or in the riots that punctuated the 1960's. It seems worth noting, however, that ethnographers like Liebow focused their attention almost exclusively on individuals who were, most likely, marginal even within their own communities. Furthermore, they chose to study men who were outside of or on the fringes of the most significant social events of that period.

This bias is even more explicit in another widely-read ethnography of the period: Ulf Hannerz' *Soulside: Inquiries Into Ghetto Culture and Community* (1969). Hannerz offers a slightly more rounded view of life in the Washington, D.C. ghetto he studies, but, again, although he appears to arrive at conclusions which are very different from Liebow's regarding the cultural distinctiveness of ghetto life (see B. Valentine 1978:150-151), the political implications of his work are possibly even more disabling than were those of Liebow.

In his introductory chapter, Hannerz states his objectives quite clearly:

> . . . the general question here is, 'What is different about ghetto living?'. . . There are
> people in the ghetto who have good, stable jobs, help their children with their home work,
> eat dinner together at a fixed hour, make payments on the car, and spend their Saturday
> night watching Lawrence Welk on TV -- to their largely mainstream way of life, we will
> devote rather little attention . . . (1969:15-16)

Here is one of the most unequivocal statements of the relationship between class/race and
culture to be found within the corpus of ghetto ethnographies: "Mainstream" Blacks were of no
interest because if they watched Lawrence Welk on Saturday night and helped their children with
homework, *they somehow weren't really authentically culturally Black.*[9] To be Black and of
interest to an ethnographer meant, perforce, to be a poor resident of the ghetto, engaging in a
lifestyle as different from that of middle-class whites as was imaginatively possible.

Hannerz was actually still in the field when Martin Luther King was assassinated, and the
community erupted into what he calls "the insurrection" (172). In the pages immediately preceding his brief description of the ensuing riot, in a section tellingly entitled, "The *Lack* of Politics"
(168; emphasis mine), Hannerz addresses the Civil Rights Movement. Hannerz claims that the
Civil Rights Movement was of little or no interest to residents of "the Washington ghetto" (168).
He feels quite free to generalize about the ghetto at large, even though his research was largely
confined to a block he refers to as "Winston Street" (Hannerz 1969: Chapter One).[10]

Hannerz writes that:

> Civil Rights groups and others carried on their work but seemed to draw little interest from
> most people in the community who agreed with what the groups did but paid little or no
> attention to them (168).

He quotes one of his informants' assessment of the up-coming Poor People's March planned
for Washington, D.C.:

> "They don't get me to walk in one of those marches and get my head busted. So where was
> King when all those people were beaten up by the police? On his way to the airport! . . .
> That's what happens every time with those protests, the leaders run off and the people who
> have been dumb enough to follow them get busted . . ." (168)

Someone, however, was at those meetings and many thousands of people participated in the
Poor People's March. On the next page, we find out who at least one of those people may have
been: "[One resident from Winston Street attended [a meeting on urban renewal, sponsored by
a local civic group], *a preacher from a storefront church who took a greater than ordinary
interest in community affairs*" (169; emphasis mine). No doubt, this particular individual also ate
dinner with his family and watched Lawrence Welk on TV, and was therefore summarily excluded
from earlier pages of this ethnography.

The first man quoted above, who expressed his skepticism about the Civil Rights Movement, was undoubtedly genuine in his remarks and his perspective certainly represented a legitimate point-of-view shared by one sub-group within that community. The actions of the preacher, however, were equally representative of another dimension of neighborhood life. In their search for the exotic "true" ghetto culture, both Liebow and Hannerz and a score of other ethnographers who produced similar works (e.g. Anderson 1976; Keiser 1969; Suttles 1968) represented Black men as members of hyper-masculine street-corner societies, who lived lives of relative isolation even within their own social environments and who were able to form successful relationships only with each other.

The production of Black male subjects, who were condemned to dwell on the social margins of the street corner, was, as Gupta and Ferguson (1992) illustrate through a series of parallel examples, in and of itself, a political act:

> In this perspective, power does not enter the anthropological picture only at the moment of representation, for the cultural distinctiveness that the anthropologist attempts to represent has already been produced within a field of power relations (Gupta and Ferguson 1992:17).

Ethnographic treatments of "Black streetcorner men" took this category of people for granted, as if they had always lived on the periphery of urban economies, in "ghettos" and "inner cities," practicing their unique and remarkable ways of life while waiting to be discovered and documented by intrepid ethnographers (cf. Gupta and Ferguson 1992:16).

In fact, the lifestyle of streetcorner men as it is represented in these ethnographies, if it existed at all, was a quite recent invention, dating back only as far as the large-scale migrations of southern Blacks to the cities of the industrial north.[11] Some would argue that this social formation was of even more recent vintage, resulting from the outmigration of the Black middle and working classes from the ghetto following gains of the Civil Rights movement, leaving behind to languish only the most impoverished of residents.[12]

In any case, the ethnograp s of ghetto life naturalized the labels "ghetto dwellers" and "streetcorner men," not stopping to consider how it was that a specific group of people, who shared some rather superficial phenotypic characteristics, happened to find themselves compelled to live "within economic spaces zoned, as it were, for poverty" (Gupta and Ferguson 1992:17). By relegating the lives of Black "streetcorner men" to the suffocating crawlspace of this unproblematized category, the possibilities for social change, and certainly for revolution, were quietly written out of the record.

Black Family Life: Biopower Operationalized

> For as long as Negroes have been in America, their marital and family patterns have been
> the subject of curiosity and amusement, moral indignation and self-congratulation, puzzle-
> ment and frustration, concern and guilt on the part of white Americans (Rainwater 1970:2).

The families of the poor, and particularly of the Black poor, have long been at the center of
social science inquiry. Indeed, some of the "ghetto ethnographies" discussed in the previous
section were undertaken in the context of larger studies concerned with African American family
life. Liebow (1966:xv), for example, collected the data for *Tally's Corner* as part of a research
project on "Child Rearing Practices Among Low Income Families in the District of Columbia."
Liebow's "brief" was to complement the contributions of other researchers on the team by
investigating specifically low-income men's relationships to women and children.

Another example is Rainwater, who in the introduction to his study of life in the notorious
Pruitt-Igoe housing project in St. Louis (1970:1) sets out his mission in the following manner:

> We will be primarily concerned in this book with private life as it is lived from day to day
> in a federally built and supported slum. The questions which are treated here have to do
> with *the kinds of interpersonal relationships that develop in nuclear families, the social-*
> *ization processes that operate in families as children grow up in a slum environment, the*
> *informal relationships of children and adolescents and adults with each other*, and, final-
> ly, the world views... arising from the life experiences of the Pruitt-Igoeans..." (emphasis
> mine).

Rainwater does draw conclusions from his study which break very decisively with the
assumptions of other ethnographies conditioned by the "culture of poverty." For example, he
writes that the work "began as a study of problems in a public housing project... and ended as a
study of the dynamics of socio-economic inequality" (Rainwater 1970:vii). Nonetheless, for him
as for other researchers, the family retains its privilege as the primary locus where poverty
commits its most visible and egregious injuries.

Concern with the supposed inadequacies of Black families erupted into a full-fledged public
debate in the mid-1960's, when Daniel Patrick Moynihan submitted his report, *The Negro Family:*
The Case for National Action, to President Johnson. Even with the passage of the Civil Rights
Act, Moynihan argued, Black communities were still likely to remained ensnared in the trap of
poverty and social pathology as a result of the fundamental "breakdown" of Black family life
(Katz 1979: 25). Moynihan concluded that although not all of the "Negro's" problems could be
attributed to the family,

> Nevertheless, at the *center* of the tangle of pathology is the weakness of the family
> structure. Once or twice removed, it will be found to be the *principle source* of most of
> the aberrant, inadequate, or anti-social behavior that did not establish but now serves to
> *perpetuate* the *cycle* of poverty and deprivation (Moynihan 1965:30; as quoted by C.
> Valentine 1968:33; italics added by Valentine).

The Moynihan report reveals the view discussed earlier, of poverty as both cause and consequence of its own self-sustaining perpetual motion machine. Moynihan targets the family as the single institution most responsible for the reproduction of the "culture of poverty."

While the work of social scientists like Liebow (1966) and Hannerz (1969), with its focus on street-corner men, may have implicitly supported the view that Black men were largely absent from households of women and children, thereby rendering these families "matriarchal" and, hence, unstable, other social scientists, not coincidentally white women, produced their own studies of Black families which would challenge the implications of the Moynihan report.

Stack (1974) and Aschenbrenner (1975) presented almost identical conclusions in their work on Black kinship. They each found that Black families were, in fact, resilient and adaptive configurations, in which the maintenance of households and the rearing of children occurred within networks of extended female kin, rather than within the confines of nuclear families, the formation touted by white middle-class "experts" as the norm. Both researchers found that the extended structures found among Blacks were well-suited to deal with the exigencies of poverty, and that, contrary to the views of Moynihan and others, such family structures did not promote disorganization or instability (Aschenbrenner 1975:139-144; Stack 1974:124-129).[13]

As pictured in the "streetcorner society" ethnographies, Black men floated aimlessly through the public domain, unmoored from the stabilizing rudder of family life. In the more family-oriented studies, Black women existed *only* within the domestic sphere, seemingly cut off from the world outside the household and the family.

The critical question here is not whether Black families "really" were/are functional or dysfunctional, culturally distinctive or making do in the midst of deeply trying circumstances; our question is, rather, why did the family become the privileged site for so many of these studies concerned with the causes and effects of poverty? Why not look more closely at workplace cultures and at structural discrimination in the job market, for example, or at the effects of housing policies or at participation in community organizations? This is not to imply that social institutions outside of the family were totally absent from this particular corpus of ghetto ethnographies, but to emphasize the fact that the principle interlocutors with whom these works were in dialogue were critics of Black family life.

Donzelot (1978) has argued that the emergence of such convictions regarding the centrality of family life was integral to the rise of "the social" as one dimension of the project of modernity:

> Since the end of the eighteenth century, a multitude of philanthropic and religious associations had made it their goal to come to the aid of the poorer classes, to moralize their behavior and facilitate their education *by concentrating their efforts toward the restoration of family life*, the first form and the most economical formula of mutual aid (Donzelot 1978:32; emphasis mine).

Donzelot refers to this process of "moralization" through intervention as "the policing of families." By policing, Donzelot (1978:6-7) means, "all the methods for developing the quality of the population and the strength of the nation" -- in other words, the family has become the site where those regimes of modernity, including such technologies as hygiene and public health which are generally referred to as "biopower" by Foucault (1978:140), are most intensively deployed.

The attention devoted to African American families in the context of the work on poverty then, illustrates the extent to which contemporary social scientists and policy-makers continued to act on the belief that families could -- and *should* -- be made to be "agents for conveying the norms of the state into the private sphere" (Donzelot 1978:58). Indeed, it is the general acceptance of precisely this kind of assumption that Moynihan demonstrates in his report:

> The family is the basic social unit of American life; it is the basic socializing unit. By and large, adult conduct in society is learned as a child. (Rainwater and Yancey 1967:127-128; as quoted by Katz 1989:25-26).

Moynihan's programmatic conclusion was that,

> A national effort is required that will give a unity of purpose to the many activities of the Federal government in this area, directed to a new kind of goal: the establishment of a stable Negro family structure (Moynihan 1965; as quoted by C. Valentine 1968:30) [14]

Social work and different forms of public assistance, psychiatry and counseling were all invoked as modes of biopower, designed to reshape the supposedly aberrant contours of the poor (and African American poor, in particular) family.

Whether the family was seen as a positive or as a negative force in the socialization process, this body of ethnographic literature reinforced the conviction that the family was, and would continue to serve, "not only as a target of interventions but as a bearer of social duties" (Horn 1988:403). In purporting to document and catalogue the behaviors and mechanisms which characterized the ways in which poor Black families functioned within their own particular socio-economic contexts, urban anthropology implicated itself in "the policing of families" (see also Horn 1992). Whether one advocated applying the preventative and supposedly rehabilitative measures recommended by Moynihan and his adherents, or one applauded the positive and adaptive functions which white ethnographers attributed to it, constructions of the poor Black family remained integral to upholding the hegemony of government by the social. [15]

The Crisis of the Social: Racializing Poverty

Deciding exactly who is poor and who is not has always been a point of contention. The concept of the "poverty line" originated with studies undertaken by Charles Booth in mid-nineteenth century London, and debates about this calculus of deprivation (was it a relative or an absolute measure?) have continued from that time up through the present. [16]

The question of exactly what standard should be used to define poverty as a status remains unresolved. I would suggest, however, that treatments of poverty in the American ethnographic literature (and certainly in the media) have come to rely on an indicator other than income-level or standard-of-living to determine who is *truly* poor: That marker is race. Beginning in the 1960's, the term "poor" became associated almost exclusively with Black ghetto communities; white urban neighborhoods on the other hand, were by definition, "working class."

In the earlier generation of urban ethnographies, communities of predominantly white immigrants and "ethnics" were clearly described as poor, their inhabitants as slum-dwellers. Whyte (1947:xv) for example, begins his study of street-corner society, "In the heart of 'Eastern City' there is a slum district known as 'Cornerville,' which is inhabited almost exclusively by Italian immigrants and their children." Zorbaugh (1929:9) describes the "cosmopolitan" denizens of the district in Chicago he studied as living in "a squalid backwater."

In 1962, Herbert Gans published his now-classic work, *The Urban Villagers,* which was a study of the predominantly white (and Italian) West End of Boston in the years immediately preceding its destruction as part of an "urban renewal" plan. His introduction to the community begins thusly:

> To the superficial observer, armed with conventional images and a little imagination about the mysteries thought to lie behind the tenement entrances, the West End certainly had all the earmarks of a slum. Whether or not it actually was a slum is a question that involves a number of technical housing and planning considerations and some value judgements. *I felt that it was not...* For the moment, the West End can be described simply as an old, somewhat deteriorated, low-rent neighborhood that has housed a variety of people, most of them poor (Gans 1962:3-4; emphasis mine).

Here, although Gans clearly recognizes the residents of the West End as poor, he resists the notion that their community is a slum. In part, this may be due to the position Gans developed in the course of his fieldwork which placed him in opposition to the planned urban renewal scheme. He writes that at the start of his research, he had no position on the redevelopment plan; later on, after he began to identify with his "informants" and to understand the nature of the social ties which bound together members of that community, he became adamantly opposed to the project and, hence, to the designation of the entire district as a slum (Gans 1962: Chapter 14).[17]

At the conclusion of his critique of the redevelopment program, however, Gans writes the following:

> [T]he West End differed from most other urban renewal projects in that it was a neighborhood of European ethnic groups. Whereas over 95 percent of its population was white, most other renewal projects have been in predominantly nonwhite areas: 80 percent of them according to one estimate. In such areas, the housing is usually of a poorer quality. *Moreover, there is probably less community life, fewer long-standing relationships between residents and less attachment to the neighborhood than in the West End.*

Therefore, my argument against clearance would often be less justified in these areas
(Gans 1962:377 emphasis mine).

Small wonder that in some circles in the 1960's, urban renewal was caustically referred to as "Negro removal." Gans echoes the prevailing belief here that poor Black communities were inherently more "disorganized" and, hence, less worth preserving than were white ethnic communities. Like the immigrants before them, Black communities now appeared to be unable to govern themselves through internalized social controls; therefore, they needed to be controlled from the outside and urban renewal constituted one form of this governance.

With the comparative dearth of ethnographies of white poverty in the United States during the later 1960's into the mid-1970's, and with virtually no studies of Black community life outside of the most impoverished blocks of the urban ghetto, race and poverty were easily conflated. "The poor" came to stand for "the Black poor," both within the corpus of social science literature and most assuredly within the domain of public policy discourse. It was easy to forget that, in fact, the War on Poverty had been launched by Kennedy initially in reaction to white rural, not Black urban, poverty (Gaventa 1980:34; Katz 1989:82).

Black poverty emerged as the greater social concern later in the decade, after the rise of the Civil Rights Movement and the urban riots had called unmistakable attention to the tenacious character of poverty in the ghetto (and to the threat of insurgency) (Katz 1989:84). By the nineteen-eighties, Black poverty had even acquired its own specific designation: "the underclass." As Katz (1989:195) notes, despite the increase in white poverty during this same period, "Two groups- black teenaged mothers and black jobless youths- dominated the images of the under-class."

As early as the late 1960's, whiteness had already become disassociated from poverty, and Blackness from worker. The American ethnography of the 1970's and 1980's which dealt with urban communities preserved this symbolic Maginot Line separating Black ghettos from white urban neighborhoods, even though in most cities, "working class white" communities and "Black ghettos" bordered on one another and shared the consequences of the same fluctuating dynamics of the housing market and economy.

Of course, it is true that in most of ethnographies of white communities during this later period (e.g. Halle 1984; Kornblum 1974; Susser 1982), poverty had not yet become nearly as pervasive or as debilitating a presence as it was in African American neighborhoods, and most of the white men at the time of these studies were still employed in unskilled jobs or in heavy industry. As Susser (1982) illustrates, however, as early as the mid 1970's, macro-economic changes began to wreak havoc on the lives of the white working class, moving this population perilously close to the boundaries which marked off the marshlands of the ghetto, where the "genuine" poor remained mired.

How then is this process of racializing poverty related to the discourse of the social? The ultimate triumph of the social was the development of the welfare state, which became the vehicle for insuring its subjects' widespread loyalty and adherence to the notion of progress:

> Now the State must aim to guide progress and become positively responsible for it so as to gain the means for securing the social promotion of society and eradicating the sources of evil, poverty and oppression which prevent it from corresponding to its ideal (Donzelot 1988:424).

The specific designation of the poor of the 1980's as "poor and Black," for which now read, "the underclass," reinforced the notion that certain populations remained resistant to the techniques of the social. Benevolent tactics, like welfare, for example, are now regarded as failures because they allegedly held the poor, and the Black poor in particular, in thrall to the dictatorship of dependency on the State.

Binding the problem of poverty to Blacks has detracted attention from the overall restructuring of the economy, a reorganization which has created possibly even greater dislocations for the [white] working class than for impoverished Blacks. A recent passage from the *New York Times*, for example, acknowledges the existence of this "new" white poverty, but still relies on references to the "working class" and on the insistence that the white poor do not live in slums to distinguish this current, and presumably transitory, poverty from "real" poverty:

> Diana Kuchenreuther, 34 years old, single, the mother of three children, has been working for two years and trying to get off the dole,[18] but she is still desperately poor. Her home is an apartment in a big rundown home *in a working-class neighborhood...*Here, poverty stays indoors. *Marshalltown is not rich, but it is barren of slums, and the poor live next to the middle class. The crime and drug problems of the inner cities are, by comparison, insignificant here* (*New York Times*, Tuesday, July 7, 1992; emphasis mine).

Notice that above, the term "inner city," has replaced the label "ghetto" as the place where the *real* poor (that is, the *Black* poor) live. The white poor, like the residents of Marshalltown, live neither in inner cities nor in ghettos. Escaping poverty thus remains possible for those like Diana Kuchenreuther, who still believes in the redemptive promise of work and who lives in proximity to the middle class. Thus, she is rendered as different from the real poor, ghetto Blacks for whom an escape from poverty is, quite simply, not possible.

Racializing poverty, whether through ethnography or through the media, has extended the construction of the Black poor as subjects who actively resist productive participation in society. It is a construction produced in the service of enforcing the hegemonic discipline of the social (cf. Terry 1991), whose rule must be preserved at all costs despite the economic crises of the current moment. Therefore, the social must be imbued with the power with which it will be able to effect its own survival and ultimate triumph, *not over inequality, but over the poor, and over the Black poor in particular.* It might be possible for whites to become poor; it is not possible, however, for them to become *both poor and Black* (Hall *et al.* 1978:244). When poverty and Blackness become detached from one another, only then will the rule of "government by the social" confront its next, and perhaps its greatest, crisis of authority.

Conclusion: Toward a Post-Social Ethnography

I have offered this essay as part of my own re-thinking about how we, as anthropologists, are educated and, how we, in turn, try to educate our students to become culture critical, and to interrogate all of the ways in which power is constantly in play, shaping the categories we use to talk about people's lives. The very process of naming groups and of defining their separate identities, based on our identification of putative differences among them, is part of the way in which we are all governed by the technologies of the social.

At this historical moment, in which we write our ethnographies and teach anthropology, the struggle of the social for survival has become ever more visible as it strives to retain its hegemony over communities devastated by the encroachments of the global economy. The recent text which most obviously illustrates the desperate lengths to which this discourse is prepared to go is Murray and Hernnstein's 1994 publication, *The Bell Curve,* which argues that I.Q. scores and income level are inextricably linked. Murray and Hernnstein then go on to claim that the location of a disproportionate percentage of African Americans on the lower rungs of the economic ladder is a consequence of their presumably biologically-determined "lower" I.Q.s.

This sort of social Darwinist "just so" story is bound to find an appreciative audience among politicians and policy-makers, who are determined to indict social programs as a failure and as a waste of taxpayers' money. What lies beneath this desperate turn to biological determinist explanations for persistent (and in fact, rapidly growing) poverty is the ever-strong attempt to shore up belief in rule by the social by continuing to attack the poor, and the visible Black poor in particular, rather than by implementing policies to genuinely address inequality (and racism). However many more white families have also been reduced to living in poverty over the past 20 years, by the withdrawal of social programs and by the globalization of labor and of capital, they may still take comfort in the notion that their superior I.Q.s leave open *for them* the opportunity for an improvement in their fortunes.

Our challenge, in teaching anthropology and in continuing to do fieldwork and to write ethnographies about poor communities, is to recognize the ways in which our portrayals of cultural "difference" in these settings may also serve to promote particular policy agendas which, in some cases, might be anathema to our own political convictions. After all, the reconsideration of the corpus of ghetto ethnographies which this essay offers does not deny that at the time when these books were written, they were composed with the best of intentions, toward the goal of greater acceptance of racial diversity in American society and with the recognition that the lifeways identified as indigenous to low-income African American communities in the latter half of the twentieth century were not necessarily self-destructive or hostile to whites.

It is only by questioning the placement of the boundaries which claim to discriminate among the domains of the social, separating community from family, public from private, and local from national that we can begin to understand the ways in which these partitions are a constructed, rather than a natural, feature of our social landscape. A view of urban communities which takes into account the influence of grassroots movements and of local-level activism and which recognizes the ways in which the hegemony of the social is constantly being challenged in ways both big and small, by those who are most severely disadvantaged by its invidious distinctions (like race), is the corrective which ethnographic work in poor communities might promise.[19] Such a discourse, which interrogates the assumptions of the social by denaturalizing notions of difference, might result in a new mode of cultural critique, which is genuinely post-social, and in which an equation of *"different and equal"* just might be possible.

Notes

1. Most of the ideas contained in this paper arose from a seminar entitled, "The Anthropology of Modernity," taught during the Spring of 1992 by Jacqueline Urla and Arturo Escobar. I am grateful to Jackie and Arturo and to all of our fellow travelers for several weeks of stimulating discussions. I first read many of the urban ethnographies discussed in this essay under the tutelege of D. Douglas Caulkins at Grinnell College during the early 1970's. I thank him for passing on to us his own deeply-held belief that good ethnography can and *should* have something to say about the critical social issues facing the day. Such thinking was also characteristic of a later mentor, Sylvia Forman. Despite all of this excellent guidance, the responsibility for any errors or misinterpretation remains my own.

2. I am aware that the term African American is now the preferred usage; I have used the term "black" in these early sections of the paper because they reflect the usage current during the period I am writing about.

3. My intention here is not to continue the tradition of marginalizing texts authored by African Americans; it is to consider the contours of the underlying agenda served by those ethnographies of Black communities, which were produced and consumed by whites.

4. Since this era, many critiques of the ethnography of Black communities from this period have been offered. These include: Harrison 1988; Maxwell 1988; Mullings 1992; B. Valentine 1978; B. Williams 1992.

5. This mode of thinking was clearly parallel to the colonialist agenda of an earlier generation of British social anthropologists.

6. The obvious misogyny in this formulation and in many of the other writings about the Black family will be mentioned in passing later in this essay. See also Mullings 1992.

7. The one ethnography I have found from this period which does take into account the influence of the Civil Rights Movement is Clark 1965. Probably not coincidentally, this is a work authored by an African American.

8. See C. Valentine (1968:94-97) on Liebow's contributions to an "anthropology of poverty."

9. See B. Valentine (1978:148-149) for a similar, but not identical, critique of Hannerz.

10. See also B. Valentine (1978:143) on this point.

11. See Drake and Cayton 1945 for a history of Black migration from the south to Chicago, from the first major influx, 1914-1918, up through World War II.

12. The question of whether or not Black urban ghettos have become principally inhabited by the "underclass" and of the significance of demographic changes in Black communities has been hotly debated. On both sides of the argument, Drake and Cayton's 1945 classic and under recognized study of the Chicago Black community is invoked as evidence for the multi-class character of ghetto communities up to the 1960's. This point is most strongly embraced by Wilson 1978, 1986, 1987. In one piece, he argues that "unlike the present period, inner city communities prior to 1950 exhibited the features of social organization -- including a sense of community, positive neighborhood identification, and explicit norms and sanctions against aberrant behavior" (Wilson 1986:2).

In contrast, Gregory 1992 contends that many Black communities continue to be multi-class in character, but that the specific reforms of the Civil Rights era privilege the interests of Black homeowners over tenants, creating class divisions within these communities. Newman 1992 also argues that Harlem is a diverse community which does not fit Wilson's model of the "underclass." She notes that the most impoverished members of African American communities have always been subject to social, but not spatial, exclusion.

13. Mullings (1992:17) points out that while African American families are represented in the literature as dysfunctional because the women are supposedly dominant and the men emasculated, Mexican American families are criticized for the exact opposite phenomenon. That is, their problems are seen to arise from an excessively patriarchal structure where the men are violent and macho, thereby allegedly rendering the women pathologically subservient.

14. See Valentine (1968: 29-42) for a summary and critical evaluation of Moynihan's proposals.

15. As Mullings (1992:17-18) has written: "Images and symbols associated with gender roles, family and race are particularly powerful... By transforming social categories into biological ones, they effectively perpetuate the view that these distinctions are part of a natural order, not a social order, that they are grounded in nature, not in the class structure of the society."

16. See Himmelfarb (1991: Chapters One and Two); also Harrington (1962: Appendix) on different measures of poverty in more contemporary times; Katz (1989: Chapter Four) up-dates Harrington's discussion.

17. I am grateful to Rick Fantasia for raising this point with me in conversation.

18. It seems worth noting that in this description of white poverty, although Diana Kuchenreuther is a single mother, the form of public assistance that she is receiving is described as "the dole," rather than as "welfare."

19. For an excellent example of this strategy in contemporary ethnography, see Gregory 1993.

References

Anderson, Elijah
1976 *A Place on the Corner*. Chicago: University of Chicago Press.

Aschenbrenner, Joyce
1975 *Lifelines: Black Families in Chicago*. New York: Holt, Rinehart and Winston.

Clark, Kenneth B.
1965 *Dark Ghetto: Dilemmas of Social Power*. New York: Harper & Row.

Donzelot, Jacques
  1979 *The Policing of Families.* New York: Pantheon Books.
  1988 The Promotion of the Social. *Economy and Society* 17(3):395-427.

Drake, St. Clair and Horace R. Cayton
  1945 *Black Metropolis: A Study of Negro Life in a Northern City.* New York: Harcourt, Brace and
  Company.

Foucault, Michel
  1978 *The History of Sexuality, Vol. I: Introduction.* New York: Vintage Books.
  1979 *Discipline and Punish: The Birth of the Prison.* New York: Vintage Books.

Gans, Herbert
  1982 (1962) *The Urban Villagers: Group and Class in the Life of Italian Americans.* New York: The
  Free Press.

Gaventa, John
  1980 *Power and Powerless: Quiescence and Rebellion in an Appalachian Valley.* Urbana: University
  of Illinois Press.

Gregory, Steven
  1992 The Changing Significance of Race and Class in an African-American Community, *American
  Ethnologist* 19(2):255-274.
  1993 Race, Rubbish and Resistance: Empowering Difference in Community Politics, *Cultural
  Anthropology* 8 (1): 24-48.

Gupta, Akhil and James Ferguson
  1992 Beyond 'Culture': Space, Identity and the Politics of Difference, *Cultural Anthropology* 7(1):6-23.

Hacking, Ian
  1982 Biopower and the Avalanche of Printed Numbers, *Humanities in Society* 5(3 & 4):279-295.

Hall, Stuart, Chas Critcher, Tony Jefferson, John Clarke, Brian Roberts
  1978 *Policing the Crisis: Mugging, the State and Law and Order.* London: MacMillan Press.

Halle, David
  1984 *America's Working Man: Work, Home and Politics Among Blue-Collar Property Owners.*
  Chicago: University of Chicago Press.

Hannerz, Ulf
  1969 *Soulside: Inquiries into Ghetto Culture and Community.* New York: Columbia University Press.

Harrington, Michael
  1962 *The Other America: Poverty in the United States.* MacMillan: Pelican Books.

Harrison, Faye V.
  1988 Introduction: An African Diaspora Perspective for Urban Anthropology, *Urban Anthropology* (Special Issue) 17(2-3)11-141.

Himmelfarb, Gertrude
  1991 *Poverty and Compassion: The Moral Imagination of the Late Victorians.* New York: Albert Knopf.

Horn, David G.
  1988 Welfare, the Social and the Individual in Interwar Italy, *Cultural Anthropology* 3(4):395-407.
  1989 Culture and Power in Urban Anthropology, *Dialectical Anthropology* 13(2):189-198.
  1991 Constructing the Sterile City: Pronatalism and Social Sciences in Interwar Italy, *American Ethnologist* 18(3):581-601.

Katz, Michael B.
  1989 *The Undeserving Poor: From the War on Poverty to the War on Welfare.* New York: Pantheon Books.

Keiser, Lincoln
  1969 *The Vice Lords: Warriors of the Streets.* New York: Holt, Rinehart and Winston.

Kornblum, William
  1974 *Blue Collar Community.* Chicago: University of Chicago Press.

Komarovsky, Mirra
  1962 *Blue Collar Marriage.* New York: Vintage Books.

Lewis, Oscar
  1959 *Five Families: Mexican Case Studies in the Culture of Poverty.* New York: Basic Books.
  1966 The Culture of Poverty, *Scientific American* 215(4):19-25.

Liebow, Elliot
  1966 *Tally's Corner: A Study of Negro Streetcorner Men.* Boston: Little, Brown and Company.

Maxwell, Andrew
  1988 The Anthropology of Poverty in Black Communities: A Critique and Systems Alternative, *Urban Anthropology* 17(2-3):171-191.

Moynihan, Daniel Patrick
  1986 *Family and Nation.* San Diego: Harcourt, Brace and Jovanovich.

Mullings, Leith
  1992 *Race, Class and Gender: Representations and Realities.* Center for Research on Women, Memphis State University.

Newman, Katherine
  1992 Culture and Structure in *The Truly Disadvantaged, City and Society* 1:3-25.

Procacci, Giovanna
   1991 Social Economy and the Government of Poverty. In *The Foucault Effect: Studies in Governmentality*, Burchell, Gordon and Miller, eds. Pp. 151-168. Chicago: University of Chicago Press.

Rabinow, Paul
   1989 *French Modern: Norms and Forms of the Social Environment.* Cambridge: MIT Press.

Rainwater, Lee
   1970 *Behind Ghetto Walls: Black Families in a Federal Slum.* Chicago: Aldine Publishing Company.

Rainwater, Lee and William L. Yancey
   1967 *The Moynihan Report and the Politics of Controversy.* Cambridge: MIT Press.

Riis, Jacob A.
   1971 (1901) *How the Other Half Lives.* New York: Dover Publications.

Rubin, Lillian Breslow
   1976 *Worlds of Pain: Life in the Working-Class Family.* New York: Basic Books.

Stack, Carol B.
   1974 *All Our Kin: Strategies for Survival in a Black Community.* New York: Harper and Row.

Susser, Ida
   1982 *Norman Street; Poverty and Politics in an Urban Neighborhood.* New York: Oxford University Press.

Suttles, Gerald
   1968 *The Social Order of the Slum: Ethnicity and Territory in the Inner City.* Chicago: University of Chicago Press.

Terry, Jennifer
   1991 Theorizing Deviant Historiography, *Differences: A Journal of Feminist Cultural Studies* 3(2):55-74.

Urla, Jacqueline
   1993 Cultural Politics in an Age of Statistics: Numbers, Nations and the Making of Basque Identity, *American Ethnologist* 20(4):818-843).

Valentine, Bettylou
   1978 *Hustling and Other Hard Work: Life Styles in the Ghetto.* New York: The Free Press.

Valentine, Charles A.
   1968 *Culture and Poverty: Critique and Counter-Proposals.* Chicago: University of Chicago Press.

Whyte, William Foote
   1943 *Street Corner Society: The Social Structure of an Italian Slum.* Chicago: University of Chicago Press.

Williams, Brett
  1988 *Upscaling Downtown*. Ithaca: Cornell University Press.
  1992 Poverty Among African Americans in the Urban United States, *Human Organization* 51(2):164-
     174.

Wilson, William Julius
  1978 *The Declining Significance of Race: Blacks and Changing American Institutions*. Chicago:
     University of Chicago Press.
  1986 *Cycles of Deprivation and the Underclass Debate*. Working Papers on Race Relations and Urban
     Studies No. 1. Chicago: Chicago Urban League.
  1987 *The Truly Disadvantaged*. Chicago: University of Chicago Press.

Wirth, Louis
  1928 *The Ghetto*. Chicago: University of Chicago Press.

Zorbaugh, Harvey Warren
  1976 (1929) *The Gold Coast and the Slum*. Chicago: University of Chicago Press.

Taken by University of Massachusetts Photographic Services, 1981.

Sylvia Helen Forman: Personal Reflections

Ralph H. Faulkingham
University of Massachusetts at Amherst

Ralph Faulkingham has been in the Department of Anthropology at the University of Massachusetts at Amherst since receiving his PhD. from Michigan State University in 1970. He was promoted from Assistant to Associate Professor in 1976, and then to Professor in 1984. Initially hired because of his interest in political anthropology and African ethnology, he has expanded his research interests to political economy and rural development in francophone West Africa. He unabashedly takes credit for the UMass decision to hire Sylvia Forman in 1972; the dean had withdrawn the position that the department had initially offered to her, and only his last ditch efforts to patch together a joint position between the School of Education and Anthropology salvaged the appointment. It took five full years for Forman to undo the curse of that joint appointment.

My heart hammered in my chest as I drove the half mile from her house to mine. Sylvia had just given me a copy of her Curriculum vitae and had asked me to draft her obituary. "I want to see it before I go, and I don't want anyone to screw it up," she had said matter-of-factly. How could I write her obituary? With her death so clearly imminent, there was no time to reflect on her past; the present was so thoroughly consuming. Sylvia and those of us in her immediate orbit at that moment were lurching, careening even, toward the "trip" she did not want to talk about.

By mid-January 1992, Sylvia had come to understand that her cancer did not give her much more time to live. A month later, she left the University Infirmary to go home to be attended to by hospice workers, her companion for the previous twelve years David Litwak, and a few friends. In the past she had talked easily about death, and had once even taught a course on death and dying. But now she used the metaphor of getting ready to go on a voyage -- a lot of technical things to be gotten through before the trip could begin.

Over the previous month, she had been "packing" furiously -- she had written dozens of personal, chatty notes to colleagues, friends, and students. She had me print out several "To Whom it May Concern" letters of reference for her PhD. students who would soon be looking for professional employment. She had invited in the director of a local funeral home to negotiate a price for the cremation of her body, and she had thoughtfully yet methodically parceled out her jewelry collection to several friends.

She and her lawyer had fussed, seemingly endlessly, over the details of her will and had established the Sylvia Forman Third World Scholarship Fund that was to be the principal beneficiary of her estate. "I want students from those areas of the world where anthropologists have done their work to come to our department to study anthropology," she had said. "They can certainly enliven our program; they might even transform the profession."

I returned in the morning with a draft, and she paused for about ten minutes from her detective novel to read the draft and to make a few editorial changes. When she was done, she said, "That will do just fine, Ralphie," and she went back to her story. The interchange, so utterly empty of the emotion we both kept at bay, reminded me of the many times, when as chair of the Department of Anthropology, she gave me drafts of memos or letters she had written and asked for my judgment about a line of argument or a turn of phrase. When she died two days later, I had only to insert the date, March 1, 1992, before sending the text to the funeral director.

A memorial service took place on the UMass campus almost two weeks later. In that long interim, I and many others mused a good deal about Sylvia. No longer were we restrained by Sylvia's explicit prohibition on expressions of emotion. The service filled Memorial Hall to overflowing and provided a forum for many to recount aloud their memories of Sylvia. As I listened that day to the speakers, I was struck with how poignant, yet different, the memories were. She had been like a precious cut stone: each of her facets reflected light in a different direction, but each ray was distinct, bright, and clear. John Nelson, a professor of English at UMass, recounted the first time he met Sylvia...

> It was some years ago when several faculty in English were first proselytizing for the new faculty union, the Massachusetts Society of Professors, and I was invited to the Faculty Club to meet pro-union people from other departments. Everyone in the little club bar was talking about the union, when I became aware of a woman sitting on a barstool with her back to the bartender, talking with a mixed group. I say "became aware" because this woman was something like a force field or a sun carrying her own planets along with her. She was wearing a lovely blouse and a short skirt and sitting in such a way, one arm behind her on the bar, a glass of whiskey in one hand, head tilted back slightly, eyebrows raised, inviting anyone who dared to enter the force field. (Few could resist.) She was engaging a number of people at once, like a grand master at chess playing five games simultaneously.
>
> Sylvia held forth on the projected conservative backlash to the union effort, but could have been talking about the Albigensian heresy for all I cared. This was a woman to be seen and heard -- in full flight, wholly engaged, at home in the rough and tumble of debate, enjoying every minute. Laughing, picking up a lost thread of argument, skewering an adversary on a point of history or logic. As she held forth, she ran a hand through her great rich tumbling profusion of reddish/auburn hair, flicking it deftly to one side and laughing again. No one in her audience could match such a combination of statement and gesture.
>
> I've thought a lot about that scene; what remains so clear is her brightness and vitality and engagement, how she loved the risks to be taken in the delight of the moment. But I also remember the great beauty of the fully realized woman, Sylvia Forman. Like Yeats' dancer at the end of his poem "Among School Children," the mystery lies there before us: how can we separate the woman from her ideas and presence and passion, the dancer from the dance?
>
> Sylvia, you have given us rare gifts: it has been our great fortune to know you and, all too briefly, to live alongside you in this community to which you gave so much of your mind, your irreverence, your spirit, your radiance, and ultimately yourself.

Sylvia Forman rarely talked about her youth. Whenever the subject came up, she tried to change it. "It's not interesting," she declaimed. Born on December 31, 1943, she grew up in the Washington, DC area, where her father worked for the federal government. Her mother had died of cancer when Sylvia was four years old. Thereafter she spent summers with her maternal grandmother (the "Irish Protestant" one) in North Carolina. She got into trouble as a young teenager, and was sent to what she called a school "for Jewish girls" in Shaker Heights, Ohio. Others called it a reform school. Later, she attended courses at the University of Maryland in the fall of 1961 and flunked every one. Then on the day of her eighteenth birthday, she packed her few belongings on a motorcycle and left for the San Francisco bay area, where she hustled odd jobs before enrolling in Oakland's Merritt College.

There she met an English instructor, Edith Jenkins, who with her husband Dave, opened their home and family to Sylvia. Their progressive politics, love of good books, passion for debate, and emotional support became an anchor for Sylvia. Even after Sylvia had established herself at Amherst, she returned at least once a year to San Francisco, often at Thanksgiving, to visit friends and to spend time with the Jenkins family.

By the mid-1960's, Sylvia had transferred to the University of California, Berkeley, where she developed a particularly close friendship with anthropologists Theodore McGowan, Patricia Lyon and John Rowe. Pat and John fostered Sylvia's commitment to general anthropology and to the life of the mind. She completed her higher education at Berkeley, even returning there for a post-doc in 1977.

I first met Sylvia Forman for an interview in Laura Nader's hotel room in New York, at the 1971 annual meeting of the American Anthropological Association. Sylvia at the time was returning to Berkeley, having just completed her doctoral research in Ecuador. Before writing the dissertation, she interviewed for a position at UMass, and we subsequently hired her.

During Sylvia's first year at UMass, the department held a day-long retreat to restructure our graduate program. Until that time, students had no voice in departmental governance, and the structure of the graduate program was considered to be sacrosanct -- perhaps having been delivered by Moses to Machmer Hall on tablets of stone. At the retreat, Sylvia was the catalyst in creating an entirely new graduate program, allowing students a much greater role in shaping their concentrations.

Her style in those early days as well as in the 1980's when she chaired our department was consultative, respectful of divergent views, and tenacious to the point of exhausting everyone. If she could not win an argument by evidence or logic, she would win it by outlasting her opponents. She was a sharp debater and parliamentarian, and had an unerring sense of the nub of an issue. For her last 15 years, she carried a tiny copy of Roberts' *Rules of Order* in her pocket book, and on more than one occasion, used it to good effect, usually to undercut an opponent.

She was even more skilled in departmental, university, and professional politics. She made it a point to write a personal note of congratulations to every woman hired to a professional position on campus, and she routinely invited administrators out for lunch or a drink. Before the annual election of faculty to various administrative and committee positions in the department for the ensuing year, Sylvia regularly "wired" the outcome by her adroit politicking before hand. "I believe in democracy," she claimed, "but I'm not stupid!"

Her politics in the university and her teaching were both rooted in liberal values about the meaning and purpose of a university education. While she worked hard for union representation for the faculty on campus, she also sought to strengthen the role of the largely anti-union Faculty Senate. As a practical matter, she saw the educational value in requiring students to do a lot of writing -- drafting, peer editing, revising -- and became a champion of writing across the curriculum in the university. It's an interesting paradox; Sylvia did relatively little scholarly writing; yet she wrote hundreds of personal letters and perhaps as many lucid memoranda, and she mentored scores of successful student writers at both the undergraduate and graduate levels.

I recall that in October 1991, I told Sylvia I wanted to nominate her for the university's Distinguished Teacher Award. She asked me not to, not because she didn't think she was deserving -- she was not shy about her capabilities. Rather, she said, "My students have come to think that they are really hot stuff, and that they've done it all on their own. Frankly, I think I've got them to think that way, and that's fine, but it means they're not likely to look at me as a hero figure, which is what it probably takes to win the Distinguished Teacher Award."

As I think about it, Sylvia was right; her students did not think of her as a hero. Faculty and students alike knew she was more demanding than any other professor in our program, and she frightened away many timid souls. But she did attract many students who -- like herself, I believe -- had a strong sense of themselves and what they wanted to do as anthropologists. Many, but not all, felt that she sustained a sharp professional -- i.e. hierarchical -- distinction between students and friends. At the same time, she taught and mentored with an unfailing commitment to excellence, and with abundant and detailed encouragements to ripen her students' own professionalism. She took enormous pride in their accomplishments, but I do not think she told them of it. Yet, they must have known.

The Faulkingham house was one of Sylvia's frequent stopping places on her way home from work. She came in through the front door without knocking and announced, "Hello," almost as a question. Invariably it was supper time, and while she almost always declined to eat with us, as she preferred to eat much later in the evening, she pulled a chair up to the table and joined in the conversation. She often wanted to talk about university issues, but she knew Linda Faulkingham detested such talk at the table. Sylvia fell back on interviewing our daughters Sarah and Lisa, often grilling them on their school work and encouraging them to challenge their teachers more often than they did.

Like a good aunt, she often brought stories and little treasures to them from her travels around the world -- stamps, coins, jewelry -- and was a fountain of sage advice. The scene that her advice conjured was filled with intrepid young women facing an illogical and unjust world, winning out by cunning and superb planning. But she played her best auntie role when she "encouraged" our daughters on the eve of their taking their driving license exam. Sylvia's straight-ahead grisly stories of drunken drivers, speeders, and tie rods about to break were more than enough to foster defensive driving, if not second thoughts about taking the exam.

We enjoyed many Thanksgiving dinners with Sylvia and David as well as the graduate students we knew who had no place to go for the day. For Sylvia and Linda, the planning began weeks in advance as they pored through her cookbook collection and recent issues of *Gourmet* magazine. Over the last three years, her "Essence of Mushroom" soup and "Composed Salad" began our feast together. On a few occasions, we celebrated her birthday and New Year's Eve.

In June 1991, Sylvia had orchestrated a surprise birthday party for David. This was no small feat, since David worked mostly at home. She had spent the Spring semester on sick leave from the university, her hair was just beginning to grow back in after her chemotherapy, and she had kept herself removed from many of her friends for some time. She chose this occasion to bring her and David's friends together to celebrate him. Sylvia, with a new lease on life, was resplendent with David's delight in being so wonderfully feted by so many friends. When I think of Sylvia, I often recall her radiance that day.

Less than a year later she was gone from us. Edith Jenkins asked that the following letter be read at Sylvia's Memorial Service:

> Dearest Sylvia,
>
> This is the letter I could not write -- could not write it when first I learned of what was to be your fatal illness, could not write it when we received from you two weeks before your death what we knew was a letter of farewell. You did not say it was that. Did not say so, I know, to spare us the pain of a communication that could in no sense really be answered. Did not say so because it was not your way. The tough/tender, no-nonsense Sylvia did not welcome displays of emotion in yourself towards yourself, and part of our contract of love was to respect your rules. Your rules did not forbid you, however, the outpouring of love and help you gave me on an occasion when I was in much need of it.
>
> We spoke often and laughed often about how we first met. It was in the shabby portable housing English Department offices at Merritt College in Oakland. You must have been nineteen at the time when I noticed your grumpy presence in the area that served as waiting space. With your long, gorgeous red hair, your shabby student garb, your irritated look, you somehow caught my attention. When I asked you what was the matter, you said, "I can't get into Mr. Baugh's English class." "You can get into mine," I responded. As we laughed about this encounter later, you claimed I kidnaped you.
>
> I remember you sitting in the first row of English 1B, waving your hand, saying indignantly, 'Mrs. Jenkins, I disagree with you.' And I remember what so distinguished you was that you had no hostages to fortune: if you could be convinced of another's

position, you had no trouble giving up your own. I remember how your intellectual brilliance and integrity were an utter delight.

I don't remember whether it was during that semester or shortly thereafter that I invited you to our house for Thanksgiving, and my husband, who had been mystified by how much I spoke about a certain student, soon understood and formed a friendship with you of his own. That was the beginning of our lasting and special relationship wherein you became what we called our foster daughter, and we became what you called your surrogate parents.

But such an abbreviated account in no way explains the rare and unduplicable qualities you have -- you had -- (how quickly we must consign to the past!). What I have loved about you is your remarkable intellect, your lack of pride in it, your generosity in making your knowledge and analyses of everything from anthropology, to history, to politics, available to me at our long and luxurious visits over lunch in San Francisco, in Amherst, in Northampton. (How I loved to exploit your knowledge to answer my questions!) What I loved about you was your lack of preciosity, your enjoyment of working people, cowboys, motorcyclists, lovely (but not fancy) blouses, jewelry, food, gardens, flowers, flower arrangements, the growing of vegetables, good parties, late night talks before you went to bed with your drink of bourbon, your historical novel or volume of medieval history. (How I would sneak into your room when you stayed with us and put out the light over your sleeping body.) What I loved about you was your fierce commitment to progressive causes, a commitment of time, of advocacy, of financial support. What I have loved was your passionate loyalty to friends, to us your surrogate family which I hope we have repaid with loyalty of our own.

A photograph of you in a bullfighter's stance waving a flag at a young heifer adorns our hall stairway. The pajamas you left for what had become our ritual Thanksgiving visits are in the closet in the guest room. I do not want to relinquish the immediacy of your presence. Sylvia, your unremitting and unqualified love has adorned our lives.

Farewell, loved one, farewell,

Edith.

CURRICULUM VITAE
of
Sylvia Helen Forman

Department of Anthropology
University of Massachusetts
Amherst, Massachusetts 01003

413-545-2221 (o)
413-545-1379 (o)
413-256-8819 (h)

Education

Graduate:
University of California, Berkeley. Ph.D. Degree, in Anthropology, September 1972. Ph.D. Dissertation Entitled: Law and Conflict in Rural Highland Ecuador.

Undergraduate:
University of California, Berkeley. Major in Anthropology, B.A. Degree, with Honors, June 1968.

Academic Employment

Chairperson (1984-90), Professor (1989-1992), Associate Professor (1979-89), Assistant Professor (1972-79), Department of Anthropology, University of Massachusetts, Amherst, Massachusetts. Also: Associate Faculty, Center for International Education, University of Massachusetts, Amherst.

Consulting Positions

National Academy of Sciences, Board on Science and Technology for International Development: Member of Panel on Comparative Factors Involved in Introducing Selected Renewable Energy Technologies in Developing Countries; 1980-82.

Solar Energy Research Institute, Economic Analysis Branch: cultural factors in successful design of solar energy demonstration projects in developing countries; February - April 1980.

Practical Concepts, Inc. and USAID: design of feasibility analysis methodology and a survey instrument for assessment of rural energy projects in Bolivia; La Paz; January 1980.

Jet Propulsion Laboratory, Social Sciences Group: cross-cultural considerations in the development of DOE's International Photovoltaic Program Plan and other energy projects; Pasadena; June - September, 1979.

Ministry of Health, Republic of Ecuador and Panamerican Health Organization: personnel training program on rural health problems and health care delivery; Quito; January, 1979.

Peralta College District: evaluation of local region oral history project; Oakland, CA; August, 1977.

Academy for Educational Development and USAID/Nicaragua: background field research on nutrition and program design for nutrition education; Managua; May, 1977.

TEMPO (General Electric Center for Advanced Studies): assessment of materials about population dynamics and economic development; 1973-75.

USAID/Ecuador and the Center for International Education of the University of Massachusetts: evaluation of rural non-formal education projects; Ecuador; December 1973 - January, 1974.

USAID/Ecuador: background field research for programs of family health, family planning and rural education; Ecuador; March - November, 1971.

Fellowships and Grants

Post-doctoral Fellow, Program in Quantitative Anthropology with Public Policy Emphasis, Department of Anthropology, University of California, Berkeley, California; June, 1977 to June, 1978. Sponsored by NIMH.

University of Massachusetts, Faculty Growth Grant for Research, 1974; ongoing study of demography in highland Ecuador.

Carolina Population Center, University of North Carolina, 1973; post doctoral training fellowship at the Summer Institute in Population; sponsored by NICHD.

University of Massachusetts, Faculty Growth Grant for Teaching, 1973; preparation and development of materials for an experimental integrated freshman year program in Global Survival Studies.

Wenner-Gren Foundation for Anthropological Research, Conference Grant, 1973; for Conference on Comparative Ethnography of Law, held September 1973, Amherst, Massachusetts.

National Institute of Mental Health, Training and Research Fellowship, 1970 to 1972.

Danforth Graduate Fellowship, 1968 to 1972.

Articles

'Verticality:' Concept and Practice, Past and Future. IN: J. Cole and R.B. Thomas, editors, Papers in Honor of Richard B. Woodbury. (Research Report #29, Dept. of Anthropology, University of Massachusetts). 1993:145-164.

The Junior Year Writing Program at the University of Massachusetts at Amherst. IN: T. Fulwiler and A. Young, editors, Programs That Work: Models and Methods for Writing Across the Curriculum. Pp. 199-219 Boynton-Cook Publishers: Montclair, NJ. 1990. (co-authored with Harding, Herrington, Moran and Mullin)

Longevity and Age Exaggeration in Vilcabamba, Ecuador. Journal of Gerontology, Vol. 34, No. 1, pp. 94-98. 1979. (with R.B. Mazess).

Occupational Status of Women in Anthropology Departments, 1977-78. Anthropology Newsletter, Vol. 19, No. 8. 1978.

Food Production in the Andes: An Alternative Strategy for Highland Agricultural Development. Proceedings of the Population and Food Policy Conference, pp. 333-336. 1978.

The Future of the "Verticality" Concept: Implications and Possible Applications in the Andes. Actes du XLII Congress International des Americanists, Vol. IV, pp. 233-256. Paris. Societe des Americanists. 1978 (Reprinted in: Allan, N.J.R., G.W. Knapp and C. Stadel, editors, Human Impact on Mountains. NJ: Rowman & Littlefield. 1987.)

Occupational Status of Women in Anthropology Departments, 1976-77. Anthropology Newsletter, Vol. 18, No. 9, pp. 10-12. 1977.

The Totora in Colta Lake: An Object Lesson on Rapid Cultural Change. Nawpa Pacha (Institute of Andean Studies), Vol. 15, pp. 111-116. 1977.

Migration: A Problem in Conceptualization. Special Issue: New Approaches to the Study of Migration. Rice University Studies, Vol. 62, No. 3, pp. 25-35. 1976.

The Siberian Peoples. An Annotated Bibliography of English Language Sources. Kroeber Anthropological Society Papers, No. 36, pp. 1-31. 1967.

Reports

Planning and Conduct of Energy Demonstration Projects in Developing Countries. Report for Solar Energy Research Institute. (In mss form)

Diffusion on Biomass Energy Technologies in Developing Countries. National Academy of Sciences. 1982. [NAS does not list authors on Panel reports. For this report, I contributed data on Latin America and assistated with substantive editing of several sections.]

Planning Rural Energy Projects: A rural energy survey and planning methodology for Bolivia. Report to USAID Mission, Bolivia and Practical Concepts, Inc. (with George Burrill and Enrique Gomez.) 104 pages and survey questionnaire in Spanish and English. 1980.

International Photovoltaic Program Plan. Report to Department of Energy. (with Dennis Costello and five other co-authors.) Solar Energy Resarch Institute, publication #TR-353-361; 2 volumes. 1979.

Employment and Hiring of Women in American Departments of Anthropology: Five-Year Record, 1972-77. Report to the Executive Board of the American Anthropological Association. (with Roger Sanjek and Chad K. McDaniel.) 25 pages. 1977.

Food Practices of Lower-Income Nicaraguans and Cultural Considerations in Changing Food Practices. Report to the Comite Tecnico de Nutricion del Gobierno de Nicaragua and USAID Mission, Nicaragua. 41 pages; English and Spanish versions. 1977.

Evaluation Study of the Colta/Columbe Facilitator Project. Report to ecuador Non-Formal Education Program (Quito, Ecuador and Amherst, Massachusetts.). 25 pages. 1974.

Nutritional Survey of Rural Areas. Report to USAID Mission, Ecuador. 28 pages; English and Spanish versions. 1971.

Reviews

Review of: Women's Worlds: From the New Scholarship; M. Safir, M.T. Mednick, D. Israeli and J. Bernard, eds. American Anthropologist 89:2:470-471. 1987.

Review of: Campus Shock: A firsthand report of College life today; Lansing Lamont. Today's Education, p. 86. November-December 1980.

Review of: Relaciones Interetnicas en Riobamba: Dominio y Dependencia en una Region and Indigena Ecuatoriana; Hugo Burgos Guevara. American Anthropologist 80:3:692-693. 1978.

Review of: Terror and Urban Guerrillas: A Study of Tactics and Documents; Jay Mallin, ed. Urban Anthropology Newsletter, Vol. 2, No. 2, pp. 110-111. 1973

Papers Presented at Professional Meetings

'Now You're Cooking with Gas:' Changing Work of Women in Rural Highland Ecuador. 87th Annual Meeting of the American Anthropological Association. Phoenix; November, 1988.

Specialization and Separation: Subfield Interaction and the Role of Linguistic Anthropology. 85th Annual Meeting of the American Anthropological Association. Philadelphia; December, 1986.

Conceptual Renewal in the Renewable Energy Field: Appropriate Technology and Participation. 82nd Annual Meeting of the American Anthropological Association. Chicago; November, 1983.

Demographic Aspects of Longevity in Vilcabamba, Ecuador. In symposium: Biological Approaches to Aging and Longevity. XIth International Congress of Anthropological and Ethnological Sciences. Vancouver, B.C., August, 1983.

Inequality and Compliance: The Heart of American Education. (with Carole E. Hill) 3rd Annual Conference of the World Future Society-Education Section. Amherst, Massachusetts; November, 1980.

The Hiring of Women in Academic Anthropology: A Summary Review. In session: Women in Academic Settings. 77th Annual Meeting of the American Anthropological Association. Los Angeles; November, 1978.

Remnant Populations: Effects of Migration of Rural Populations. (with Charles Drucker). 22nd Annual Meeting of the Kroeber Anthropological Society. Berkeley; May, 1977.

Food Production in the Andes: An Alternative Strategy for Highland Agricultural Development. Population and Food Policy Conference (Capoon Springs Public Policy Series, No. 2), sponsored by the Population Food Fund. Washington, D.C.; February, 1978.

Turning Anthropology Toward the Future. 75th Annual Meeting of the American Anthropological Association. Washington, D.C.; November, 1976.

The Future Value of the "Verticality" Concept: Implications and Possible Applications in the Andes. In symposium: Organizaction Social y Complementaridad Economica en los Andes. XLII International Congress of Americanists. Paris, France; September, 1976.

Migration: A Problem in Conceptualization. In symposium: New Approaches to the Study of Migration. 74th Annual Meeting of the American Anthropological Association. San Francisco; December, 1975.

Ethnographic Research Methods. Panel presentation, by invitation. Law and Society Research Colloquium. The Law School, State University of New York. Buffalo; 1975.

Indian and Mestizo Fertility Differences: A Comparison from Ecuador. In symposium: Anthropological Studies of Fertility. 141st Annual Meeting of the American Association for the Advancement of Science. New York; January, 1975.

"To Make the Balance" - Revisited in Ecuador. In symposium: Law in Question. 72nd Annual Meeting of the American Anthropological Association. New Orleans; November, 1973.

Birth Control in the Boondocks, or How to Say "IUD" in Quechua. 137th Annual Meeting of the American Association for the Advancement of Science. Philadelphia; December, 1971.

Justice of Function? 70th Annual Meeting of the American Anthropological Association. New York; November, 1971.

Indian Diet in Highland Ecuador. 13th Annual Meeting of the Kroeber Anthropological Society. Berkeley; May, 1969.

Other Papers, Lectures and Workshops

Discussant, Invited Symposium on "Teaching as Praxis: Race and Ideologies of Power," 89th Annual Meeting of the American Anthropological Association. November/December, 1990.

Organizer and Co-Chair, Open Forum on "Teaching About Race and Gender," 89th Annual Meeting of the American Anthropological Association. November/December, 1990.

Organizer and Co-Chair, Open Forum on "Teaching About Race and Gender," 88th Annual Meeting of the American Anthropological Association. December, 1989.

Organizer and Chair, Invited Symposium on "Integration or Dis-Integration?: The History and Implications of the Reorganization of the AAA," 86th Annual Meeting of the American Anthropological Association. December, 1987.

Panel Chair, Conference on "The Public University as a Source of Democratic Values," University of Massachusetts. December, 1987.

Conducted training workshop for faculty on "Teaching Writing Across the Curriculum," Mt. Wachuset Community College. Gardner, MA; January, 1987.

Conducted an Open Forum on "Anthropology and the Public," 84th Annual Meeting of the American Anthropological Association. November, 1985.

Conducted training workshop on "Collecting Information in Villages" for a group of Guatemalan rural educators (USAID sponsored). Amherst; June, 1986.

Conducted training workshop for faculty on "Teaching Writing Across the Curriculum," Keene State College. Keene, NH; May, 1985.

Panelist in symposium on "Beyond 1984: Options for the Near Future;" University of Massachusetts, Amherst. May, 1984.

Conducted training workshop for faculty on "Writing Across the Curriculum," Greenfield Community College. Greenfield, MA; April, 1983.

Conducted an Open Forum (with J.B. Cole) on "General Education and Curriculum Reform: What's the Role of Anthropology," 81st Annual Meeting of the American Anthropological Association. December, 1982.

Panelist in Great Decisions Program on "Central America: Fire in the Front Yard," broadcast on WFCR Radio. February, 1982.

Panelist in symposium on "The U.S. in the U.N.," Amherst College. October, 1981.

Presented lecture on "Renewable Energy: Issues in the Third World," University of Colorado, Boulder. April, 1980.

Presented lecture on "Notes on the General Relationship of Schooling to Societal Structure," in Seminar on 'Manipulation of Conciousness Through Schooling,' Center for the Study of Public Policy, Cambridge, Massachusetts and the Rockefeller Brothers Fund; Cambridge, MA. May, 1980.

Presented lecture on "The Demography of Vilcabamba," International Workshop on the Longevous Population of Vilcabamba at the National Institutes of Health; Bethesda, MD. February, 1978.

Presented lecture on "Non-Formal Education: Cross-Cultural Perspectives," Public Lecture Series of the Committee on Modernization and Development, Purdue University; Lafayette, IN. October, 1975.

Editorships

Program Editor for the 80th Annual Meeting of the American Anthropological Association (November, 1981; Los Angeles, California).

Associate Program Editor for Social/Cultural Anthropology for the 78th Annual Meeting of the American Anthropological Association (November, 1979; Cincinnati, Ohio).

Editor, Kroeber Anthropological Society Papers, Special 20th Anniversary Issue; 1969.

Field Work and Professional Travel

Field research in highland Ecuador on demography and on changes in women's economic conditions; February-May, 1988.

Travel in Belize, representing Five Colleges, Inc.; June 1987.

Travel in People's Republic of China, representing the University of Massachusetts, Amherst; March-April, 1981.

Travel in Cuba, as member of delegation of the Association of Black Anthropologists to the Cuban Academy of Sciences; July, 1980.

Field research in Bolivia on rural energy use, as consultant; January, 1980.

Travel in Cuba with University of Massachusetts student group; December 1979-January, 1980.

Field research in Nicaragua on food practices and diet, as consultant; May-June, 1977.

Field research in Andean Ecuador on evaluation of projects in rural non-formal education, as consultant, and as continuation of previous studies; July-August, 1974.

Field research in Andean Ecuador; general ethnography and study of conflict management in Quechua-speaking Indian villages; dissertation research; July 1970-November, 1971.

Field research in Andean Ecuador on dietary practices among Quechua-speaking Indians; June-September, 1968.

Offices and Memberships in Professional Organizations

American Anthropological Association (Fellow)

Chair of the Search Committee for Editor-in-Chief of the American Anthropologist, 1988-89.

Member of Organizing Board of the Association for Feminist Anthropology, 1987-88.

Member of the Executive Committee of the Board of Directors, 1986-88, and Chair of the Administrative Sub-Committee, 1987-88.

Member of the Board of Directors, 1984-88.

Chair of the General Anthropology Division, 1987-88.

Chair-elect of General Anthropology Division, 1984-86.

Chair, General Anthropology Organizing Committee, 1983-84.

Chair of the Committee on the Status of Women in Anthropology, 1976-77, and member, 1975-78.

Member of the Planning and Development Committee, 1969-70.

Society for Applied Anthropology (Fellow):

Member of Nominations and Elections Committee, 1984-86.

Member of Publications Policy Committee, 1982-84.

Association of Political and Legal Anthropologists:

Secretary-Treasurer, 1980-83.

Kroeber Anthropological Society.

    President, 1969-70.

    Secretary, 1966-69.

American Association for the Advancement of Science.

Sigma Xi (elected to membership, Massachusetts Chapter, 1973).

Association of Black Anthropologists.

Society for Medical Anthropology.

Association for Feminist Anthropology

Other Professional and Service Activities (1978-88)

1987-88 Organized and chaired an invited symposium "Integration or Disintegration?: The History and Implications of the Reorganization of the AAA," at 1987 Annual Meeting of the American Anthropological Association.

    Reviewed grant proposals for Wenner-Gren Foundation, NSF and University of Alaska.

1986-87 Member of Search Committee for Coordinator (CEO) of Five Colleges, Inc.

1985-86 Presented lecture on "Stag Parties: Middle Class Images vs Economic Realities," to the Amherst Club; January.

    Presentation on teaching writing, University Parent's Day, University of Massachusetts; April.

1984-85 Discussant, session on "Anthropology of Food Habits," NEAA Annual Meeting; April.

    Invited participant in seminar of the American Council on Education/Women in Higher Education Program; March.

    Presentations in two faculty workshops on teaching writing, University of Massachusetts; September and January.

1983-84 Presentations in several faculty workshops on teaching writing across the curriculum, University Writing Program, University of Massachusetts.

Participant in campus-wide faculty "Working Group on Quality of Work Life," year-long.

1982-83 Presentation in faculty symposium on "Human Relations in the Curriculum," University of Massachusetts, November.

Chaired session on "Exercise of Political Power," 81st Annual Meeting of the American Anthropological Association; December, 1982.

1981-82 Presentation in "Toward the Year 2000: Educations and Vocations," symposium sponsored by Cooperative Education Program, University of Massachusetts; May.

Presentation in Human Futures Series, Mount Hermon School; April.

Member of Search Committee for Chancellor of University of Massachusetts at Amherst.

1979-80 Reader, Danforth Foundation, on Reading Committee for applications for Danforth Graduate Fellowships; January.

Organized Plenary Session, "The Emergence of Global Society," 78th Annual Meeting of the American Anthropological Association. November.

Regional reviewer for postbaccalaureate applicants for Danforth Graduate Fellowships. Fall.

1978-79 Reader, Danforth Foundation, on Reading Committee for applications for Danforth Graduate Fellowships; January.

Official Representative of American Anthropological Association at inauguration of E. Kennan as President of Mount Holyoke College. October.

Regional reviewer/endorser for postbaccalaureate applicants for Danforth Graduate Fellowships. Fall.

MEMORANDUM

This is the memo which Sylvia Helen Forman prepared when she applied for promotion to full professor at the University of Massachusetts, Amherst in 1989. It is included here as a clear statement of her own priorities and her personal assessment of her strengths as a scholar, teacher and academic. Sylvia was promoted to Full Professor in 1989 and held that rank until her death in 1992.

To: Donald Proulx, Chair, Personnel Committee, Dept. of Anthropology

From: Sylvia Forman (1/5/89)

Re: Personal Statement on my Promotion to Professor

As you and our colleagues on the Personnel Committee assess my candidacy for promotion to Professor, I would like to offer you my own interpretation of my professional activities. My intent here is not to replicate my vita; rather, I would like briefly to summarize and highlight some specific elements of my work which I think merit your attention. Your review concentrates on my performance since I was awarded tenure and promoted to Associate Professor, and thus I restrict this document also to the period from 1979 to the present.

TEACHING. I have consistently devoted much, if not most, of my professional effort and attention to teaching and advising. I think it is fair to say that, by a variety of measures, I have been and am an effective and productive teacher at both the undergraduate and graduate levels. Although the Department Chairship carries a reduced teaching load, I averaged more than one classroom course a semester since 1984, and have maintained a full share of advising activities.

a) Course Teaching. As indicated in the appended roster of the classes I have taught since 1979, my repertory of courses is relatively large, ranging from introductory level (104) to courses for majors (333, 364, 479, 524) to graduate seminars (671, 740, 755). Almost all of my courses since I became Chair have been at the undergraduate level. Students' evaluations of my courses are consistently positive, with emphasis on the fact that they are challenging and demanding at the same time that they are well organized and intellectually exciting.

I developed the department's Junior Year Writing course (333), and have taught it three times in four years. Anthro. 333 has been held by the Writing Program as a model of a junior year writing course. Yet, when experience indicated some problems with the format of that course, largely due to increased enrollment, I initiated a revision of the requirement and worked with Dr. Faulkingham to redesign both the writing and theory components of the requirements for the major, developing our new combined, year-long course (364/365).

My applied anthropology course (479) has, I think, been a particularly valuable addition to the department's curriculum. It enables senior majors to undertake a substantial field research project which closely approximates real applied social research. Students master important techniques of data collection and analysis and gain experience in research design. They also benefit from learning how to collaborate effectively with each other and with community organizations. The reports students write in this course must -- and do -- follow the professional formats and meet the standards of clarity of consultants' reports. They are submitted to the community agencies with which the students have coordinated their projects, as well as to me. Many of the reports have seen serious use in community planning and program development efforts, and most of them have been of significant value to the students after graduation, as evidence of their skills and competencies.

I regularly offered an Honors section with Anth. 104, and in 1982, I taught a STPEC Honors seminar. Along with J.B. Cole, I developed the course on "Women in Cross-Cultural Perspective" (524) and with Keene a series of 1-credit courses on "Anthropology through Literature." For the Spring 1989 semester, I am preparing to teach the General Education course in "Inequality and Oppression" (205), as a four-credit, enriched Honors class.

In addition to classroom courses, I have supervised tutorial courses almost every semester. Altogether I have given 27 undergraduate and 17 graduate readings, independent study and practicum courses in the last decade. All of these tutorials have required a contract of formal expectations and regular meetings and papers. They have been tailored to the needs and interests of individual students, but have met the same standards of quality as my regular classes.

In these and other undergraduate courses, I have emphasized student development of critical analytic skills and clear, professionally-oriented writing. I have successfully encouraged students to be active participants in class, to take a high degree of responsibility for their learning and to effectively share their capabilities with each other (through such activities as peer critique of papers). I have regularly revised all of my courses, both to keep up to date with relevant materials and to incorporate new pedagogical approaches as appropriate.

Given my commitment to contributing to the undergraduate curriculum, my opportunities to offer graduate seminars have been limited since I became Chair. I have offered 524 and a 1-credit seminar on applied anthropology (597). I have worked closely with graduate students in other settings.

b) Advising and Non-course Teaching. I take very seriously my teaching role outside the classroom, especially that part of it concerned with students' preparation of theses and dissertations. As indicated in the attached list, I have worked with numerous students on their Honors, MA and PhD. committees over the last decade. Many of the graduate students with whom I have worked are in departments other than anthropology. I have also served as an advisor for four UAW students, four BIC majors and four Women's Studies majors/certificate students, as well as anthropology majors.

I have been successful in helping the graduate students on whose committees I have served to obtain scholarships and research funding and to attain professional employment after completing their degrees. All five of the students who have completed their doctorates under my direction since 1980 received funding for their dissertation research and currently hold faculty positions. Since becoming Chair, I have served as an informal advisor to many graduate students who do not work directly with me, especially regarding their career plans. I have taken initiative in helping all of our graduates identify and obtain professional positions, with, I believe, a fair degree of success.

I am especially proud of my role in establishing and co-instructing our departmental training program for teaching assistants. Our day-long teaching workshop is one of the few TA preparation programs on the campus. One indication of its worth is that experienced TAs return to participate in it year in and year out.

RESEARCH. My research interests and activities have been rather diverse, although they are linked by a common theme of my applied anthropological orientation. In the period 1978-82, I engaged in a series of applied (consulting) projects, in association with distinguished organizations, on alternative energy in the developing world. A combination of factors (the Reagan administration's approach to development aid, my increased involvement with the American Anthropological Association, and then my becoming Department Chair in 1984) has precluded my maintaining this type of research more recently.

Since becoming Chair, I have virtually ceased to publish scholarly work based on new field research. However, I have maintained some scholarly activity through the presentation of papers at professional meetings and participation in a variety of symposia, panels and workshops. I also, with some regularity, review grant proposals for NSF, Wenner-Gren, and other agencies and manuscripts for the American Anthropologist, American Ethnologist, and other journals.

With a sabbatical leave in Spring 1988, I was able to return to the site of my earlier research in highland Ecuador. During the three months I spent there, I made progress on two projects: a re-census of this Indian/peasant village, to be used comparatively with the census data I have from 1971; and, a series of life histories of women of the community, with a focus on changes in their economic roles over a generation. I presented a paper at the American Anthropological Association Annual Meeting in November, 1988, based on the second project.

My research plans for the present and immediate future include: (a) editing for publication the papers -- including my own -- from the 1988 AAA symposium on 'Women's Changing Economic Roles'; (b) a return to Ecuador during the summer 1989 to continue the fieldwork begun last year. Having the data, from additional field research, to comparatively examine fertility, mortality, migration and education over the time span of nearly a generation will permit me to carry out a type of analysis of demographic change, at a fine scale, which is rare for rural Third World settings. I anticipate having more time and energy to devote to scholarly preparation of these materials when my term as Chair ends in 1990.

SERVICE. A complete inventory of my service activities since my previous promotion is part of/appended to my vita. Some of these contributions have overlapped significantly with other aspects of my professional life: both teaching and research. I think that the list of such activities is relatively lengthy and indicative of my professional standing both on and off campus. It is also indicative of my view of the appropriate role of a professional and a faculty member at a public university. Some of my service activities can also be taken as another form of applied anthropology: an effort to dedicate disciplinary expertise to the practical issues of the institutions with which I am involved.

a) Departmental Service. My colleagues have regularly elected me to positions of administrative responsibility. In 1982-83, I was a member of the Personnel Committee and in 1983-84 the Director of Undergraduate Studies. This is my fifth year -- second term -- as Department Chair, in which capacity I work closely with all other departmental officers and committees and represent the Department to other campus units.

b) University and Five College Service. The highlights of my campus and Five College service contributions are: two years as Chair of the Rules Committee of the Faculty Senate and two as Vice-President of the MSP; membership on the search committees for the Chancellor, the Director of the Honors Program, the Director of Nursing, the Assoc. Vice-Chancellor for Affirmative Action and the Five College Coordinator; membership on the Task Force on Residential Academic Programs, Junior Year Writing Program Task Force, Honors Committee, the Committee on Revision of Professional Search Procedures, and the Quality of Student Life Committee. I have taken a leadership role in drawing the anthropology programs of the Five Colleges back into a more integrated and communicative relationship. Over a number of years, I have been quite active in helping to prepare faculty in other departments to teach junior year writing courses.

c) Professional and Public Service. Since 1983, I have devoted much time and energy to work with the American Anthropological Association (AAA). When the AAA underwent a complete reorganization, starting in 1982, I was asked by the officers to lead the effort to organize the General Anthropology Division of the Association, the largest and most diverse segment of the AAA. I successfully undertook that task, and then served a four-year term as Chair-elect and Chair of the Division. As Chair of the General Anthropology Division, I was also a member of the Board of Directors of the AAA and of the Executive Committee of the Board and thus involved in a wide array of AAA actions and decision-making events, including the selection of a new Executive Director. While my term of office in the Division has now ended, I was elected last spring by the Executive Committee to serve as Chair of the Search Committee for a new Editor in Chief of the American Anthropologist, an assignment which currently requires my attention.

I have also served the profession as Secretary-Treasurer of the Association of Political and Legal Anthropologists (1980-83) and as a member of the Publications Policy Committee (1982-84) and the Nominations Committee (1984-86) of the Society for Applied Anthropology. Most recently, with two colleagues, I undertook to organize a new unit of the AAA -- The Association for Feminist Anthropology -- which was approved by the Board of Directors in November, 1988. (I managed, however, <u>not</u> to become an officer of this new Association for the time being.)

I believe I have been elected to these positions not only because I have a reputation for getting the work done but also because my understanding of the discipline and my judgement concerning the directions of the profession are appreciated by my peers.

List of Graduate Students

This list, generated from the alumni database of the Department of Anthropology at the University of Massachusetts, Amherst, represents all alumni who meet either of the following conditions:
SHF was the MA chair (coded MA)
SHF was the PhD. chair (coded PhD.)
There were in addition, other students who worked closely with Sylvia although she was not officially the chair of their committee and they are not included in this list although they certainly consider themselves her students. We have done our best to be inclusive and apologize to anyone who has been omitted.

Betsy Chadwick (MA - 1989)
3 Riverview Road
Rocky Hill CT 06067-1524

Javed Chaudhri (MA - 1976)
(no address)

Mary E. Crandon-Malamud (PhD. - 1980)
(deceased)
Dissertation Title: Changing Faces of the Achachilas: Medical Systems and Cultural Identity in a Highland Bolivian Village

Elizabeth Falkenthal (MA - 1979)
276 State Street
Northampton MA 01060

Karen Gaul (MA - 1990; PhD.- 1994; Brooke Thomas replaced Sylvia in 1991)
Dissertation Title: Negotiated Positions and Shifting Terrains: Apprehension of Forest Resources in the Western Himalayas
49 Conway Street, #4
Greenfield MA 01301

Susan B. Hyatt (PhD.; Jackie Urla replaced Sylvia in 1991; Sue is now writing the dissertation)
Van Mildert College
University of Durham
Durham DH1 3LH
ENGLAND

Barbara C. Johnson (PhD. - 1985)
Dissertation Title: Our Community in Two Worlds: The Cochin Paradesi Jews in India and Israel
325 Cascadilla Street
Ithaca NY 14850-3476

Barbara R. Johnston (PhD. - 1987)
Dissertation Title: The Political Ecology of Development: Changing Resource Relations and the
    Impacts of Tourism in St. Thomas, U.S.V.I.
1115 Lennon Way
San Jose CA 95125

Ann Kingsolver (MA - 1987; PhD. - 1991)
Dissertation Title: Tobacco, Toyota and Subaltern Development Discourses: Constructing
    Livelihoods and Communication in Rural Kentucky
136 Hagar Court
Santa Cruz CA 95064-1035

Nancy K. Lundgren (MA - 1980; PhD. - 1987)
Dissertation Title: Socialization of Children in Belize: Identity Race and Power with the World
    Political Economy
608 North Fountain Avenue
Springfield OH 45504

Makaziwe Mandela (PhD.- 1992; Ralph Faulkingham replaced Sylvia in 1991)
Dissertation Title: Gender Relations and Patriarchy in South Africa's Transkei
Deputy Registrar
University of Witwatersrand
Johannesburg, South Africa

Lisa B. Markowitz (PhD.- 1992; Brooke Thomas replaced Sylvia in 1991)
Dissertation Title: Pastoral Production and its Discontents: Alpaca and Sheep Herding in
    Caylloma, Peru
Department of Rural Sociology
University of Missouri
Columbia MO 65211   (relocating -- University of Kentucky)

Irma McClaurin (MA - 1989; PhD. - 1993; Ralph Faulkingham replaced Sylvia in 1991)
Dissertation Title: Women and the Culture of Gender in Belize, Central America
538 10th Avenue
Grinnell IA 50112-1411   (relocating -- University of Florida, Gainesville)

Thomas McGuire (MA - 1990)
PO Box 44
Greenfield NH 03047-0044

Melba M. Sánchez-Ayéndez (PhD. - 1984)
Dissertation Title: Puerto Rican Elderly Women: Aging in an Ethnic Minority Group in the
    United States
Via Bernado #1 Monte Alvernia
Guaynabo, Puerto Rico 00969

Dena Shenk (MA - 1976; PhD. - 1979)
Dissertation Title: Aging Christian Lebanese-Americans: Retirement in an Ethnic Context
Coordinator, Gerontology Program
Department of Sociology, Anthropology and Social Work
University of North Carolina at Charlotte
Charlotte NC 282223

Carolyn A. Smith (MA - 1986)
Ft. Lucas Road
Box 397
Colrain MA 01340

Melissa Smith (MA - 1976)
(no address)

Patricia Suprenant (MA - 1976)
(no address)

Sue Perkins Taylor (PhD. - 1978)
Dissertation Title: Aging in Black Women. Coping Strategies and Lifeways Within an Urban
    Population
Department of Sociology & Anthropology
Box 987
Howard University
Washington DC 20059

Catherine M. Tucker (MA - 1987)
278 Chester St.
Chester NH 03036

Lynn B. Wilson (PhD. - 1993; John Cole replaced Sylvia in 1991)
Dissertation Title: Speaking to Power: Gender, Politics and Discourse in the context of United
    States Military Priorities in Belau, Western Micronesia
P.O. Box 61156
Honolulu HI 96839